WORKING WITH PARENTS

Working with Parents

A Practical Guide for Teachers and Therapists

ROY McCONKEY

CROOM HELM
London & Sydney

BROOKLINE
BOOKS
Cambridge, MA

© 1985 Roy McConkey
Croom Helm Ltd, Provident House, Burrell Row,
Beckenham, Kent BR3 1AT
Croom Helm Australia Pty Ltd, First Floor, 139 King Street,
Sydney, NSW 2001, Australia

British Library Cataloguing in Publication Data

McConkey, Roy
  Working with parents: a practical guide
  for teachers and therapists.
  1. Home and school
  2. Title
  371.1'03

  ISBN 0-7099-3503-X
  ISBN 0-7099-3543-9 Pbk

Published in the USA and dependencies,
Central and South America by
Brookline Books, 29 Ware Street,
Cambridge, Massachusetts 02138

Library of Congress Cataloging in Publication Data

McConkey, Roy.
  Working with parents.

  Bibliography: p.
  Includes index.
  1. Home and school—Great Britain. 2. Parent-teacher
relationships—Great Britain. 3. Compensatory education—Great Britain. 4. Home and school—United States.
5. Parent-teacher relationships—United States.
6. Compensatory education—United States. I. Title.
LC225.33.G7M33   1985   371.1'03   85-3744
  ISBN 0-914797-13-1
  ISBN 0-914797-14-X (pbk.)

Typeset by Columns of Reading

Printed and bound in Great Britain by
Biddles Ltd, Guildford and King's Lynn

Contents

For my parents, Florrie and Sam McConkey, in gratitude

About the Author

Roy McConkey has a PhD from the University of Manchester and is Senior Research Officer with St Michael's House in Dublin, Ireland. St Michael's House is an organisation providing a full range of services to people who are mentally handicapped and to their families.

He graduated in psychology at the Queen's University, Belfast, and worked at the Hester Adrian Research Centre, University of Manchester, on a government-funded, parental involvement project. This topic is one of the major themes of his present research programme, which has been supported, in part, by grants from UNESCO. Over the past twelve years he has instigated many developments in the field of parent education. These have been reported in various international journals and described in five books, including *Teaching the Handicapped Child* and *Making Toys for Handicapped Children* (published by Prentice-Hall in the USA and Souvenir Press in the UK).

Dr McConkey is also involved in the training of special education teachers, speech therapists and psychologists, and has spoken at international conferences in Europe, India, Canada and New Zealand.

Acknowledgements

Books that claim to give practical guidance can never be the product of one mind. Hence, I gladly acknowledge the debt of gratitude I owe to David Kenefick and many other colleagues in St Michael's House and to former colleagues at the Hester Adrian Research Centre, University of Manchester; in particular Dorothy Jeffree, Cliff Cunningham and Peter Mittler.

I have also drawn upon the writings of many other British and American authors but I must acknowledge espᵉcially the books written or edited by Gillian Pugh, Barbara Tizard and her research team, and Peter Mittler and Helen McConachie. My thanks to them and their publishers, respectively National Children's Bureau, Grant McIntyre and Croom Helm, for permissions to use quotations.

I am indebted to my wife, Pat, for transforming my untidy handwriting into a neat typescript; a task which only love not money could reward.

The preparation of this book was sponsored by the Research Committee of St Michael's House and to the Chairperson, Dr Barbara Stokes, I would like to say thank you for her constant encouragement and, in this instance especially, for her example. Nearly 30 years ago, she and a group of parents came together to organise the first day services for mentally handicapped children in Dublin. Out of that partnership grew the organisation I am privileged to be part of today. I trust this book lives up to the aspirations embodied in the original name of our service: the Association of Parents and Friends of Mentally Handicapped Children.

Preface

> The means then to advance humane learning, and the
> reformation of schools, is to elaborate certain treaties
> and to put them that they may be made use of by all. The
> first of these treaties should be a discovery of the defects
> and of the disorders in teaching and educating children,
> with the intimation of the remedies thereof, and of the
> manner of applying the same unto the disease, which
> should be done briefly and substantially. The second
> should be a direction for parents, how to implant into
> their children the seeds of vertue and to beget in them a
> disposition towards learning.
> [John Drury, 1642; cited by R.F. Young, in *Comenius in
> England* (London, 1932)]

Working with parents is more often preached than practised.
Government committees and departments have consistently
stressed the importance of parental participation in all children's
education and in some countries — for example the United States
and Britain — their rights are now detailed in legislation. Eminent
child developmentalists, such as Jerry Bruner, Urie Bronfenbrenner, John and Elizabeth Newson, have lauded parents with
titles such as 'the only true educators'. Furthermore extensive
research has shown conclusively that many benefits accrue to
children when their parents are interested and involved in their
education. There is plenty of evidence too that most parents want
to be involved. At least two in three is the commonly cited figure.

Why then is the involvement of parents with teachers and
therapists still thought of as exceptional rather than accepted
practice? Service systems may vary in style and substance across
the developed world, but they have in common a philosophy of
'professionalism' that has failed to embrace parents. This is as
true for Britain, Ireland and Continental Europe as it is for the
United States of America. Our services for children with special
needs exude an aura of 'it's our job: leave us to get on with it';
an attitude inherited, I suspect from our institutional, hospital
and educational systems. It is not that staff are actively blocking
the involvement of parents, rather in their system they cannot see

themselves coping with it. Nor can the fault, if that is the correct word, be wholly theirs. It is amazing that the evangelical zeal with which parental involvement has been preached has rarely been matched by practical assistance for staff as to how they could make it a reality within their service.

In this book I draw together many examples from both Europe and the USA as to how professionals (psychologists, nurses, doctors but especially teachers and therapists) can work with parents. My concern has been to give practical guidelines for action. A reply, if you like, to the hesitant questioner who asks 'but what can I do?'.

Although particular emphasis is given to working with parents of preschoolers or children with disabilities, the principles described can be applied to all.

The book is mainly written for the young professional in training or newly graduated. They need to see work with parents as an integral part of their job and one for which they have been prepared. I hope the book proves acceptable to their tutors and that they will use it in conjunction with some form of practical experience for their students. Of course I am conceited enough to believe that experienced professionals will benefit from reading it, although, for them too, I advocate some form of training workshop so that they can have a stimulant and support for their new endeavours.

The four sections of the book are designed to be self-contained. At the beginning of each one, there is an *overview* of the topics covered. Reading these will quickly give you a feel for the scope and style of the book. Each chapter then contains a range of practical suggestions; from those requiring little additional work to ones which necessitate a radical reappraisal of your professional lifestyle. I trust there is something for everyone.

We live in an era when our professional expertise in overcoming disabilities is expanding at a tremendous rate and at a time when parents are arguably more available to work with us through increased leisure time, better education and smaller family size. Our generation of teachers and therapists has therefore a unique springboard from which to make John Drury's second treatise a reality: albeit over 300 years late.

PART ONE

Working with Parents

OVERVIEW

Most of this book is for readers who want to work with parents. I hope that includes you. If it doesn't or you're not sure, then don't give up on me just yet because this first section is specially for you. In Chapter 1, I outline three reasons why I believe it is worthwhile for parents, teachers and therapists to work together. If you don't share these beliefs, and it's your judgement that counts, then let's part as friends. Simply put the book back on the shelf and, as the song says, 'you'll go your way and I'll go mine'.

But if you're inclined to walk along with me to Chapter 2, you might then care to sample what I believe are the ingredients for an ideal working relationship. These, I suspect, will be rather hard for some of you to stomach. If so, as you leave, 'tread softly, because you tread on my dreams' (with apologies to W.B. Yeats).

The third chapter is for those of you who prefer to get down to the nitty-gritty. Here I've culled as complete a listing as I can of all the many ways 'working with parents' can be seen in practice. Most of these will be explained in further detail in subsequent chapters of the book but the compilation is there for those who like to have a foretaste of the main course. I'm prepared to take the risk that some of you will not want to stay for dinner.

The final chapter of this section is a dessert called 'humble pie'. It's offered as an antidote to those readers whom I may have lulled into a false sense of confidence and for those readers who, from the outset, were rather cocky or blasé and wondered what all the fuss was about. Here I identify four groups of parents with whom working relationships are *generally* harder to attain: fathers, single mothers, low-income families and immigrant families. If you are prepared to take on these and other challenges, then you're a real 'pro'.

To the survivors of these initiation rites, and indeed to those previously initiated by dint of their labour with parents, my heartfelt plea is both simple and succinct: please buy the book!

1

Why Should I?

(The title is a favourite phrase of my daughter; often
spoken when her mother or father makes an unwelcome
demand, such as washing the breakfast dishes. Somehow
it seemed strangely appropriate when I started to think
of the reasons usually given for not working with
parents.)

Reason 1: 'I don't Usually Work with Parents, so why Should I?'

You are a teacher or therapist, or in training to be one, right? So
what's your main function with handicapped children or, to put it
more crudely, what are you paid to do? Teach; administer
therapy . . . ye . . . es, but with what result? The children
learn/develop/overcome their difficulties/master new skills etc,
etc. Exactly; you are there to help the children.

I wonder if you are doing that to the best of your ability? My
guess is that sometimes you do, but more often you do not. You
see I believe the evidence is quite overwhelming that:

*CHILDREN LEARN MORE WHEN PARENTS, TEACHERS
AND/OR THERAPISTS WORK TOGETHER*

If you are not working with parents, then the children must be
losing out. You are doing a second-rate job. But don't just take
my word for it.

During the late 1960s and early 1970s, the most ambitious
attempt ever to help preschoolers learn was launched in the
United States under the title 'Head Start'. Special preschool
facilities with new, and old, teaching methods commenced in
many low-income areas, with the aim of eliminating the
disadvantages these children frequently have on entering formal
schooling. The outcomes, however, were mixed. In some cities

19

gains in the preschool years seemed to be lost after a few years in regular schools. The head start was 'washed' out. But in other places, these programmes had lasting effects: fewer children failed a grade or required remedial education; the children's confidence and self-image improved and their parents' aspirations for further education and employment were high. So why the difference? The extensive evaluations that were built into these programmes provided a clear answer. The most effective ones were those in which both parent and child participated, often with teachers visiting the home regularly alongside attendance at the preschool.

Urie Bronfenbrenner[1] summed it up thus:

The involvement of the child's family as an active participant is critical to the success of any intervention prc̥ ̃amme. Without such family involvement, any effect of intervention, at least in the cognitive sphere, appears to erode fairly rapidly once the programme ends. (p.252)

Another eminent researcher in child development, Burton White,[2] is even more radical in his conclusions. On reviewing a lifetime's research, which culminated in his directorship of the prestigious Harvard Preschool Project, he stated:

We came to believe that the informal education that families provide for their children *makes more of an impact on a child's total educational development than the formal education system.* If a family does its job well, the professional can then provide effective training. If not, there may be little the professional can do to save the chlid from mediocrity. This grim assessment is the direct conclusion from the findings of thousands of programmes in remedial education. (p.4; his italics)

These insights were not new, rather they were discovered anew. Ten years earlier British investigators had come to somewhat similar conclusions. A national study of health and development involving all British children born during one week in March 1946, was well positioned to explore differences in the educational achievements of eight and eleven year olds. The project's director, J.W.B. Douglas,[3] summarised their findings thus:

> At both eight and eleven years, but particularly at eleven, the highest average scores in the test are made by children whose parents are the most interested in their education and the lowest by those whose parents are least interested. This is partly a social class effect . . . but the relationship between the children's scores and their parents' attitudes persists within each social class.
>
> The influence of the level of the parents' interest on test performance is greater than that of any of the other three factors: size of family, standard of home and academic record of the school . . . and it becomes increasingly important as the child grows older. (pp.84–5)

Twelve years later Ron Davie[4] and his colleagues began to monitor the progress of some 11,000 British children in a second national child development study. They described the striking disparity between children from different social backgrounds that was already apparent by the age of seven years. In the case of reading performance there was a gap of over four years between the most and least advantaged children. They go on . . .

> Furthermore the most potent factors were seen to be located in the home environment. The most obvious implications to be drawn from this are, first, that equality of educational opportunity cannot be achieved solely by improving our educational institutions. (p.190)

All-in-all, the evidence from national studies in Western countries is pretty unanimous: the home has more influence on a child's learning than does school.

Parents and Handicapped Children

Thus far the data have been derived from ordinary children and may not apply to those with handicaps. Peter Mittler[5] thinks otherwise: 'there is evidence that this relationship (between home and learning) is likely to be even stronger in handicapped children.' (p.9) However, here we have to rely on a different sort of evidence, because we do not have data from national longitudinal surveys. Instead we can examine children's development under different circumstances: for example, children reared in institutions, rather than with families, or when the parents participate in home-teaching programmes.

Janet Carr's[6] developmental assessments of Down's syndrome children clearly shows significant advantages to home-reared infants which are apparent even at the second year of life. Moreover, when the amount of one-to-one contact within institutions was improved the children's progress advanced. This was true for both non-disabled and disabled children.

During the 1970s reports appeared regularly in the literature of the benefits which accrued to handicapped infants when they and their parents participated in special developmental programmes. Cliff Cunningham[7] ends his review of these studies thus:

> Taken together, the results of early intervention studies with mentally handicapped infants clearly suggest that it is possible to facilitate both developmental rate and management. Parents gain considerable support from such activities and generally are capable of learning techniques and content. (p. 14)

Nor is it just babies who benefit. For instance, Jean Cooper and her colleagues[8] at the Wolfson Centre, London, worked with language-delayed children ranging in age from two to four-and-a-half years and spanning a diversity of aetiologies. They contrasted the efficacy of conventional weekly speech therapy sessions with the outcomes of parent-administered therapy at home and placement in a special language class. They found that the children's progress was much more marked in the last two conditions, although individual weekly sessions with a therapist were better than no treatment. Jean Cooper continues the story:

> Although the success rate for the children in the parent programme was less striking (than language classes), it was still very high and this is clearly the most economical way of using resources . . . Language education is incorporated into daily living activities by parents who are guided by a session with the speech therapist every six weeks. Seeing three children in a day in this six-weekly programme enables each speech therapist to carry a case load of 90 children, giving

constant help via the parents. This is more than twice the number that most speech therapists can manage on weekly therapy. (p.68)

If you don't Usually Work with Parents, Shouldn't you Think Again?

All these studies come to a unanimous conclusion; if you want children to develop better, get the parents involved. By all means spend money on better schools and clinics and employ more staff, but remember the likely pay offs will be nothing like as good than if these resources were channelled into homes and parental involvement. Urie Bronfenbrenner's[1] logic is irrefutable:

> The family is the most effective and economical system for fostering and sustaining the development of the child . . . The involvement of the parents as partners in the enterprise provides an on-going system which can reinforce the effects of the programme while it is in operation and help to sustain them after the program ends. (p.252)

The implication for all professionals who are concerned with helping children grow up, is that parental help is necessary if they are to do their job efficiently and effectively. Shouldn't you think again about working with parents, even if you don't usually do so?

Reason 2: 'The Parents have never Asked me to Work with them, so why Should I?'

Barbara Tizard and her colleagues,[9] as part of her research on involving parents in nursery and infant schools, asked teachers what might stand in the way of increased parental involvement. She found 'the obstacle most frequently mentioned was the parents' unwillingness': said one teacher, 'the main obstacle is the parents. They may be shy or afraid of the school or have to work or they don't speak English but, anyway, they don't come.' (p.47)

Yet I believe there is sufficient evidence to justify this assertion

MOST PARENTS WANT TO BE INVOLVED IN FURTHERING THEIR CHILD'S LEARNING

In writing this, I am well aware that I am directly contradicting the views of many therapists and teachers. Could it be that you don't know your parents as well as you think you do?

For instance, Barbara Tizard's team interviewed teachers and parents about nursery-school activities.

> The staff considered that parents could best help their children by playing with them; reading to them and developing their language. But except in the middle-class units, they doubted whether many parents did in fact help in these ways and six of the 14 staff thought that the parents made no positive contribution to their children's education at all.

One teacher went so far as to say 'To be frank, the children are better off in school.' (p.46)

But when the team interviewed the parents, they discovered that, 'In every school between two-fifths and three-quarters of parents were, unbeknown to the staff, trying to teach their child to write, count and in some cases, also to read.' (p.47)

Larger-scale studies have found similar results with ordinary infants. The Plowden Committee's survey (1967)[10] found that 73 per cent of parents with six and seven year olds helped their child with school work and John and Elizabeth Newson[11] report over 80 per cent of working class parents in Nottingham assist their seven year olds with their reading.

Moreover, when Teresa Smith[12] interviewed mothers in Oxfordshire with preschoolers, she found that

> more than half wished to play a larger part in their children's preschool group. More than two in three parents who were not involved would have liked to be, but they had not been asked or their offers of help had not been taken up by the staff running the groups. (p.174)

Barbara Tizard's interpretation is unequivocal. 'This evidence suggests that whatever the reason for the lower educational achievements of working class children, it is not lack of interest on the part of parents.' (p.12)

How then does one account for the teachers' mistaken perceptions of parents' willingness?

Ron Davie[4] and his co-researchers speculated that,

> quite apart from their educational ethos, schools are middle-class institutions. The staff are middle-class by definition and, by and large, this can be seen in their speech, their dress, their values and attitudes. Any social barrier can serve to intensify the social discomfort. (p.137)

This parent put it rather more graphically:

> When you're sort of lower-class and you get a person speaking really posh, you feel — I don't know how to put it — there's a wall. People can talk nice and it comes natural, you know that it isn't put on; but then you get another person talking really lah-di-dah and you feel they're putting on an act. They speak as though they know more than me about my own child or they know better than me about my own child. They won't accept what I have to say. That's what people in authority are like. (quoted by Fox,[13] p.14)

If teachers or therapists don't listen to your needs, why bother talking to them?

In Chapter 4 I shall return to the theme of working with 'reluctant' parents.

Families with Handicapped Children

The plethora of specialists and services for disabled children is eloquent testimony that these families need extra help. Moreover, many parents are prepared to go to extraordinary lengths if it will help their child. Even so, a minority may be unwilling for involvement. For example, in a survey of over 240 families with three- and four-year-old, severely mentally handicapped children in the Greater Manchester area, Dorothy Jeffree and I[14] found that one-third of parents were unwilling to become involved with a university-based project. We could find only two things that distinguished willing from unwilling parents: the further they lived from the university, the less inclined they were to be involved and, secondly, working mothers (either full-time or part-time) were less likely to express interest.

You have to remember, too, that there is no absolute percentage of parents who are willing to be involved. Rather the proportion will vary according to the type of scheme they are offered, for example a home-based scheme might attract more interest.

> Moreover, we have to accept that some parents will wish to opt out of whatever type of involvement we offer, either through force of circumstances (gross overcrowding of homes, severe social or marital problems, sheer emotional and physical exhaustion) or from a desire to lead a life of their own.

And as Peter and Helle Mittler[15] go on to add 'If we are serious about helping parents to choose, we must allow them to choose not to be involved at the level of detailed collaboration which some professionals are now offering.' (p.12)

In the field of disability a rather more subtle influence can operate which dampens the willingness of parents to be involved. Alan Sutherland[16] presents the view of one disabled lady, but I am sure she echoes many a parent's reaction too.

> They [professional workers] reduce our ability to function independently. Because they give you the impression that they're the only ones who know what's good for you, they reduce your belief that you can solve your own problems. They therefore reduce your motivation to get things sorted out in your own life. So then they'll produce somebody who'll come and deal with your lack of motivation. (p.182)

Bob van Zydirveld,[17] a social worker, summed up the attitudes of Dutch parents thus:

> It is our experience that parents in Holland are less interested than parents in Britain and some other countries, in contributing directly to what they consider to be the field of professionals . . . They expect the experts to known the solution to any problem, to train the child and to check

systematically on its psychological education. (p.210)

Thus the very growth of professional services could well decrease parents' motivation to share in your work.

If the Parents have never Asked you to Help them, Shouldn't you do the Asking?

It is not only teachers who believe that parents should take the initiative in seeking involvement. It's the view of most mothers and fathers whether their child is disabled or not. However, as Teresa Smith[12] discussed in her preschool survey, 'a large number of parents said they would like to help but had not been asked or their offers had not been taken up.' For example:

> I did ask her if there was any help she wanted, but she said no . . . They've got the time to do it themselves . . . There are three of them and they seem to be so happy; and I've noticed that the children start playing up when they see the mums. (p.119)

Maybe you will consider your perception of parents' willingness and perhaps ponder on this. Should there only be one willing parent, isn't that the beginning for working with parents? And you'll never know who it is, unless you ask.

Reason 3: Nobody Expects me to Work with Parents, so why Should I?

Working with parents will change your professional lifestyle, sometimes quite profoundly. The process of change is, at best, unsettling, at worst, traumatic. There is the risk, too, that the end result could be much less satisfying to you personally or that your hopes are not realised and you are made to feel a failure. All of which can be avoided by keeping on with the old familiar work routines.

And if we were really honest, should a boss come along and order you to work with parents, you could probably find ways of avoiding it. As Sally Tomlinson[18] argued,

All the professionals involved in special education should, despite their undoubted concern for individual children, recognise that much of what happens in special education is as much to do with their own particular vested interests as with the 'needs' of children. (p.277)

This is far removed from the third belief which I feel should underpin professionals' work with parents, namely

THE CUSTOMER IS ALWAYS RIGHT

This old maxim of shopkeepers was an overstatement, I admit, yet the fundamental philosophy it embodies about their relationship with customers rings true. I use it to jolt you into thinking about the relationship you have with your clients.

As a professional you are exhorted and expected to be objective, impartial and wise, three worthy attributes; summarised by my dictionary as 'not an amateur'. Interestingly, the definition it gives of amateur is 'one whose mastery is only superficial'!

Latterly somewhat more worldly attributes have accrued to the notion of professionalism, which run counter to consumerism. Barbara Tizard[9] noted three features:

- A central tenet of professionalism is the belief that, because of the professional's specialist knowledge, critical comments on his work cannot be made by laymen.
- Each profession tries to prevent laymen from encroaching on its territory. It is considered unacceptable for a professional to share or teach his professional skills to laymen or to allow laymen to carry out his tasks.
- To maintain professional status, it is also considered unacceptable for the professional to admit ignorance to the laymen or to ask him for opinion and advice.

In this scenario, the maxim changes to '*the shopkeeper is always right*'. The consequences for customers, however, are quite serious, as Jack Tizard and Susanna Mantovani[19] point out:

a purely professional service will not be able to provide for more than a fraction of the children who would benefit from it;

and by leaving out parents, such a service is likely, on the one hand, to weaken, rather than strengthen, their confidence and ability to act as good parents and, on the other hand, to enhance, rather than alleviate, mothers' feelings of depression, anxiety and low esteem. (p.31)

And, although they were talking particularly about preshool child care and education, their comments apply equally to handicap services. The reality, I suppose, is that neither the shopkeeper nor customer is *always* right; perhaps the word should be *usually*; it certainly could be *sometimes*. But to admit that both parties are *sometimes* right, allows for the truth of the converse: sometimes both are *wrong*. In my experience parents find this so much easier to admit than teachers or therapists:

He has tantrums at the training centre because they make him do things which is quite right. He needs discipline and he does not get it at home: I get it if I insist on him dressing himself; he raises Cain and I can't stand it so I give him a hand, which is wrong, I shouldn't do it. (Mrs Davis, quoted by Charles Hannam,[20] p.76)

It is no surprise then that some parents use experts as a cure for their uncertainties and lack of confidence. Professional omnipotence could be as much in the eye of the beholder as in the self-image of the 'expert'. But whatever its source, it is still an illusion. 'If you prefer illusion to realities', wrote George Santayana, 'it is only because all decent realities have eluded you and left you in the lurch.' So how can parents and professionals capture a decent reality?

Teresa Smith[12] concludes her book on *Parents and Preschool* with the suggestion:

If parental involvement is to mean more than communication or sharing information . . . then we must work hard for a more participative approach. We must recognise the boundaries that exist between the role of parents and professionals in many groups, whether subtly or openly, and experiment far more boldly with different ways of putting partnership between parent, child and professional into practice. (p.176)

Barbara Tizard's[9] conclusions at the end of her project on involving parents in nursery and infant schools, were strikingly similar:

> The need to uphold professional status by creating social distance between themselves [the teachers] and the parents prevented some of them from asking parents into the staffroom and most of them from developing out-of-school relationships with them. The advantages of this social distance for the teachers are obvious but a serious disadvantage is that it prevents them knowing much about the children's families, their lives out of school and the local community. (p.107)

Philippa Russell's[21] analysis of family needs from the parents' perspective and how they should be met, ends with these words:

> The fundamental problem lies in the creation of a genuine dialogue between the professional agency and the family. . . . The acceptance of the philosophy of parental involvement is seldom openly questioned but the nature of the partnership is one which needs further debate. (pp.57–8)

Removing boundaries, reducing social distance, the creation of a genuine dialogue: all challenging and daunting prospects; hard to visualise. The implication is probably caught best in Eric Midwinter's metaphor. Teachers (and others) will have to forsake the image of 'riding through enemy-occupied territory at 9.00 a.m. to man foreign-legion-type fortresses'.

A New Professionalism

If your image of professionalism does not square with what I have described thus far, perhaps you will read a little further before parting company. Professionalism is an evolving concept and here are some visions of the type of professionalism needed for the twenty-first century:

Peter Mittler[22]

> The highly trained professional must in future share and communicate his skills to others — to parents and families, to volunteers, to paid staff without training and qualifications. We must learn to give away what skills we have — indeed

learning to give away our skills is one of the most difficult skills that we ourselves have to learn and that we shall have to teach future generations of our students to learn. (p.16)
Jack Tizard and Susanna Mantovani[19]
Working with parents should mean enlisting the active participation of parents in the day-to-day life of the nursery, learning from, as well as teaching them, working together. To learn how to do this is perhaps the hardest skill of professional people to learn and practice; yet without this partnership the nursery is impoverished, and will always be short-staffed. (p. 48)
Patricia Potts[23]
The problem with the slogan, 'Parents as Partners', is that it implies that parents *are* partners, that things are all right now and that the improvement has been easy. But making permanent changes in client–professional relationship is far more difficult. (p.185)

'Most difficult' . . . 'hardest skill' . . . working with parents is not an easy option. That's why I believe it should not be forced on professionals against their will. It has to be their own decision. But in the last analysis, it all boils down to a question of parental rights and hence duties on the part of service providers. This notion has been developed most clearly in the United States.

Public Law 94-142, The Education for All Handicapped Children Act, passed in 1975 by the US Congress, included specific provisions for parental involvement in, and consent for, the educational programme developed by schools for handicapped children. The parents must be included in a planning team that considers the results of the assessments and develops the educational plan for their child, and must sign the plan to indicate their agreement. If they refuse to sign the plan, they can appeal the school's proposed plan to an administrative hearing convened by the state department of education, and later file suit in the US Federal court to revise it. Clearly the specific provisions of the Act indicate the importance placed by the US Congress on the positive participation of parents in the education and training of their children with special educational needs.[24]

Recent British legislation makes similar proposals. As the song says, 'the times they are a-changing'.

Your Decision

To sum up then, if you believe that:
● children learn more when parents, teachers and/or therapists work together
● most parents want to be involved in furthering their child's learning
● current images and styles of professionalism need changing
then I think you will find this book helpful, because it tries to give you practical guidance as to how working with parents can become a reality, a decent reality, for you.

On the other hand, if you are inclined to dispute some or all of these beliefs, then I guess you will perceive the remainder of the book as idealistic, irrelevant or infuriating, depending on your disposition or mood. Equally, of course, I am likely to regard you as prejudiced, egocentric and old-fashioned. And there, in a microcosm, is what this chapter is all about. The failure of two parties with a common purpose, failing to share, negotiate or learn from each other; surrounded as they are by mistaken perceptions.

2

What Does it Involve?

Human experts and rabbits have much in common.
Firstly, they multiply at a prolific rate. Secondly, they are
both highly susceptible to infection; rabbits catch myxo-
matosis and experts catch expertosis. The symptoms are
common to both: the head swells and the patient goes
blind.
(Cliff Cunningham)

It is easier to recognise when professionals are *not* working with
parents, than to give a precise definition of what it involves. I
readily accept that you may be convinced intellectually of the
need to work with parents but that your hesitations come from
uncertainty about what you will have to do. In part, the
confusion stems from the variety of terms used: some talk of
'parental *participation*', others of '*collaborating* with parents'. We
have had parental *involvement* projects, others have spoken of
training parents. The current vogue phrase is undoubtedly
'*partnership* with parents'.

There are some who would draw a distinction between these
various terms. For instance, Peter and Helle Mittler[15] write:

Parents may be productively involved in the work of
professionals and collaborate in the work of schools but this
may fall some way short of true partnership. Partnership can
be seen as an ideal, a goal towards which we should be
working . . . it involves a full sharing of knowledge, skills and
experience in helping children with special educational needs
to develop as individuals. (p.7)

Perhaps they are right: there may be different levels of grace
in our strivings for nirvana. Yet I can't help but think, moving
now from the sublime to the ridiculous, that this song has more

than a line of truth, 'it's not what you do, it's the way that you do it — That's what gets results.'

In this chapter, I'm *not* going to describe what you'll have to do: you'll get enough of that from page 79 onwards. Rather I shall focus on the way you do it and try to paint a picture of the manner, style and ethos entailed in working with parents.

Flexibility

The danger with a slogan like 'working with parents' is that it implies you are dealing with a uniform human species, of single mind and purpose. The individuality of John and Mary, Peter and Louise, is submerged once they don the mantle of parenthood. Nonsense!

No two parents are alike; even a husband and wife can differ in their attitudes and aspirations. Hence you cannot transpose a style that has 'worked' with one family on to another.

Helen McConachie[26] put her finger on the problem:

> Many professionals seem to find it easier to have a model parent in mind: one who sees her or his handicapped child as a special responsibility and a special challenge, who gives a lot of individual attention to the child and who is eager and organised to do special teaching and play sessions . . . [but] further progress in developing services for young mentally handicapped children is crucially dependent on understanding and respecting the range of different ways in which families think and live their lives. (p.125)

Even with the best of intentions, professionals can easily fall into the trap which Cliff Cunningham[25] describes:

> As we visit more families in the course of intervention programmes, we increase our confidence and expertise and with this the risk of expertosis. Suddenly we begin to pre-empt and short cut parents' questions. We stop manifestly working through developmental problems with parents, explaining our observations and analyses as we go; instead we recognise some increasingly familiar cue and are likely to produce an increasingly familiar recipe for action. (p.97)

Peter and Helle Mittler[15] conclude that, 'if professionals want to establish comfortable and productive relationships with parents, they will need to explore with each family afresh, what the situation means to them and how each family can "learn to live with" the handicapping condition of one member.' (p.49)

These are high ideals for newly graduated professionals to attain. Neither their tender years nor their college training will have prepared them adequately for such an adventure. Dorothy Jeffree,[27] in her usual common sense way, proposes an admirable solution: 'making relationships with parents obviously takes time, because making relationships with people takes time'.

It will, of course, come quicker with some parents than with others and you'll probably have your failures as well as your stunning successes. In summary, then, my advice is

AVOID UNIFORMITY: WELCOME DIVERSITY

Common Purpose

'Partnership is a word with many shades of meaning' wrote Freddie Brimblecombe.[24]

> In its best sense, it implies sharing — but sharing for a purpose which is creative. In this sense a partnership is formed because the participants believe that the product . . . will be enhanced through partnership to an extent which none of the participants would have achieved in isolation. (p.88)

It may be an exaggeration but generally most teachers and therapists are quite confident about what they are doing with children and why. This is less likely to apply to most parents, although it can apply to some. But even with confident parents, do they and professionals share a common purpose and are the 'unsure' parents always convinced that your goals are the right ones for their child?

It is probably another symptom of 'expertosis' that we have had so little research into parents' opinions, for instance, about what they feel their child should be learning in schools. A notable exception, a recent one, is the work of Barbara Tizard[9] and her colleagues, Jo Mortimore and Bebb Burchell. They asked parents and staff what they saw as the aims of nursery education. The majority of staff referred to furthering the children's intellectual development through stimulation or by enriching their language, usually through the medium of play. Parents had different views:

> Most of the mothers appeared unaware that the teachers were concerned with the children's intellectual development. They saw the nursery as a place where children learn to mix together, learned rhymes and songs, drawing and painting and, in the case of Asian children, English. A substantial minority was critical of this curriculum and thought that their children were 'just playing about at school'. Between a half and a fifth of parents in all the visits would have liked the children to start on reading and writing. Others mentioned swimming and music. But few parents expressed these views to the teachers. (pp.44–5)

Helen McConachie[26] interviewed parents of handicapped children and came to this conclusion:

> Advice [to parents] needs to be based on a full knowledge of the parents' own ideas and desires. There are many difficulties in gathering such information in a way which does not distort it . . . Programmes which respect the current organisation at home will be more successfully taken up than those which unwittingly demand changes in routine or ignore current family structures of child-care. (p.133–5)

The implication for professionals is

BE PREPARED TO LISTEN, OBSERVE AND NEGOTIATE

This is the only way to achieve a common purpose. But I must also admit that with some parents this will be an elusive goal.

Mariet van Hattum,[28] a Dutch parent, expresses the dilemma this way . . .

> The relationship between parent and child, differs fundamentally from the relationship between a teacher and child: for one thing, it is lifelong. Children occupy a central place in a teacher's work and the teacher has chosen to do this job.

However, should we take for granted that the child will have a central place in the parent's life? Parents have not chosen to have a handicapped child. (p.136)

The centrality of the child in the parent's life, is threatened when other concerns predominate: poor housing, ill-health, marital and social problems. The handicapped child's progress could be the least of a parent's worries and hence they see your overtures as irrelevant. Equally, other parents may well opt to lead a life of their own and they can rightly expect to experience some 'relief' both practically and emotionally when their child starts school or attends a therapist.

For most parents, though, there is no doubt that children, whether handicapped or not, do occupy a centrality in parents' lives which can extend far beyond 'reasonable' care. Many in their eagerness to help are only too willing to accept unquestioningly the inappropriate demands of a professional, only to suffer anew the shock of disillusionment and failure.

Finally, let's not forget that there is a trio involved in defining the common purpose: the handicapped person joins the parent–professional duo. Family Focus,[29] a group of Coventry parents with handicapped children, rightly perceived the extra negotiation this involves:

Professionals and parents should try to see the child as part of that partnership too, particularly where an older child is concerned. To that end, we [the parents] have to recognise that our views are not always congruent with their views about their needs. (p.194)

Mutual Respect

The success of any partnership lies in mutual respect. If one partner is suspicious or distrusting of the other, then the relationship will soon deteriorate.

It strikes me that there are two presumptions frequently made here, (1) that parents invariably have respect for professionals, but (2) that professionals' respect for parents needs to be built up. I think both are exaggerations, even if they basically are correct. Some parents don't have much respect for professionals and sometimes a professional's respect for parents is so overwhelming, that they give the family little or no help.

Parents' Respect for Professionals

You cannot take it for granted that a parent will respect either you or the work you are trying to do, simply because you have a title and draw a salary. Respect has to be earned. More often than not this is frighteningly easy to win. Parents can be embarrassingly grateful for the smallest amount of consideration and often their respect for a professional's authority and power is such that they would not dream of questioning his or her decisions: 'the teacher must know best'. Other parents may not want to seem 'pushy' or get a reputation for being 'awkward'. Consequently, professionals are often sheltered from their client's reactions.

It is a salutary experience for professionals to read some parents' experiences at the hands of their colleagues. For instance: Charles Hannam's[20] compilation of eight parents' experiences, entitled *Parents and their Handicapped Children*.

What will gain you the respect of parents? Two American researchers L.N. Huang and L.J. Heifetz[30] asked a sample of parents with 'organically damaged' children to recall the most helpful and the least helpful professional they had come across and to give a description of each. They found striking differences.

> The most frequent type of response dealt with *personal relatedness*. The most helpful professionals were typically recalled as being 'warm', 'interested', 'concerned', 'understanding' and 'sensitive'. Whereas the least helpful professionals were 'discouraging', 'insensitive' and 'cold and business-like'. The next most important dimension dealt with *parent–professional collaboration*, e.g. 'involves you in decision-making', versus 'doesn't listen to what you have to say'.

> Interestingly they discovered that

> the least most important item (although still statistically significant) in distinguishing the two groups, mainly involved *intra*personal (as opposed to interpersonal) qualities of the professionals. This included their experience, confidence and efficiency. (p.430)

In summary, the parents' respect grows as a *relationship* develops. And that, of course, is a two-way process, as the nursery-school teachers involved in Barbara Tizard's[9] research discovered.

> When we asked the staff what activity they thought had been the most worthwhile, the majority mentioned occasions which they considered fostered friendly staff–parent relationships; 'home-visiting', the 'Mother and Toddler Club' . . . 'coffee mornings'. Thus, despite the teachers' initial expressed concern to increase parents' understanding of nursery education, it was clear that what they most valued was the development of a feeling of personal trust between teachers and parents. (p.84)

Professionals' Respect for Parents

The reports of British governmental working parties are an excellent source of 'quotable' quotes, even if their recommendations for action are confined to oblivion. The Court Report[31] of an enquiry into child health services, did us all a great service when they wrote, 'We have found no better way to raise a child than to reinforce the abilities of his parents to do so'.

There in a nutshell is the kernel of professional respect: you are dealing with competent people. As Helen McConachie[26] observed, 'Parents have views on bringing up children which are not happened on by chance but have been worked out through considerable experience.' (p.133)

The implications though for practice have been slow to sink in. Here's how Cliff Cunningham[25] has tried to embody them in his Down's infant programme

> We do not attempt to 'transplant' professional skills into the home so that professional therapies, *per se*, are maintained and extended via the parent. Instead we offer parents what we feel is the necessary information for them to live with and help their infant with Down's syndrome. They then select from this according to their current needs and in their own time . . . Thus the parent is the consumer and like any consumer, can reject our 'goods'. This model ensures we remain firmly in the servicing and advising role and do not fall into the trap of 'professional authoritarianism'. (p.96)

Likewise, Sally Beveridge[32] highlights the need to develop parents' consistency and confidence in their own approach to the child:

> Some parents are naturally more creative than others in their approach, and prefer to intervene actively and to prompt their child's activities. Others are less directive and prefer to set up activities and then sit back and see what their child will do. We have attempted to respect the parents' preferred style of interaction, and take account of these and other differences between parents in developing an individualised approach to parent-teaching work. (p.120)

Finally, it is no comfort to an insecure unconfident parent to be told by a well-meaning but overwhelmed professional that they are doing a 'marvellous' job which couldn't be bettered! It is *mutual* respect that's needed and, in this instance, the parents' respect for the professional probably nose-dived. In essence what it is, all boils down to is, you must

CONSULT THE PARENTS AT LEAST AS OFTEN AS THEY CONSULT YOU

Shared Feelings

> We go and I never quite know if Mr X is taking in what I'm saying. There is never any reaction from him. I often wonder if I went in there and stripped off in front of him, if I would get a reaction then. He's completely passive and he nods and says 'Good' and 'Yes' and that's about the stretch. So it's good in that the child's seen regularly and Mr X has got an excellent reputation, but not so good in that you go wanting to know how he's getting on and you come out with a vague feeling that you never went. (p.127)

Those are a Scottish mother's words as reported by Neill Richardson,[33] but she could have been speaking for many other parents throughout the length and breadth of the land. Elizabeth Newson and Tony Hipgrave[34] devote the final chapter of their excellent handbook to the theme of feelings and this is the advice they give to parents, professionals are not *immune* from feelings — in fact if you meet a professional who really seems to have no natural feelings or emotions, this probably means that he has quite serious emotional hang-ups about whether he is doing his job properly. Some professionals are afraid to show the feelings they have. (p.100)

They go on to add that the result is that 'the parents often have to bear the extra stress' which in some cases leads them to blame themselves. For instance, here's another mother's answer to Neill Richardson's[33] question about her visits to a clinic.

Depressing. I suppose you are always looking for something good. But you know you get 'he hasn't made much progress'. And that's that. I come back crying and depressed. He's a very nice man, but he's just very frank. It must be me. I'm always looking for good news. (p.127)

In fact, professionals have too readily 'blamed' parents and described them variously as over-anxious, guilt-ridden, anxiety-laden, over-protective and rejecting. Elizabeth Newson and Tony Hipgrave[34] assert that these labels 'can very seldom be justified' and go on to add:

It's a great pity when it happens, because it not only makes the professional faulty in his judgement of parents but also gets in the way of proper communication. In this sort of case, it may sometimes be worthwhile for parents, *calmly*, to ask the professional whether this *is* what he is thinking. (p.103)

Rod Ballard[35] is well qualified to take up this theme, writing as he does both as a parent and as a professional.

If you have a handicapped child, you have got to learn a lot about yourself very quickly and it is possible that this process will be facilitated if the professional people around can recognise that crises can create growth in one's ability to cope, provided that it is used in a constructive way. What seems to happen . . . is that the bits of the coping parts of one's personality get shaken up at times of crises and if there are people around at the time able to offer supplies of warmth and caring, these bits fall together in a new arrangement which is better ordered to deal with all the stresses and strains which life brings. (p.101)

Likewise, Peter and Helle Mittler,[5] from their experiences too as parents, advise professionals to share

their initial reaction to handicap and early difficulties and failures because it may make parents more comfortable in expressing their own doubts and worries. Similarly professionals and parents can help each other through difficult periods when little progress is being made and it is only too easy to be discouraged. (p.46)

Strangely enough, the hardest feelings of all for professionals to express seems to be a sense of enjoyment and satisfaction with the child. Neill Richardson's[33] report contains the following comment,

When asked: 'Tell me the sort of thing you enjoy about N?' one mother, probably speaking for many, responded, 'Nobody has ever asked me that before . . . you know, I don't think it ever occurs to you sort of people that we might like our kids!' (p.48)

BE OPEN ABOUT YOUR FEELINGS SO THAT THE PARENTS CAN BE OPEN ABOUT THEIRS

Exchange of Knowledge

Partnerships are based on the premise that two heads are better than one. However, sharing the knowledge each has is not an easy thing to do. Israel Scheffler,[36] an educational philosopher, distinguishes between information and knowledge. He wrote:

Knowledge requires something more than the receipt and acceptance of true information. It requires that the student earn the right to his assurance of the truth of the information in question. New *information*, in short, can be intelligently conveyed by statements, new *knowledge* cannot. (p.126)

For professionals, this means that no amount of listening to parents' experience or reading about them can convey a complete understanding of what it is like to be the mother or father of a handicapped child. Many a parent has proposed that each new professional should spend at least 24 hours living with the family to experience for themselves what the parents feel they describe inadequately.

Equally, the parents have a knowledge of their child that certainly no therapist and few teachers could rival, for all their expertise and training. As such, they are an invaluable resource for professionals. Elizabeth Newson[37] put it this way:

> We should start from the basic assumption that parents in fact have information to impart; that parents are experts on their own children. This is not to say that they know of their children in any systematic or integrated form; one cannot ask the parent to bring along an ordered case history . . . None the less, they know more about the child, on a very intimate level, than anyone else does; the fact that their knowledge may be diffuse and unstructured does not matter, so long as it is available. It is the professional's job to make it available; structuring can come later. (p.105)

Later, she goes on to recount an incident that illustrates clearly the importance of action in conveying this knowledge:

> 'I don't think I'd let her get away with that' said one mother, when the psychologist, tentative with a child he did not know well enough yet, was 'kid-gloving' to avoid a tantrum. 'Show us how you would handle it' was the reply and with a rapid switching of roles, the mother proceeded to do so, teaching us in the process more about what her daughter could do with a little pressure. (p.108)

Interviewing might convey information; actions transmit knowledge. I shall return to the need to watch parents interacting with their child in the next section. (p.92)

Professional's Knowledge

Just because teachers and therapists learn from being with parents does not mean that this is the best way for parents to share in the professional's knowledge. For instance, a welcome development has been the opportunity for parents to sit in on an assessment of their child or to spend some time in the classroom. But if they aren't given the rationale for what's going on, they could possibly end up more confused than enlightened.

Teresa Smith[12] ends her study on parents and preschools with this recommendation:

> Open access and shared experience, even when they are achieved, do not necessarily on their own bring about a better understanding or greater knowledge about an educational role in the interaction between parent and child. Parents may need far more explanation and discussion than they are given at present at every level about the group, their children and their role. (p.175)

Barbara Tizard[9] reports a very similar conclusion:

> Our evidence suggests that unless efforts are specifically directed to explaining what the teacher sees to be the purpose of play materials, most mothers will think the activities are to keep the children amused. Visiting or helping in the classroom will not, in itself, bring parents closer to the teacher's point of view. What the mothers saw was children filling bottles of water; what the teachers saw was the children acquiring the foundations of science. (p.66)

Sometimes the misunderstandings have a humorous side! After a psychological assessment, during which my colleague naturally enough made reference to the test manual, one mother commented to me, 'he had to keep consulting his book to see what the results of the different tests meant. I feel he should not have to look it up'.

The solution, according to Cliff Cunningham,[25] is threefold:

> It is essential that the parent is constantly encouraged (1) to understand why the activity is important for the child; (2) to invent and augment the ideas of how it can best be carried out; (3) to observe for themselves the progress being made from which to make their own decisions for change.

He adds, 'It is too easy and too comfortable to provide packaged recipes for action which do not require parental involvement at these levels.' (p.97) The latter runs the real risk of *increasing* rather than decreasing parents' dependence on specialist help and, by implication, eroding parents' autonomy and self-confidence.

So what pithy comment will help stick these messages in your mind? I recall Marion Blank's assertion that of all the questions teachers can ask children, the most demanding are those which begin 'why?' They are a real test of a child's understanding. Hence my advice to you is:

ALWAYS ASK WHY

Kurt Vonnegut expressed it more poetically:

> Tiger got to hunt, bird got to fly,
> Man got to sit and wonder, 'Why, why why?'
> Tiger got to sleep, bird got to land;
> Man got to tell himself, he understand.

Joint Decisions

Although I come to this last, it is no reflection of its importance. Quite the opposite. Joint decision-making epitomises a partnership in action. When one or other partner starts making all the decisions, the partnership has dissolved. Two outcomes then ensue, either each goes his or her own way, or one falls in line behind the other. The first is, by and large, the role which parents have been expected to fulfil in relation to experts. Indeed, Patricia Potts[23] would argue, that the new era of partnership with parents is largely window-dressing on the part of professionals. The underlying message, the 'internal memo of the professional gang', she imagines reads something like this:

> Keep parents in the classroom, playroom or sitting room and off the management committee; second, let parents support the work of the professionals rather than question it; third, as parents do not have the specialised skills and knowledge to help their children on their own, professional jobs need not be

threatened; fourth, working with parents prevents them from organising themselves too well into a separate force and can actually extend the professional role. (p.185)

There certainly is a wariness among professionals about involving parents; Barbara Tizard[9] writes:

> All but two of the staff saw potential dangers in trying to increase parental involvement. Some were concerned about their authority. 'You must be firm. Otherwise if you give them half a chance, they'd take over the place.' (p.48)

The researchers then interviewed both teachers and parents about whether or not parents should be consulted over certain special issues such as school rules, curriculum and selection of teachers. They found that one-third of teachers were prepared to listen to parents' opinions on the curriculum — 'I'd be prepared to discuss with the mothers. I'd tell them my reasons and justify them but in the end I'd decide.' But two-thirds of teachers thought this was the sole preserve of teachers.

As for parents:

> Just under half would like to be asked for opinions on the curriculum . . . but the majority parent opinion was summed up by one mother, 'No, teachers are trained to know these things'.

The research team concluded:

> While we found little evidence then, that parents want to take over schools, we did find that about half the parents would like to be asked for their opinions and suggestions about school matters. The other half of the parents interviewed argued that what went on inside the school was the teacher's business. The proportion of mothers who wanted to be consulted was the same in middle-class and working-class areas. (p.89)

Perhaps paranoia is an occupational hazard of professionals. Joint decision-making, which is in the best interest of all three parties (children, parents and professionals), should follow naturally if the previous five features of a successful partnership are maintained. And, as Barbara Smith,[38] a teacher and parent, wisely observes:

> There will be those parents who do not wish to engage in any form of joint involvement with the school. I believe that this is a right which parents have and which should be recognised by professionals. (p.147)

But to come back to those parents who want to be involved in decision-making, we should not underestimate the difficulty this presents to *professionals* whose training and job experience has emphasised both their autonomy and expertise in deciding what's best. Helen McConachie[26] writes:

> It is often still the case that parents are told what the child's programme should be, without involvement in the decision-making, even if they are to be the main agent in carrying out the programme. Once a programme has been entered into by parents, they may feel they have no alternative but to drop out if it fails to take account of their present situation. (p.134)

The solution she envisages is echoed by many others:

> The important thing is not the invention of new structures of services but rather flexibility in responding to each individual family over time. And that requires professionals to really listen to parents and siblings. (p.134)

Finally, another scenario is possible when one partner takes all the decisions: they split. The 1970s saw a remarkable resurgence in parent-run services and in parent-consumer bodies. Groups such as the Preschool Playgroups Assocation (PPA) now offer a much more extensive service than that provided by the state and one which its proponents argue is a better service, simply because it is parent-managed. Jerry Bruner[39] pays them this accolade:

> The principal genius of the playgroup world is in the zest and autonomy of its local PPA groups to whom the parent organisation provides point of view, training and advice . . . National PPA remains at a discreet distance; it neither formulates policies for local groups nor attempts to change

practice by any save indirect means. (p.194)

The winds of change can also be felt in services for handicapped children, although the fewer numbers, greater vulnerability of families and greater geographical spread has blunted their effectiveness as a separate force.

Nevertheless, in the United States, a major provision of the recent Education for All Handicapped Children Act (Public Law 94-142; 1975) is that parents serve on the Individual Education Program Committee with status equal to that of the committee's professional members.

In Britain, too, Barbara Tizard[9] notes

> a growing belief that public services and professionals should be held accountable to their clients. As Halsey has put it, we have moved into a world 'in which all social relations are increasingly subjected to the authority of negotiation'. (p.19)

Cliff Cunningham[25] cites one example of the impact his work with families has had on the statutory services:

> Recently several professionals and students who have short attachments to the programme have expressed surprise at the parents' questions and dealings with them; as one social worker put it, 'They have obviously been well trained at coping with us.' (p.48)

Both he and others note in particular the impact on schools of a family's prior involvement in home-based teaching schemes for preschool children. Gillian Pugh[40] writes of one such scheme in Wales:

> Relationships with schools have in the past presented some problems, particularly for parents who have become closely involved in their child's development and in planning further goals and who find their enthusiasm viewed with some suspicion by teachers. (p.48)

Joint decision-making, the natural outcome of working with parents, has far-reaching consequences for the structure and style of services we offer families and children. The tidal currents within our society are submerging old models of authority and bringing with them a new egalitarianism. Young professionals unfettered by the anchors of tradition and habits, have a much greater chance of swimming with the tide, provided that they remember:

DON'T GO IT ALONE

Have you the Qualities Needed for Partnership?

It's at this point, that I could have asked you to complete a questionnaire along the lines of those in popular magazines, so that you could determine your score on the 'will I make a good partner' test. I decided against, not because it would have cheapened the tone of this learned volume, but because it's *not* what you are now that counts but what you're prepared to become: be it through training, practice or experience. If you are prepared

- to avoid uniformity and welcome diversity
- to listen, observe and negotiate
- to consult as well as be consulted
- to be open about your feelings so that your partners can be open about theirs
- to ask why and to answer why
- *not* to go it alone

then you'll find working with parents a rewarding experience.

And should there be any parents who have read this far and are rather smugly thinking 'Yes, why can't they all be like that?', remember all these six characteristics apply to you as well and some parents don't score too high either. Both partners need to dance to the same rhythm.

3

What Can I do?

First, say to yourself, what you would be; and then do
what you have to do.
(Epictetus, second century BC)

Never argue with a Greek philosopher is my motto. Having dealt
with the first part of his admonition, I will now hasten on to
describe what working with parents can mean in practice. This
could vary depending on your profession. The opportunities for
teachers will be different from those open to therapists,
psychologists or doctors. However, in the listings which follow, I
have made no distinction because increasingly 'traditional' ways
of working are, or should be, blurred.

Rather I have chosen to group parent–professional activities
along three dimensions: first, those which focus on an individual
family versus those aimed at groups of parents, both small and
large; secondly, the point of contact, whether it is primarily face-
to-face between parent and professional or at a distance; thirdly,
activities designed to increase family-to-family contact. This
results in five categories of activities but, needless to say, the
same activity can occur within more than one category. I should
stress, too, that some activities will suit some parents more than
others. They are included as possibilities, not prescriptions, for
all.

The resulting lists are not my invention. Rather I have
summarised activities that have been used successfully by various
professionals in a range of settings. These have been described in
the writings of Barbara Smith,[38] Peter and Helle Mittler,[15]
Gillian Pugh,[40] Barbara Tizard and colleagues[9] and to which I
have added a few experiences of my own. Many of these
activities will be described and discussed in more detail in later
sections of the book. However, at this point, I simply want to
show you the tremendous range of possibilities which exist in
developing a closer working relationship with parents. Some of
these require little extra effort on your part but all need to be

endued with the ethos described in the previous chapter. You might like to use the tables as a checklist, marking off those items which you have done already; those that appeal to you and those that you definitely could not, or would not, do!

As I began with a Greek philosopher, I might as well end with another, Aristotle. He reminds us where the power of decision lies: 'What it lies in your power to do, it lies in your power not to do'. The choice is yours.

Table 3.1: Individual Parents: Face-to-Face

- Professional visits the home
    - sees home surroundings
    - meets the family: father and siblings
    - hears about child's out-of-school activities
    - answers parents' questions
    - observes family's ways of teaching/handling child
    - demonstrates teaching/handling strategies

- Parents visit professionals
    - observe professionals working with child (e.g. sits in class or is present during assessments)
    - answers parents' questions, explains, discusses
    - observes parents' ways of handling child
    - video-records the parents and analyses the playback with them
    - shows parents video examples to get the message across

- Arranges for 'interpreter' with immigrant families

- Gives parents developmental charts/skills checklist to complete for their child; compares parents' ratings with theirs

- Parents attend case conferences on their child

- Helps parents select books, toys, teaching equipment for home use

- Organises review sessions to discuss the child's progress

- Gives parents a written report of the results of assessments

- Leaves the parents a written summary of recommendations for home activities

- Lets parents see the file on their child and discusses content with them

- Invites parents to help in the classroom; brings them to the school staffroom

- Arranges for parent(s) to talk to students or existing staff about their experiences and views on services, etc.

Table 3.2: Individual Parents: at a Distance

- Comments exchanged via home–school diary (weekly or fortnightly)

- Therapist–home diary used when child sees a therapist regularly

- Write term reports on child

- Personal letters from teacher/therapist to the parents

- Telephone contacts: parents provided with the home phone number of professionals and vice versa

- Loan video-programme to parents for home-viewing

- Make audio-recordings for less-literate parents or have translations done for immigrant families

- Send home toys, books, teaching equipment

- Have parents complete development chart/skills checklist

- Recommend 'homework' they could do with their child

- Provide 'holiday kit' of activities that parents can use with their child

- Let parents have access to their child's file

- Send home copies of new songs or rhymes learnt in school

- Suggest television programmes the parents and children could watch together, e.g. those with an educational slant

Table 3.3: Work with Groups of Parents: Face-to-Face

- Meeting of children's parents in your class to share information, review progress and discuss future plans

- Give a talk and answer questions at parents' meetings

- Organise a parents' 'Workshop' with talks, role-play, practical activities at home

- Devise a course for parents on a specific topic or use existing parent courses such as those of the Open University

- Show the parents video-recordings or slides of the children at school and explain why the activities are used

- Have an open session in class

- Hold open days or evenings for the school

- Organise a Parent–Teachers Association to arrange social events

- Involve parents in planning and organising special events at festival times like Christmas

- Encourage parents to form a rota to 'lend-a-hand' with activities such as horse-riding, swimming or on mini-excursions to the shops, local schools

- Interview parents about their reactions to services received and about changes they would like to see

Table 3.4: Work with Groups of Parents: at a Distance

- Provide a school prospectus: details of teachers, school routines, etc.

- Give parents a leaflet about therapy: how to contact therapists, etc.

- Prepare a class newsletter which is sent home regularly

- Organise book or toy exhibitions for parents

- Write out suggestions of home activities or possible outings

- Prepare leaflet describing assessment procedures and how results are arrived at

- Loan parents books or arrange for them to borrow photocopied extracts

- Send a questionnaire to ascertain parents' views

- Have a notice-board or blackboard outside class or in waiting room giving 'news' items

- Write articles for local newspapers or magazines

- Make a video-programme for parents

- Write a manual or handbook giving suggestions for learning activities which parents could use at home

Table 3.5: Encourage Parent–Parent Contacts

- Initiate 'baby-sitting' circle among a group of parents

- Arrange for experienced parent to visit family with a new handicapped baby

- Organise mother and toddler group within school

- Have a parent's den within the school or clinic

- Nurture parent self-help groups: evening meetings in each other's houses

- Invite fathers to help make or repair equipment

- Ensure there are parent representatives on the management board and planning teams of the school or service

- Encourage parents to be involved in the work of community health councils and health boards, either in lobbying officials or standing for election

- Promote membership of parent voluntary organisations, e.g. Down's Syndrome Association, Mencap

- Assist parents to organise leisure pursuits for their children, e.g. youth clubs, holiday schemes

4

How do I Cope with these Parents?

A smooth sea never made a skilful mariner.
(English proverb)

After a talk to a professional audience about working with parents, I am very often asked a question like, 'How do you work with fathers or single parents or low-income families or those from minority groups?' I like to think that the questioner is eager for fresh challenges, even though battle-scarred from current experiences, but my cynicism sometimes gets the better of me and I suspect my interrogator is trying to prove that if you can't work with this sort of parent, then it isn't worth working with parents at all because they are the only ones who need it.

I hope the answers outlined in this chapter are an adequate reply to both types of questionner. I don't want to underestimate the extra difficulties you are likely to encounter but in recent years, especially, we have gathered the know-how of getting a foot in the door. I also want to explore what the opposite concept might mean, that of the 'willing parent', and, finally, point out some ways whereby you can get support which helps to maintain your stamina for work with parents.

The concept of professionals working in partnership with parents is a new departure, barely a decade old. We have only just begun to test its possibilities and potential. Inevitably there will be difficulties and disappointments, perhaps even distress. The seas will certainly not always be smooth.

Fathers

The importance of the mother–child relationship has been so much stressed in recent years, that it almost seemed fathers

need merely to provide material things for their offspring. Work with handicapped children has shown how mistaken this view is. Where the father shares responsibility of upbringing and care, there is a much better chance of the child's triumphing over his disabilities than if the mother is left to cope by herself.
(Mia Kellmer-Pringle,[41] p.62)

The positive contribution that fathers can and do make to their child's upbringing, has been a recent theme in the developmental literature; another plus for woman's liberation! Mia Kellmer-Pringle rightly points out the extra benefits that accrue to children with disabilities, presuming, of course, that the father is willing and able to share in the responsibility.

David Wilkin[42] interviewed 120 families in the Salford area near Manchester in the north of England and explored the fathers' involvement in the caring routines of their handicapped son or daughter. He discovered that there were only two tasks in which more than half of fathers were described as participating equally with wives: lifting and carrying the child (a necessity because of the weight of some of the older profoundly handicapped children) and in baby-sitting. In other areas of physical care, dressing, washing and feeding, fewer than one in four regularly participated. Those most likely to be involved were the unemployed, those in higher social classes (skilled non-manual and above) and fathers aged between 31 and 40 years.

Likewise, in a survey of 67 Dublin families with a severely mentally handicapped child between the ages of two and 15 years, John McEvoy and I[43] found that only 49 per cent of fathers had a daily play session with their child, compared with 85 per cent of mothers. The percentage playing at least weekly was 30 per cent for fathers and 12 per cent for mothers.

David Wilkin compared his results with those found with families of ordinary children and concluded that fathers of handicapped children

were not very different from most ordinary fathers in the extent of their contribution but the difficulties faced by their wives were much worse than those faced by most other mothers. (p.133)

He goes on to argue that we need to re-examine the paternal role in child-rearing, although cautions that the way this is tackled requires careful consideration. Part of the problem may be fathers' lack of know-how:

Some fathers, although prepared to mind the handicapped child, did not know what to do with him or her. The father's role in the upbringing of normal children tends to mean he has little experience in the sort of play and learning activities appropriate to very young children. The severely mentally handicapped child often remains at this level, thus making it difficult for the father to become involved. (p.134)

Helen McConachie[26] pinpoints other reasons as well:

[Fathers] may feel left out of the process of getting and giving information, through being at work during the child's probably numerous clinic appointments or visits by educational home visitors. They have less chance to talk about their feelings and may not easily meet other parents in the same position. They may feel incompetent with this child who is 'different' and so tend to give up. They may feel bitterly disappointed that their ambitions for their child will not be realised. (pp.128–9)

If this analysis is correct, then there are some obvious steps which professionals can take to provide fathers with the opportunities for more involvement.

John Hattersley and Laurence Tennant[44] argue that these should be available right from the start. As part of their parent workshop programmes in Worcestershire special schools, they arranged evening meetings once a month for fathers to meet to discuss their child's progress with the head teacher and psychologist and to explore the implications for them of the workshops which were held in school hours, attended by mothers. But only a handful of fathers ever turned up. Their confession could be echoed by many another eager organiser, 'It was clear that we had not produced the right formula for involving the majority of fathers'.

So what's the right formula? They suggest:

Perhaps the only way to change this position is to offer help to families long before their children start school so that fathers can be helped to avoid adopting a passive or minor role with respect to their handicapped child. (pp.80–1)

I'm sure they're right, although unlike them I wouldn't put all my eggs in one basket and see it as the only way. Indeed, Cliff Cunningham's[25] experiences on the Down's Babies Project, suggest that the beginning can be a particularly trying time for fathers:

> My experience suggests that fathers are more likely to have difficulties in accepting the condition and . . . many fathers seem to prefer discussing the problem of adjustment with a man during this first phase [i.e. shock]. I would also note that whilst we see both parents together at the first visit, it is often useful to see parents separately by discretely managing one's visiting. (p.100)

Helen McConachie[26] cautions against a blanket exhortation for fathers to be more involved with their handicapped child. She predicts that the 'primary effect could be to increase the burden on the mother, through feeling that it is their failure if the father is not involved.' (p.129) She goes on to point out the need for more information about the father's role in the family, and in her study with 19 fathers found 'striking' differences in the extent of their interaction and involvement with their severely handicapped children. Five couples shared time and responsibility for the child at weekends, whereas in eleven the mother was always the primary caretaker. She suggests:

> In some families it seems an obvious step to involve fathers as well as mothers in planned programmes. In other families we may need to proceed more carefully. The present routine will have its own momentum which we might threaten by suggesting unrealistic changes. (p.131)

There is some controversy among parental-involvement researchers as to whether the involvement of fathers does affect the outcome of the treatment programme with the child. Bruce Baker[45] concludes his review thus:

> While having a spouse is predictive of success, it does not

seem to matter whether he or she is involved in the intervention program, a finding that seems at odds with theories of family process.

He rightly goes on to speculate that

> it does seem possible, none the less, that there are unmeasured delayed benefits of having both spouses involved if only to prevent such a strong alliance between the teaching parent and handicapped child that the rest of the family is excluded. (p.362)

Mia Kellmer-Pringle[41] sees benefits for mothers in having fathers who are supportive if not actively involved.

> The mother herself probably receives reassurance in her maternal role from her husband's support, so that he 'reinforces' not only the child's but her own feelings of adequacy and self-esteem; this in turn increases her confidence in her mothering which communicates itself to the child. (p.61)

So what does this boil down to in practice?
● Get to know the *family*: fathers as well as mothers, other brothers and sisters
● Time your contacts so that fathers have a chance to talk to you
● Personally contact fathers if you are particularly eager to involve them: a telephone call or letter to both '*Mr & Mrs*'
● It may seem chauvinistic, but some fathers will relate better to men, especially when talking about their feelings
● Provide leaflets or written notes so that fathers can be kept up-to-date

The distinction between encouraging fathers to avail of the opportunities you provide and pressuring them into accepting is more real on paper than in practice, mainly because it has to vary according to each family. This is where your professional judgement will be tested.

Finally, if present trends continue, at some point in the future, much of this discussion would be centred around involving mothers and finding ways they can support fathers in their child-rearing responsibilities! If so, the same strategies will still apply because our goal is to make allies of both parents.

Single Parents / Working Mothers

Many children now live with only one parent, generally the mother. Unsupported mothers have special problems, although special financial incentives in the form of grants [welfare] are available, these are rarely adequate to provide help with the day-to-day task of looking after a home and caring for and working with a handicapped child.
(Peter and Helle Mittler,[15] p.13)

Most single mothers are forced to find work, either part-time or full-time. This obviously reduces their availability and energy to work alongside professionals. Bruce Baker and his colleagues[46] analysed the characteristics of parents who had enrolled in and completed his parent-training programme at the University of California in Los Angeles, USA. They, and others, have found that

single parents have been less likely to complete training programs. Moreover, those who have completed training were less likely to demonstrate lasting benefits. In a follow-up study of 83 families with retarded children, the likelihood that a parent who began training, completed the program, attained proficiency and followed-through some during the subsequent six months was only 14 per cent for single parents compared with 59 per cent for parents with intact marriages. (p.361)

As the Mittlers hint, a realistic allowance paid to these mothers would solve some of their financial worries and arguably could be cost-effective if a crisis was to be averted: for instance, the children having to come into care. Professionals can lobby politicians on this issue.

In the short-term though, we need to tailor our demands to the parent's availability. Again, each one is different. Some will be keen to extract the maximum benefits from the time they spend with their child and will be eager for your advice and support. Remember, too, the practical difficulties facing working mothers which could give the impression that they were disinterested. For instance, evening or weekend meetings will suit them better.

Bruce Baker[45] suggests that a critical dimension is not being single *per se*, but lacking another person who will provide support: recall Mia Kellmer-Pringle's comments on the need to bolster a parent's feeling of adequacy and self-esteem. His team initiated a policy of encouraging single parents to bring a friend or relative with them to the meetings; most did and the drop-out rate reduced. This is a role that a trusted professional could fulfil, particularly one who visited the home regularly, or you could invite the people who care for the child while the mother is at work to come with the mother. You might initiate 'aunty' or 'granny' schemes. In these, a person from the community befriends the family and lends a hand in caring for the child so that the mothers can have a break.

Finally, social changes in our society have meant that more mothers opt to continue working rather than be tied to the home for all or part of the day. They want to lead their own lives alongside parenting their children.

In fact, David Wilkin[42] found that the majority of mothers he interviewed in Salford in the north of England expressed a desire to go out to work or to work for longer hours if they were already working. The reason given most frequently was for more social contacts (the extra income was secondary). Some mothers have argued persuasively that they are all the better parents for having a break from their child:

> 'Quite honestly, it lets me recharge my batteries, I can appreciate and enjoy him all the more than if I was with him day in, day out.'

As Teresa Smith[12] points out, professionals have not always been too sympathetic to working mothers

> We heard a number of comments about mothers going back to work 'too soon' or playgroups not being in business to cater for mothers to 'dump' their children. Working mothers often regretted the difficulty of being involved or felt guilty about not putting in their full share of effort. (p.164)

Maintaining the role of parent and worker entails extra negotiation both within the family as well as with outside agencies. Old stereotypes and routines have to give way to the new reality, although as yet we have a limited picture of how this will look. Potentially the biggest asset is that more and more professionals are themselves working mothers.

One head of a day centre told Caroline Garland and Stephanie White:[47]

> 'We have to give an awful lot to those mums — They've got a lot on their plate, and I know what it is like because I am working too.' (p.102)

Low-Income Families

> Families willing to be involved in parent intervention programs, tended to come from the upper levels of the disadvantaged population. Research findings indicate that at the most deprived levels, families are so overburdened with the task of survival that they have neither the energy nor the psychological resources necessary to participate in an intervention program involving the regular visit of a stranger to the house.
>
> (Urie Bronfenbrenner,[1] p.250)

Even the Head Start programmes, that made intensive efforts to involve disadvantaged parents, had their failures. The families referred to in the above quotation require resources far beyond the scope of one helping professional. Among those outlined by Urie Brofenbrenner are increasing the number and status of part-time jobs available to disadvantaged parents, introducing parent-apprentice programmes in schools to engage older children in supervised care of the young and creating patterns of mutual assistance among disadvantaged families living in the same neighbourhood.

But let's not forget that many low-income families do cope, not only with these and other social pressures but they provide loving care for a handicapped child. The label 'low-income' implies a uniformity which does not exist.

One ironical truism well known to every helping professional is that the very people generally in need of statutory services are the least likely to avail of them. For instance, in the British National Child Development Study,[4] it was found that children from unskilled working-class families were least likely to be brought to 'toddler' clinics or to child guidance services. Yet at seven years of age, their educational standards were lower and their school adjustment poor and many had signs of delayed development. But still their parents tended not to seek a discussion with the teachers. 'The answer,' according to Ron Davie,[4] 'must surely be that either the statutory services are not in general seen by these parents as being relevant to their child's welfare; or else there are barriers, physical or psychological, to their attending.' (p.392) Among the latter, he includes the 'inevitable social distance' between the helpers and the helped. Or as Michael Harrington wrote, 'people who are much too sensitive to demand of cripples that they run races, ask of the poor that they get up and act like everyone else in society.'

So how can we ever adapt the working relationship that suits us to one that these parents will value? Bruce Baker[45] collated the evidence from the research literature in relation to encouraging parents to attend meetings:

● choose a venue that is central and familiar to the parent's home
● provide child-care facilities
● reimburse travelling expenses or arrange pick-ups
● organise a 'lottery' with prizes, toys, plants and foodstuffs, and give tickets for attendance and completed home assignments. Award diplomas at completion of the course (apparently these schemes work well with middle-class Americans too)
● utilise videos or demonstrations rather than talks or written materials. Make it less like school and more like entertainment
● when arranging a systematic course, allow parents to work through at their own pace, ensuring they master each step before moving on to the next.

But by far the most frequent solution for engaging low-income families in services, has been based on the premise, 'if they won't come to us, we'll go to them!' By now, most western countries have their own experience of educational home-visiting services in disadvantaged areas. Indeed, some have been so successful that they were lifted lock, stock and barrel and applied to other needy populations, such as parents of mentally handicapped children, for whom they were never designed. The Portage Project in Wisconsin, USA, is a good example. Here home teachers were employed to visit familes in rural areas who had no access to preschool facilities. They instructed parents — usually mothers — in the selection of appropriate teaching tasks, on how to present them and on how to adapt them according to the child's progress. This model of service provision to families has since been successfully implemented in other parts of the US and in many other countries.

The key element in their success has been the *regular* visits by a professional worker, variously described as a 'home visitor/ teacher/therapist'. Their role, as Philippa Russell[21] points out, is much wider than their title would imply and certainly extends far beyond dishing out a teaching recipe from the curriculum packages which are mistakenly seen by some as the core of the programme.

● They can adjust the demands of the home intervention programme to what is possible with a particular family and the level of commitment that is likely to be forthcoming.

● The practical needs of the family can be served. Washing machines and tumble driers purchased from special grants may be critical to the success of any programme, if they can give the mother *time*.

● Places can be arranged for siblings in playgroups or other preschool facilities.

● Advice can be given on aids and adaptations.

● Transport can be arranged for hospital or other clinic visits.

● The home visitor might accompany parents on visits to clinic and to other professional consultants and act as an advocate, intermediary, translator or support as necessary. This element has been highlighted by the Honeylands Scheme in Exeter, which is described in Gillian Pugh's[40] book.

● Parents can talk to a professional whom they see regularly on sensitive personal areas which they might hesitate to share with a 'one-off' team visit or a busy hospital doctor.

All of these points apply equally well to better-off families, but they do have a particular significance with disadvantaged parents. As David Wilkin[42] discovered, mothers in lower social classes were less likely than other mothers to express need for additional support in child-care and household tasks, although in material terms they were probably worse off. As Philippa Russell[21] wisely observed:

> Since most of us who are parents wish to appear competent, it may take the objective eye of a professional to observe what the practical needs really are and to seek to alleviate them. (p.50)

I do not want to leave the impression that home visiting is in itself a panacea. Indeed as Sarah Sandow[48] describes, it can be quite a trial for a home teacher to work with the child, 'surrounded by three generations of a mutually hostile family, in an atmosphere composed of equal parts cigarette smoke, sweat and old chip papers'. Reconciling the needs of a child with those of the parent remains an elusive art towards which we strive, although few have mastered.

Immigrant Families

Not infrequently the families of coloured immigrant children are large and have a low income; their housing conditions tend to be unsatisfactory; family relationships may be more often impaired . . .; language and hence educational handicaps are also bound to be more frequent; in certain groups, at least, one-parent families are prevalent. But, worse still, coloured immigrant families must adapt — to a greater or lesser extent — to quite different cultural, social and climatic conditions, often with little prior preparation.
(Mia Kellmer-Pringle,[41] p.147)

The difficulties faced by immigrant families are as much social and economic as they are cultural and linguistic. Hence many of the points made previously apply equally here. However, it cannot be denied that these families have special needs, particularly in relating to professional services.

In the past decade valuable experience has been gained by workers on the ground about the needs and how best they could be met. Unfortunately, this has been rarely written down or collated so that it can be shared with others. Moreover, we lack detailed representative information that surveys can provide. In fact the recent ones carried out in cities and regions with significant immigrant populations, Glasgow,[33] Salford[42] and Manchester,[14] make no reference to the families' cultural background. As I was associated with one of those surveys, I take no pride in noting this omission. And, of all the books published recently on partnership with parents, only one devotes a chapter to working with immigrant families; the remainder rarely, if ever, mention them. Perhaps that is a reflection of how much we still have to learn.

The exceptional book is by Barbara Tizard and her colleagues[9] and you will recall their primary concern was involving parents in ordinary nursery and infant schools. They noted that the teachers assumed either that immigrant parents were not interested in their child's education, because they rarely responded to the school's overtures, or that they were so overwhelmed by social problems, that it was unreasonable to expect these parents to be involved. But as Barbara Tizard goes on to point out, there is

> much evidence which suggests that the opposite is the case. For many parents the wish to obtain a good education for their children was a major factor in their decision to emigrate. In general, truancy rates are lower and the proportion of children staying on at school after 16 higher among minority group children, and their parents tend to have higher aspirations for them. (pp.221–2)

She goes on to identify two main barriers: the obvious one of no common language and the more subtle cultural differences. An instance of the latter is that,

> in their countries of origin, the teacher was likely to be no stranger to them but someone who lived in their community and with whom they were in daily contact outside of school. The British situation in which parents are expected to visit and even spend time in the school, but the teacher tends to hurry away from the neighbourhood as soon as school finished, is unfamiliar to many minority groups. (p.223)

The research team went on to explore possible ways of working with minority-group parents. Among the approaches they found to be successful are:
● film shows about the children's activities at school (issue invitations in the parents' own languages, encourage them to bring other relatives, repeat the film at hours to suit shift and night workers)
● mothers from a number of different cultures made illustrated books for the class in their own languages, relating tales from their own childhood. This was preceded by a researcher visiting the home to explain why and how
● individual appointments for mothers to visit the school and

watch the class in action
● ensure interpreters are available and arrange to have notices, newletters, etc., translated.

However, they were also aware that more radical changes are required to ensure that these parents have real opportunities to share their knowledge of their children and cultures and to be fully consulted about the way they are educated. They go on therefore to propose

● Serious efforts need to be made to recruit a proportion of staff from the minority groups concerned.

● The curriculum followed and the teaching resources used should be multicultural: choice of play material, pictures and books.

● Professional staff must make the first move to forge the real links with the community: visiting the children at home, using the local shops and cafes and asking for invitations to visit the families' places of worship and social centres.

Many of these conclusions are echoed in a recent report by Martin Powell and Elizabeth Perkins[49] on the use of the Portage Scheme in west Birmingham with eleven Asian families who had a preschool mentally handicapped child. In particular, they emphasise the provision of a named person who is a mother-tongue speaker, as the only way of overcoming the families' lack of understanding of the services they were receiving and of their failure to use the range of services and benefits to which they were entitled.

As regards the child's development, it was found that nine out of eleven families desired advice on teaching their child and the majority wanted someone to visit at home. However, some significant cultural differences were noted, e.g. only a minority of mothers mentioned playing with their child. None the less, the investigators were able to make this conclusion:

The picture that emerged was of a modest expectation that children could be taught early developmental skills and that mothers, particularly, played an active part in this process. However, if the process is explicitly labelled as 'teaching', and if a teacher is available, mothers may . . . see this as being a teacher's responsibility. (p.51)

The words from the Court Report[31] take on a whole new meaning when applied to immigrant families, 'We have found no better way to raise a child than to reinforce the abilities of his parents to do so.'

Willing Parents

The implication of much of the foregoing is that certain parents are 'unwilling' or 'reluctant' to become involved with teachers and therapists. The corollary, willing parents, must not be overlooked. But what is the essential feature? From past experience we can say they are likely to be better educated, have smaller families, enjoy a larger family income and have higher social status. While these factors may give them more time and energy to work alongside the professionals, they cannot provide the whole answer because many poorer families can be equally enthusiastic and willing. There must be a deeper meaning.

John McEvoy and I[50] contrasted the characteristics of 38 mothers who enrolled for a course on nurturing the play of handicapped children, with a random sample of 29 mothers who refused an invitation to participate. Alongside traditional variables, such as age, education and social status, we had the mothers complete questionnaires regarding their attitude to play and toys; we interviewed them about their feelings when interacting with their child in special situations (play, shopping and dressing) and we collected details of their child's play at home. Rather surprisingly, we found no differences between the two groups in terms of mother's age, socio-economic status, family size or educational level, nor did they differ in terms of the children's characteristics: aetiology, age, degree of handicap. However, there were striking differences between their reports of child's play activities and in their attitudes to the child.

The main distinguishing features of mothers who enrolled for the course were, first, a feeling that they could be better parents, particularly in situations such as shopping, and a feeling that it was important for their children to play and for them to join in their activities. By contrast, the course refusers felt comfortable about their role as parents but gave the impression that their children did not play and that they, the fathers, or the other children were less likely to play actively with the handicapped child. This presents a paradox; the mothers who enrolled felt they needed help, yet they already appeared to be doing much to nurture their child's play, whereas those mothers who did not join the course were not active players with their children and yet felt they were doing a good job as parents.

Hence a central issue in the concept of parental willingness is their presumptions about children's development. Our work as therapists and teachers is based on two beliefs which apparently some parents do not share,

● the behaviour of a handicapped child is modifiable
● parents' interactions can affect their child's development.

Similar observations have been made by the team involved in the Honeylands Project, Exeter:[51]

> Some parents involved in the project were slow to accept that they could actually bring about progress in their child by working with him and the therapist had to exercise considerable skill in showing parents what to look for and how to respond. (p.25)

Likewise, the Hornsey Intervention Project in London directed by Chris Kiernan[52] 'found some difficulty in making them [parents] believe that they *could* make a positive contribution at home and could affect how their child behaved by changing their own behaviour.' (p.15)

It is much easier to relate to parents who are on the same wavelength as ourselves but, unless we try to see the world through the eyes of those who have a different outlook, then our efforts at 'tuning in' will be ineffective. In the short-term, professionals need a greater sensitivity to parents' feelings about the effects their interactions have on their children while, in the longer run, we will have to break down the mistaken myths and routines about children that are handed down from one generation to the next. As Elizabeth Newson[53] put it, 'the child born into the lowest social bracket has everything stacked against him, including his parent's principles of child upbringing.' (p.115)

Mia Kellmer-Pringle[41] advocates preparing all of our young people to be parents:

> Modern parenthood is too demanding and complex a task to be performed well because we all have once been children ourselves. Those who have been deprived of adequate parental care, thus not having had an opportunity to observe

even those parental skills which were practiced a generation ago, have little chance of becoming in turn responsible parents themselves. (p.157)

A beginning though is for all professionals to observe and listen to parents. That makes possible the sharing of knowledge.

Helping you to Cope

'The trouble with some parents is that they forget we're not miracle workers.' And I guess that exasperated social worker would also have included with the parents, authors of books like this one. No one expects you to work miracles all the time; just one or two, now and again.

What's even harder, though, is to have your miracles go unrecognised or your labours come to nought. So in this final section, I want to explore three ways in which you can get advice and support that may help you cope if the going gets rough.

Team Work

The plethora of disciplines involved in handicap services is a constant reminder to each of us of our own inadequacies. The ideal of having one professional with all the necessary expertise is an unobtainable dream. The compromise is a team drawn from different disciplines, variously known as inter- , multi- or trans-disciplinary teams. Having the back-up of such a resource group seems to be a crucial feature to the success of home-visiting schemes, such as those based on the Portage model or the Honeylands Scheme in Exeter. Peter Wilcox[54] writes:

> Weekly staff meetings have a major problem-solving function and allow home teachers to discuss families with whom they are having difficulties of any sort. In this way they can draw upon the experience of other staff but, if things continue to go badly, another member of staff will visit the family with them to advise. (p.36)

In the Honeylands Scheme the entire support team and home therapists meet once a month for a morning. Gillian Pugh[40] reports that:

In the early days, the discussion centred on general topics and in the organisation of the project but, as time went on, they focussed on specific children and their families and this was found to be an invaluable way of sharing experiences. (p.23)

A flavour of these sessions is conveyed in a parent's observations:[55]

> It was more a meeting of people with common aims than a group of professionals from different fields. The willingness of the professionals involved to voice doubts, to question and criticise one another and, above all, share their expertise with parents, contributes much to the success of the project. (p.107)

Likewise, teachers can have the support of colleagues, the head teacher and visiting specialists, such as psychologists. The old saying rings true: 'a trouble shared is a trouble halved'.

There is, however, one danger inherent within the concept of teams and one which often surfaces to fulfil Mark Twain's wry observation that 'half the results of a good intention are evil'. Professionals disagree with one another. 'Conflicting advice from professionals usually causes parents a great deal of anxiety and can lead to disillusionment with or even rejection of service provisions.' (p.95)

That was Cliff Cunningham's[25] view and here are Sally Beveridge's[32] recommendations:

> It is vital that effective links are established with all professionals who are involved with a family so that the particular expertise which can be offered by one professional is neither duplicated by nor confounded by the input of another and that families do not feel overwhelmed by a multiplicity of information and advice. (pp.121–2)

The favoured solution in the preschool years has been to designate one person as the 'key worker' or 'named person' for a family, a procedure recently endorsed by the Warnock Committee[56] in Britain and one designed to avoid the wasteful over-visiting that can occur among social workers, home teachers, health visitors and therapists. Alastair Heron and Mary Myers describe[57] the brief of a key worker thus:

> an individual known to the disabled person and already involved in some way with him or her on a professional, social or domestic basis. The 'key worker' would be responsible for maintaining contact and for acting as a linking co-ordinator between the client and all the agencies involved in his or her total care. It is their responsibility to ensure that things happen that are meant to happen — and to know where and how to apply the necessary pressure to obtain action. (p.90)

During the school years, it appears to me that the person best suited to fulfil this role, at least in relation to a child's development, is the class teacher.

Implementing a 'key worker' scheme should reduce the pressures on you because families are shared out among the different professionals on the team. But its success depends largely on the trust and respect which the team members have for one another's expertise and competence and on their willingness to allow others to advise on matters which traditionally have been their preserve. Hence health visitors may give basic physiotherapeutic advice or the psychologist could advise on speech matters. Perhaps a willingness to share knowledge with colleagues is a precursor, maybe even a prerequisite, to sharing with parents.

Apprenticeship

One of the fallacies of preservice training for teachers and therapists is that the graduates are prepared for their professional responsibilities. But when it comes to working with parents most are ill-equipped and their early attempts will be like learning to swim in the deep end. One of the best lifebelts or life-jackets is to apprentice yourself to an experienced colleague. I have chosen this term quite deliberately because you are in the business of acquiring practical skills and the traditional way — observing the master-craftsman at work and examining the skills he uses — is far superior to any amount of talk, discussion or reading, even when they are dressed up with a fancy title like, 'inservice training'.

Equally your apprenticeship is a chance to get constructive criticism of your own attempts: a period too when you are excused your shortcomings, provided that you learn from them.

I won't pretend that finding knowledgeable tutors is easy. Few would be brash enough to call themselves 'masters'. However, it is worth advertising your interest in having a link, even if you end up with a self-help group of contemporaries.

Resources

A third source of help is the growing number of resources which you can draw upon for your work with parents. There are many books aimed at parents, but which, I suspect, are appreciated more by professionals (see p.290) and an increasing range of audio-visual materials and some ready-made training courses (see p.231).

Articles in journals and professional magazines describe how others have coped in the past and books like this should spark off some new approaches to old problems. All-in-all you have many more resources open to you than ever before.

And Finally

My intention in this first section of the book was to explore what is involved in working with parents and to give you a foretaste of how you could approach it. I hope that I will have encouraged you to set sail on what is not quite a voyage into the unknown but one which is, for all of us, a voyage of discovery.

PART TWO

Working with Parents Face-to-Face

OVERVIEW

The 1970s witnessed the emergence of a new phenomenon in services for families of 'at risk' or handicapped children: the home visitor. The basic premise underlying their deployment was simple, 'if the families are not interested or able to come to us, then we will go to them'. The various Head Start programmes in the USA which employed home visitors soon realised their worth. The idea quickly caught on and spread to Britain and other European countries as well as the developing world. This radical reappraisal of service delivery to families and young children dealt a fatal blow, albeit unintentionally, to a previously held tenet of services, namely the need for specialist centres and facilities. Now it had been proved that the family living room could easily become a consulting room for a therapist or a classroom for the teacher.

The home visitor's primary concern was to nurture the child's development through planned activities carried out by the parents and/or family at home. He, but more often she, called weekly or monthly, spending around one-and-a-half hours with the parents; usually the mother. This new type of job was neither designed to be, nor did it become, the domain of any one professional. In one English city alone (Exeter) the team of home visitors consisted of physiotherapists, paediatric nurses, a speech therapist, a psychologist, a teacher of the blind and an ordinary mother of three normal children. In other cities social workers, health visitors/public-health nurses, special-education teachers, occupational therapists and mentally-handicapped trained nurses have been recruited as home visitors. The eagle-eyed may have spotted one omission from this listing: doctors. Joyce Carlyle,[51] the project leader of one home-visiting scheme, and herself a consultant paediatrician, had this to say, 'Doctors may be seen as too high powered and are just not available for this intensive home-based work.' She goes on to add, 'that motivation is stronger, accountability higher and empathy greater when home therapy is done by those professionally trained in the "helping" disciplines rather than medicine.' (p.23) Moreover, the team[58] who instigated a home-visiting scheme in the Wessex region of southern England, came to this conclusion:

> There was no support for the Court Report's recommendations for a new speciality to deal with handicapped children, for the provision of expensive new facilities, or for new curricula for training. On the contrary, the project shows that . . . existing professionals who are already visiting families, can work very effectively with multiply handicapped children.

Home-visiting services had redefined the role of, and blurred the boundaries between, professionals. First, it was now 'respectable' for therapists and teachers to visit the home, but, secondly, and less tangibly, the concept of a 'good' professional changed. No longer were they evaluated solely in terms of the technical expertise, rather they were to be judged on their qualities of relating to families. For instance, the research team[52] associated with one home-visiting scheme in London that used social service staff, listed the most important ingredients for success as a home visitor: 'motivation, enthusiasm and sensitivity to the family's need'.

Joyce Carlyle[51] gave a more expanded listing:

> intelligence and common sense, several years' experience with children and families, the ability to listen and reflect positive elements in parents' attitudes, empathy, willingness to admit failure and answer questions accountably and a lack of the need to dominate. She will set a positive approach for parents who can see no goals or future. Professional skills and knowledge of early child development are highly desirable . . . (p.21)

Note what comes last. It is the knack of getting on with people that comes first. Re-read that description and ponder on each of the 13 qualities she cites.

A Model for the Future

I have dwelt at some length on 'home visitors' because they are probably the clearest example of how working with parents face-to-face can become a reality and of the consequent benefits it brings to children and families. I hasten to add, however, that this is not to imply that all teachers and therapists must visit the house regularly nor that no one was working effectively with parents until home visitors came on the scene. Rather I want to extract the ingredients that have made these schemes a success and explore ways whereby teachers and therapists can incorporate them into their professional lifestyle.

It strikes me that there are six features present in all successful home-visiting schemes. These are summarised below but I shall examine them in more detail in later chapters.

● *Regular contact* The visits to the home are often on a weekly basis, although other schemes have experimented with fortnightly or six-weekly calls. Visiting can commence soon after the birth of a baby with a known handicapping condition and may continue until the child goes to school, around five years of age.

● *Child's abilities* The emphasis is on what the child *can* do and, based on this, the selection of specified learning goals which are likely to be attained within days rather than weeks or weeks rather than months.

● *Aid learning* Parents are told about, and shown ways of, helping the child to learn. Sometimes these are presented as specific instructions to be followed, as in the Portage Curriculum Guides.[59] Other schemes prefer more eclectic, play-based activities. Daily 'teaching' sessions lasting up to half an hour are recommended.

● *Family-centred* Home visitors will try to involve brothers and sisters or extended family members in the learning activities, as well as parents, although they need to be equally conscious of the dangers of too much time and attention being paid to the handicapped child to the detriment of the other children.

● *Wider needs* Although the prime focus has been on the child, and nurturing his or her growth, invariably home visitors have had to cope with the family's wider needs, ranging from aids and allowances to emotional problems. Some schemes have a rough rule of thumb that half the time on a visit is for the child and half for chatting to the mother, father or family. Needless to add, home visitors will call in other professionals to help the family as necessary.

● *Support teams* All the schemes invariably include a back-up team that home visitors report to regularly, usually weekly, and with whom they can discuss any problems they have encountered.

Typically the support team includes a psychologist, therapists and the home visitor.

The outcomes of these schemes are impressive: the children's development is enhanced and parental motivation is high. For instance, in the Wessex study,[58] no families dropped out and on only one out of 236 visits was a parent not at home when the visitor called. Moreover, these schemes have proved effective with families from a wide range of cultural backgrounds, including those for whom English is not their first language.[49]

Common Difficulties

However, these successes can easily mask some common difficulties which all, or nearly all, home visitors have had to work through.

(1) Some parents were very slow to accept that they could actually affect their son's or daughter's progress by teaching and playing with them.

(2) The developmental delays or abnormal behaviour patterns perceived by the home visitor, were not always obvious to the parents and hence the importance of therapy was not appreciated.

(3) Information on the handicapping condition and the future prognosis, needed to be talked through many times.

(4) The pressure on the mother to undertake daily 'teaching' sessions could prove too much, when added to the many other demands on her.

(5) Some parents may make unrealistic demands on the child or have impossible hopes for them (see point 3 above). This is more likely after short-term inputs, during which the parents see rapid progress but the spurt is not maintained.

(6) Parents' feelings of inadequacy may be increased, especially when the child's development seems to have 'plateaued' and they blame themselves for 'not doing enough' or 'not the right things'. Cliff Cunningham's[25] solution is to forewarn parents about these 'consolidation' periods in development and that, during them, they should try 'to extend the skills sideways (i.e. horizontal) rather than seek to establish the next step up the developmental ladder'. He adds, 'parents are very relieved to understand that it is not their poor teaching or lack of effort that is causing the apparent halt in development, but the child's own maturational programme.' (p.106)

These difficulties are not peculiar to home visitors; they are likely to occur when any teacher or therapist embarks upon a partnership with parents. Nor is this listing exhaustive. Other issues that have arisen include how best to phase out regular contacts and ways of making parents more autonomous in selecting objectives and learning activities.

Potentially the most serious difficulty, though, comes from unresolved disagreements between parents and professionals. These inevitably hinder a productive working relationship. They can occur at many different levels and over diverse issues; some can be easily worked through, whereas others are more intractable. Foremost among the latter could be disputes about school placement. On this issue, recent legislation in the United States and Britain has given parents the right of appeal against decisions made by professionals, although several commentators[23,60] have voiced their scepticism and question whether parents are really in a stronger position. However, the acrimony engendered by such long disputes is hardly conducive to reconciliation, no matter who is the victor.

Recourse to law is not a solution; it is a safeguard. In most instances it can be avoided if both parties are willing to listen to each others' views and to concede that their opinions could be mistaken. In fact these two maxims could resolve most disagreements. Even so, it is inevitable that sometimes some professionals clash irreconcilably with some parents and this has to be put down to 'personality conflicts' or 'philosophical differences'. The solution is to separate gracefully.

The chapters in this section of the book will explore, in more detail, ways of overcoming some of the difficulties likely to be encountered in working with parents face-to-face and, indeed, ways of preventing problems from occurring.

Chapter 5 examines how parents and professionals can develop shared outlooks in nurturing the development of handicapped children through listening and observing each other and by analysing their interactions with the child in more detail.

Chapter 6 reviews ways of involving parents in the assessment of their child's abilities and the keeping of simple records.

Chapter 7 explores ways of selecting learning objectives with parents; how to devise, with them, suitable teaching activities for their child and methods of giving parents feedback which will enable them to become more effective teachers.

Obviously, the *content* of what you do with parents and the way you organise your contacts will be determined by the child's needs, the family's expectations, your expertise and the opportunities provided to you by your employers. Hence in this section I can only present general strategies for working with parents, albeit illustrated by specific examples. It is up to you to adapt them to your own situation.

But let me stress again, the core skills for successful work with parents are the personal and interpersonal attributes of the teacher or therapist, which I outlined in detail in Chapter 2:

● flexibility to cope with a diversity of people and needs
● a willingness to listen, observe and negotiate
● a respect for parents' viewpoints that is shown by you consulting them at least as often as they consult you
● being open about your feelings so that parents can be open about theirs
● a willingness to answer parents' questions and listening to the answers they give to your questions
● sharing responsibility for decision-making with the parents.

The one word that recurs most frequently in writings about successful parental involvement schemes is trust, mutual trust. It is invariably mentioned by parents and professionals alike. It was Emerson who wrote: 'Trust men and they will be true to you; treat them greatly and they will show themselves great.'

5

The Way I Look at it

Lynn Johnston, the talented Canadian cartoonist and astute observer of parents and their children, has a cartoon in which a young boy is showing his latest artistic efforts to a puzzled mother and saying, 'It's not a nice doodle, mum . . . it's God eating a carrot.'

Each of us, parents, professionals and children, have our own ways of looking at life. Diversities and discrepancies can be tolerated as long as we are going our own way. Once the journey becomes a shared event with common goals, then differing perspectives can cause misunderstandings, duplication of efforts and less than successful outcomes. Hence I begin by exploring ways whereby parents and professionals can develop shared outlooks in nurturing the development of handicapped children.

Shared Outlooks

Sad to say, the number of ways for sharing our outlooks are quite limited; perhaps that is why it can be so difficult. I can think of only three

- *listening* to other peoples' explanations
- *observing* their actions
- *analysing* their behaviour.

Let's look at each one in turn.

Listening

You need to make time to listen to parents and equally they need time to listen to you. Easier said than done. Therapists will no doubt recognise this scenario, recounted by Elizabeth Newson:[37]

85

I used to see them [parents] in my office; the child would play on the floor with a few toys and the mother and I would talk over his head. Eventually the child would become bored with the toys on the floor and would start wandering round the room touching things, fiddling with my typewriter, playing with the bits and pieces on my desk. And soon his mother would stop listening or talking to me, and would be constantly interjecting 'Don't touch that' or 'Come away'. She would be anxious and distracted and useless as an information resource because she did not know how far I was prepared to let the child go; it was an uncomfortable situation of uncertainty for her, however much I might reassure her. (p.112)

A similar scenario can prevail in classrooms, only here it is the teacher who has to keep interrupting to attend to the children. Meeting parents outside the classroom is an obvious solution, provided that someone else is available to look after the children. However, the alternative most frequently used, that of 'open evenings' with opportunities to meet the teacher, is not to be recommended. As Barbara Tizard[9] notes:

These interviews are often disappointing, the setting is usually public, with other parents waiting their turn, and there is neither the time nor the privacy for adequate discussion of the parent's anxieties, or for a full exchange of information. Parents must make do with a brief report, couched in vague terms — their child is doing 'well' or is 'slow', 'average', 'untidy' or a 'chatterbox'. (p.209)

It does not take much imagination to improve on these scenes.
- *Privacy* A room where you won't be interrupted.
- *Child cared for* Can you arrange for someone to keep an eye on the child, at least for part of the time?
- *Time* Try not to hurry through the interview; leave time for the parents to think and express themselves. Don't be afraid of silences. Nor should you rush away, because, as Cliff Cunningham[25] noted, 'our experience has indicated that the issue which is really worrying the parents is often raised as one is about to leave'. (p.100)
- *Asking the right questions* In your conversations with parents

you want not only *information*, but also some indication of their *feelings*; an appreciation of the *explanations* they give for their child's behaviour and the *reasoning* behind the way they handle the child. One session may be insufficient to achieve these goals but it does no harm bearing them in mind from the outset.

As regards how best to extract information from parents, I return to Elizabeth Newson,[37] who has had a wealth of experience in framing questions. She pinpoints three different types of questions that have rarely let her down: 'Has your child ever surprised you, for instance by telling you something you didn't think he could tell you?' This question gives parents the opportunity to talk about their child's best efforts and gives you an insight into their expectations.

The second type of question is rather more open-ended: 'What do you think is his biggest problem from *your* point of view?' which is immediately followed by 'What is his biggest problem from *his* point of view?' These questions give you some idea of the parents' priorities but at the same time the parents are asked to empathise with the child.

The third type of question invites the parents to think about what they would do if . . . For example, 'If I said it was really important for you to get a word out of him this afternoon for us to hear, how could you go about it?' Here the parents can reflect on what they *might* do without the pressure of having to do it.

There are many other questions you could ask, depending on the child, the family and your concerns. Owen Hargie and his co-authors[61] identify some 16 different functions of questions, give examples of different ones and their likely effects in interpersonal exchanges. They go on to add that, 'there are no hard-and-fast rules about which type of question to use in particular social encounters, since research in this area is as yet in its infancy.' But they also caution that, 'although, at first sight, questioning would seem to be one of the simplest of all social skills, upon further examination it can be seen that in fact the skill is quite complex.' (p.91) They argue that practice helps either in role-play with colleagues or through video-taping an interview with a parent and re-viewing it in the company of an experienced and trusted colleague, who will help you appraise yourself. Their excellent text will give you further details. And should you wonder which question to ask parents, Rudyard Kipling's verse may prove helpful:

I keep six honest serving men,
They taught me all I know
There names are what and why and when
And how and where and who.

Lastly, there will be some parents, the less verbally proficient, who may find it very difficult to answer more abstract questions, such as 'why?' The ideas listed in the section on 'observing' may help.

● *Answer the parents' questions* Leave time for the parents to ask you questions but, more than this, try to create an atmosphere that will encourage them to question you. Assure them that there is no such thing as a trivial question . . . leave gaps in the conversation . . . or share your thoughts and feelings . . . repeat some of the questions that other parents have commonly asked you and then go on to answer them. But, above all, don't ask question after question; interpose with other comments. Generally the more relaxed and friendly you can make the 'interview', the more open parents will be in both their questions and answers.

Needless to say, your answers to their questions should be as comprehensive and honest as you want their answers to be to your questions. And if you don't know the answer to their question, it's better to say so straight out. Bluffing rarely succeeds.

Making this a Reality

There are a number of ways whereby teachers and parents can have the opportunity to listen to each other.

● *Teachers* can arrange to meet the parents of each child individually, at least once a year but preferably each term, to discuss their son or daughter's progress. This can take place during school hours if there are assistants or student teachers available to look after the class. Alternatively, the head teacher or another teacher might help out. Some consultations will need to take place out of school hours to suit working mothers or to involve fathers.

● *Therapists* should make available time when they can have an uninterrupted conversation with the parents, e.g. the child returns to the classroom if you meet at school; or is looked after by a colleague or volunteer helper in the clinic.

● You can obtain information from groups of parents by having

Figure 5.1: A Sample Questionnaire to Parents

NAME OF SCHOOL

QUESTIONNAIRE FOR NEW PARENTS

Child's name ....

Date of birth ....

(1) (a) Please put a tick against any of the following areas of work or behaviour which you think are important for your child:

Speech and language:
Reading:
Writing:
Number work:
Physical activity and control:
Swimming:
Drama:
Art:
Music and singing:
Religious knowledge:
Self-help skills (dressing, washing, hygiene, etc.):
Health education:
Housecraft (practical household skills):
Good manners at meal times:
Good manners at other times:
Consideration for other people:

(b) Also please *underline* any of the above items which you think are *especially* important

(2) Please state any activities not listed above which you think are important for your child:

(3) Do you think that an overall aim of the school should be to help its children achieve more normal standards of work and behaviour so far as possible?

(4) Please add overleaf any further comments or suggestions you wish to make about the kind of education you want your child to receive at this school. Please continue on another sheet if necessary.

Signed .... Date ....

Source: Reproduced from *In Search of a Curriculum* by the staff of Rectory Paddock School.[62]

them complete a simple questionnaire. Figure 5.1 is a sample of one used in Rectory Paddock School,[62] London, for children who are mentally handicapped. This keeps teachers in touch with parents, if they are unable to meet regularly.

● Parents should be encouraged to call in to school or telephone if they have a query. Indeed teachers and therapists might give their home phone numbers to parents. Barbara Smith,[38] a teacher and the parent of a teenager who is handicapped, makes this observation:

> There have been rare occasions when I have felt my right to privacy has been impinged upon once a parent knows my phone number. However, as a parent, I have greatly valued being able to relieve my son's frustration at his inability to communicate something 'vital' about his day at school by a short phone call to his teacher. (p.150)

Other professionals comment on how rarely parents actually call teachers or therapists at home but there is the reassurance in having a number and the act of giving it says a lot about your willingness to listen.

● *Home-school diary* Although this is not as effective as face-to-face meetings, it does at least give the parents some idea about what is going on at school and may encourage some parents to telephone or call in to the school. It is worth leaving space for parents to write in their 'news', although relatively few make full use of it. However, for those who do, it will keep you in touch with what is happening at home.

A diary is highly recommended when teachers or therapists and parents are working on a common teaching programme (see p.127). Fuller details about diaries are given in Chapter 12.

● Parents who help out in the school on a regular basis should be invited to the staffroom. Barbara Tizard[9] writes:

> We found on our project that parents helping in the school usually resented being excluded from the staffroom at coffee time, so we asked both parents and staff whether they thought this practice was correct. Two of the heads thought it was necessary to protect the staff's privacy but all the other teachers and all but four parents thought it was impolite. Some parents also saw visiting the staffroom as a chance to get to

know the staff better. (p.90)

And we might add: the staff will get to know the parents better.
● You could set up a lending library of toys and/or books. As parents drop in to arrange a loan, you will have a chance for a chat and they can ask your advice if anything is troubling them.
● Social events, such as outings, dances, parties are a good way of getting to know each other. When the ice is broken, it is easier for both parties to get together to talk.

Observing

A picture is worth a thousand words, so they say, and this truth is certainly borne out when it comes to learning about people.

Observe the Child

Elizabeth Newson[37] writes of the child as being a 'visual aid' for both parents and professionals in sharing their knowledge and expertise. As they jointly observe the child playing freely or in the company of another adult or with other children, the parents may point out the particular behaviour that puzzles or worries them. Or you can ask the parents for more details about the things you see the child do: is that usual for him? why do you think he did that? Your questions, coupled with the child's actions, can trigger off important recollections of past events that might otherwise have been forgotten.

It isn't easy though to find the right blend of circumstances that will give you a chance to observe children in this way. The 'ideal' conditions would include one or all of the following:
● Another adult 'plays' with the child so that you and the parents can jointly observe and share your thoughts, without being part of the action. Therapists in clinic settings can get around this by arranging 'joint' sessions with a colleague: for instance, a psychologist and speech therapist may arrange to see a family together rather than separately. Alternatively, a secretary or volunteer helper might be recruited. In schools, this should be less of a problem. The child might play happily alongside other children or there may be an assistant who is free to help. Likewise at home, older brothers or sisters may be available, or it's likely that the child will be content to play alone, as he or she is on familiar territory.

● A one-way screen facility can be very useful, as it means the child is not distracted by the parent's presence and they in their turn are 'distanced' and relieved of the responsibility of reacting to the child. It also precludes the anxious parent from intervening unnecessarily: an occurrence that can easily happen if they are in the same room. Watching through the glass panels of a door can sometimes be an acceptable substitution for proper one-way screens.

● Another alternative is to make a video-recording of the child during the visit to the clinic or on a previous day in school. This can be re-viewed with the parents. Video, like the one-way screens, gives parents the chance to view their child more dispassionately: more as they would a stranger and, in so doing, their appraisal of the child's abilities and behaviour could be more realistic.

● Children behave differently in different situations. While we professionals have readily accepted the truth of this, we have been less willing to act upon a corollary of it: namely, the need to observe children at home as well as in the clinic or school. If this experience gives you new insights into the child, and it's likely it will, then it can be especially beneficial for parents to observe their child outside the home, in classrooms or playgrounds.

● There remains the problem of capturing the child's real-life behaviour, uninfluenced by the presence of observers or visitors. Some enterprising teachers and therapists have loaned parents video-equipment to record particularly significant events at home: how the child behaves at mealtimes or what he's like during a temper tantrum. As video-equipment becomes more available in homes, these recordings will not be such a rarity.

Hence there are various ways in which you and the parents can take a fresh look at a child and, in so doing, learn more about each other's assumptions and interpretations of the child's behaviour.

Observe Parents with their Child

You can learn much from seeing parents interacting with their child. Arguably the most favourable circumstances for doing this are in the familiar surroundings of home, when parents are likely to be more at ease than they would be in a strange clinic or classroom.

Here you can see how parents and child react to the spontaneous occurrences during your visit: one I well remember is the child up-ending the coal bucket. The parents' reactions, and those of the other adults in the house, will give you some insight into what the child's home life is like, particularly as you will also see at first hand the environmental constraints the family has to live with.

It is also worth observing the parents and child interacting in a more structured way, for example, playing with some novel toys you have brought along. I find it is useful to have a mixture of 'creative' type toys, such as dolls and accessories, lego or crayons, and those with a definite outcome, such as formboards, ringstacks or dominoes. (The toys should be chosen to accord with the child's developmental level.)

I try to take the pressure off the parents by emphasising my interest in the child's actions but I do encourage them to join in the play and to help their child as much as they like.

You will quickly get a feel for the parents' style of interaction: are they forceful or reserved?; do they direct the child or prefer to follow his lead?; do they introduce new ideas and variety into the play?; how much talking do they do?; what strategies do they use to get and hold the child's attention? This information will not only be valuable in the future but it can be used as a stimulant for discovering more about the parents' feelings and attitudes. This is especially so if you are able to play back a video-recording and have them share with you their feelings . . . reasons . . . or expectations at various points in the scene. Video also gives them a chance to see their own behaviour, warts and all, and they may spontaneously resolve to change there and then: 'Did I really do that much talking?' was one mother's reaction.

If you haven't video available, an audio-recording or written records will help to jog your memory as well as the parents' during the discussions.

Parents Observe the Professional and Child

Many parents have commented on how valuable it was for them to see a teacher or therapist interacting with their child. On reflection it is not hard to see why. It is a *novelty* for all parents to see another adult in sustained and uninterrupted interaction with their child because this is a very rare occurrence in everyday life. Secondly, they will be intrigued to see their child's reactions because the adult's demands and style are likely to be different from theirs. Thirdly, they like to see an 'expert' at work.

Hence, if the parents come to the school or clinic, give them a chance to see you or a colleague interacting with their child. Moreover, if you are visiting the home, it is worth having a play session with the child which the parents can observe. Even if you are familiar with the child, you might discover that he or she reacts differently in the home.

Once again, a video-recording can be most useful when you want to highlight the child's significant behaviours and your reasons for doing what you did.

But, whether or not you have video, such debriefing sessions are essential. Recall Teresa Smith's[12] conclusion that merely letting parents observe what goes on in classrooms or clinics does not necessarily 'bring about a better understanding or greater knowledge about an educational role in the interaction between parent and child. Parents may need far more explanation and discussion than they are given at present.' (p.105)

Finally, Cliff Cunningham[25] gives a salutary warning 'The home intervener must give the parent the confidence to cope, not prove how good the intervener is with the infant at the expense of the parent.' (p.105)

Making it a Reality

Opportunities to observe parents and children and for them to watch you can come about in the following ways.

● Visiting the family *at home* on at least one occasion to get a feel for the home surroundings. This is especially recommended to teachers, just before a child starts school. It could also occur when the child moves class or when the child is first referred to a therapist.

Why is home visiting not more common? Barbara Tizard[9] writes:

> we have found that teachers can be very nervous of home visiting, fearing perhaps that they will be faced with hostility or in some way find themselves unable to cope. However, in our project, of the four teachers who did home visits, none ever received a hostile reception. And in answering our questionnaires, parents had only appreciative comments to make about home visits. (p.131)

Another important reason is the lack of time available to teachers and therapists for home visits. In the case of school staff an assistant might be able to look after the class while the teacher calls at home or has time off in lieu of visits made during the weekend or in the evenings. These are the best times for catching the whole family together.

Therapists could come to similar arrangements. Nor should they think of home visits requiring extra time, as some are inclined to do. This presumes that the same work could be equally well done in the clinic, and that is rarely the case. Hence it is *essential* time, if the therapist is to do the best possible job. (The theme of reappraising job descriptions and role expectations of teachers and therapists, will be taken up in Chapter 13.)

A few practical tips. Warn the parent in advance of the day and time you will be calling, give a brief outline of why you are coming and, before setting out, make a list of the topics you want to raise with the family and the information you hope to obtain. Beware of staying too long and causing excessive disruption to the family routine; if need be, arrange another appointment.

● Parents can be invited to observe the therapist working with the child, either through one-way screens or by being present in the room with you. If you are concerned that this will be a distraction, forewarn the parent that she should ignore the child's advance; he or she might pretend to be engrossed in a book or magazine. Then it's up to your ingenuity to keep the child's attention.

It is a great waste of opportunities always to leave a parent in the waiting room while you see the child.

● Teachers, likewise, could invite the parents to spend time in the classroom (e.g. an hour or so, once a term), observing what goes on and possibly helping out. Indeed some parents might be prepared to do this regularly, once a week. A rota could be drawn up so that activities which require lots of helpers could then become part of the curriculum: horse-riding, swimming, mini-outings around the neighbourhood, etc.

Paradoxically, the latter suggestion gets a more ready acceptance from teachers than having parents observing in the classroom. Once again, their fears may be part of the reluctance: 'What if all hell breaks loose?'; 'Will they misunderstand what I'm trying to do?'; 'Will the parents distract the other children?' Generally, these fears prove groundless. The practical difficulties can be harder to surmount: the lack of space in some classrooms being the most obvious or the teacher finding time to brief the parents before and after the visit.

Parents, however, speak glowingly of how valuable the experience was for them. For example, here are two mothers' comments to Teresa Smith:[12]

> Once I did stay . . . I was sat at the lego table and it fascinated me watching them and what they were doing.

> I got a greater knowledge of children — the scope of ideas to do at home with them. I would never have thought of giving a two year old jigsaws. It widened my ideas about young children.

And one mother who hadn't ever been to the playgroup, had this to say:

> I didn't really know what they taught, what their teaching method was. If you knew, when you were at home, you could sort of carry on what they were doing and it would make their job easier.

Assuring parents that they are welcome to drop into school anytime, is probably not sufficient. If you really want to get parents along, you will need to do more than this: arrange a definite day and time, at least for the first visit, and make sure the parents are aware of the procedures; should they go straight to the classroom or call first on the head teacher? Some schools have set aside a room as a parents' den, a place where mothers can meet or where teachers and parents can chat. It is also a comfortable place for parents to wait, rather than standing in corridors or entrance halls.

● If it is difficult for you or the parents to meet and observe one another with the child, then you might consider making a video-tape or cine-film (home-type movie) of the children in school and discussing it with the parents. This idea is particularly effective at encouraging parents to attend evening meetings but you could also do this on a one-to-one basis (see Chapter 11).

Alternatively, you could show parents videos or films that illustrate teaching techniques or play activities for use at home. Give parents an opportunity to discuss the content afterwards.

Analysis

This third level of sharing is probably the most effective in that it combines the previous two, listening and seeing, with the third, action. By analysis, I mean taking a detailed and fine-grained look at the child's behaviour, such as the frequency of certain actions, what elicits them and the consequences which follow. Also, examine the effect that adults have on the child, for good or ill. These analyses can be crucial in highlighting significant relationships that are easily overlooked and in drawing our attention to things we didn't see, perhaps because we didn't want to see them.

This is the level we will have to work at to advance the child's development. Hence I will devote the next two chapters to ways of working with parents in analysing and developing their child's behaviour. These will cover assessing the child's developmental level, observing the child's behaviour in more detail, selecting learning objectives, planning teaching programmes, monitoring the teacher's behaviour and evaluating progress.

The presumption is that during these activities, teachers, therapists and parents will be in regular contact, either face-to-face or via home/school diaries, telephone, etc. It is possible that such contacts could be maintained for months or even years; however, for most teachers and therapists I guess they will be rather more periodic. For instance, you might have regular contact for three months, then only occasional contacts for a year or so, when you might resume regular links for another period of time. The family's needs will determine this, in negotiation with the other demands on your time.

Some of the thornier issues which occur during this form of intensive work are the following.

● How frequently do parents and professionals need to meet, weekly, fortnightly or monthly?

● Do they always need to meet face-to-face, could telephone contacts or home/school diaries suffice? Could you save time by seeing parents as a group?

● How do you keep other interested parties informed about what is going on. For example, therapists who work closely with parents of school-going children, should keep the teacher up-to-date with what is happening.

● After a period of intensive work with parents, how can the teachers or therapists phase themselves out and hand over more responsibility to the parents?

There are no ready-made answers to these issues; you will have to come to your own conclusions.

However, the advice of colleagues should prove helpful on these as well as the many other issues which will arise, some well beyond your competence. Hence I end this chapter with examining the need for all teachers and therapists to have the support of a back-up team of colleagues from their own and other disciplines.

Support Teams

I am convinced that the success of the home-visiting schemes described in the introduction is due, at least in part, to the multi-disciplinary support teams.

Often these were formally constituted from the specialists who were involved or responsible for the child and family, psychologists, therapists, doctors, etc., and the team met regularly (usually weekly) with the home visitors.

I want to examine first the benefits of these teams and some potential disadvantages. Then, for those teachers or therapists who have no ready-made support team to consult, I shall give some suggestions as to how they might seek assistance from their colleagues.

The benefits of support teams can be succinctly summarised as follows.

● *Access to a wider range of expertise* The home teacher or therapist can get advice from the specialists or arrange for the child to be seen by them.

● *Opportunity to discuss difficulties and plan solutions* Explaining your work to others, forces you to clarify your own thinking and a fresh mind may spot aspects you have overlooked or bring a new perspective to the issue. Nor should you shirk from the criticism that will be implicit or explicit in these discussions. As Joan Key[55] put it, 'the willingness of the professionals involved to voice doubts, to question and criticise one another and, above all, share their expertise with parents, contributes much to the success of the project.'

● *The chance of a second opinion* Members of the team can meet with the parents and child and pool their ideas. In fact, Cliff Cunningham[25] suggests that the best home-visitor service is built around a team who have shared skills and close communication. Each has a case load and is the primary visitor, but visits by other members are systematically built into the programme. The rationale being that the 'new' visitor would often raise some queries over the stimulation programme, suggesting alternative approaches or making novel observations. (p.94)

● *The family is the team's responsibility* The family's need for help may go far beyond the expertise and experience of a teacher or therapist. You should not take on the responsibility for dealing with matters outside your competence. That is not to say that you then ignore these 'non-educational' needs. Gillian Pugh[40] notes that in the Wessex Home Teaching Project

it was gradually decided that some problems — such as a bad relationship between the parents, or father leaving home, or conflicting advice to the parents from the different agencies with which they were in touch — were in fact hindering the main teaching objectives. It was therefore decided that a more appropriate response would be to take the problem to the next staff meeting and ask for advice on how to deal with it, or which other sources of help to involve. Using the same behavioural approach, with activity charts and careful monitoring, the parents' questionnaires report that the procedures used for dealing with non-educational problems were effective for almost all of them. (p.52)

If you have no access to a support team, then your best alternative is to put the family in contact with the appropriate service or personnel. Of course, you may need to continue urging for action to be taken; sometimes other agencies will not share your sense of urgency. Hence there will be times when you feel frustrated and angry.

Support teams are not without their problems. Foremost of which can be disagreements among the members on the best way of providing services, e.g. integration versus special services, or on their attitudes to sharing professional skills with parents. Dana Brynelsen,[63] in describing these difficulties in the context of an Infant Developmental Program in British Columbia, Canada, goes on to add:

Although there have been no simple resolutions to these

problems, positive changes are occurring: many agencies which were antagonistic are now referring children; more professionals are sharing skills, if for no other reason than the current economic climate, which inhibits growth; and research is providing us with a strong rationale and the tools to enhance parent–professional working relationships. (p.89)

Changes will come over time, if you persevere. However, speedy resolution of any dispute is desirable, if not easily obtained. Cliff Cunningham[25] gives these reasons:

The importance of a consensus of method and philosophy must be emphasised. Conflicting advice from professionals usually causes parents a great deal of anxiety and can lead to disillusionment with or even rejection of service provisions. (p.95)

Creating Your Own Support Team

Here are some ways in which you might get advice and support from your colleagues.
(1) You could arrange to see the child and family with a colleague present. Afterwards you will have somebody with whom to discuss your thoughts and plans. Or it may be possible for you to observe other professionals working with the child and parents, e.g. psychologists and therapists, and they in turn can see how you work. These joint sessions are not always easily arranged due to the difficulty of finding mutually convenient times and venues. However, teachers and therapists who have succeeded, speak highly of their value, provided that they plan the sessions in advance and make time to discuss them afterwards.
(2) If you do not have regular staff meetings in your school, or meetings with other professionals based in your clinic, you might take the initiative in getting them started, albeit on an experimental basis. The main function initially might be to exchange views on how best to deal with particular children's difficulties.
(3) Teachers could invite the other professionals (for instance, psychologists, social workers, therapists) who are in contact with the family to come along to your termly or yearly review meetings (see p.153). This will be a chance for them as well as

you to discuss the child's progress with the parents and to listen to the parents' viewpoint.

Issues Facing Teams

There are two other issues that teams may have to face.

Parents Attending Case Conferences. This is a natural consequence of the philosophy of working with parents. However, some of your colleagues may object to this on the grounds that the parents' presence will inhibit their freedom to discuss freely all the issues involved. Or, put another way, parents could be hurt or embarrassed by what was said. This strikes me as a curious argument, especially as they are the people who are going to be most affected by any decisions made at the case conference and they will have to be told about them sooner or later. I do concede that there may be some occasions when delicate issues are better handled in a more intimate way but, with most families, the norm should be that parents are invited and facilitated in attending case conferences unless there are very good reasons for their exclusion.

Incidentally, some of the problems of including parents in case conferences, have nothing to do with parents but with the value of case conferences at all, which in Patricia Potts'[23] words sometimes are nothing more than 'ritualised competition' between professionals. However, that's another day's work.

Access to Information on their Child's File. This creates no problem if the parents have been actively involved in gathering the information contained in the files, which will then, in a real sense, be 'joint records'. In fact, the British Department of Education and Science[64] in a recent circular was eager to foster this:

> Assessments should be seen as a partnership between teachers, other professionals and parents, in a joint endeavour to discover and understand the nature of the difficulties and needs of individual children. Close relations should be established and maintained with parents and can only be helped by frankness and openness on all sides. (para.6)

Again, though, some of your colleagues may be reluctant to grant parents access to their reports on the grounds that the contents may be painful to them. If they knew parents were going to see their records, then they would not go into detail and hence the records would be of less value to everyone.

These issues are not easily resolved. Some self-deception may be present. In Patricia Potts'[23] words:

> Records are frequently speculative, vague or irresponsibly brief. And they can also be casually damning . . . It is often the case that information of confidential files is not much used even by the professionals; it is by no means automatic that teachers, for example, get to see reports written by psychologists on children in their class. (p.190)

Perhaps a way forward is for professionals to write all reports in the knowledge that the parents will read them and only in exceptional circumstances restrict their reports or parts of them, for the 'eyes' of colleagues only.

I recommend that therapists provide parents with a written report of their assessments and plans. Likewise, teachers should give parents a written report of the child's progress in school, at least annually. Indeed, in the US this became a requirement for schools with the passing of the Education for all Handicapped Children Act. Moreover, Public Law 94-142 requires that parents have access to all records pertaining to their child. If the spirit as well as the substance of the law is to be met, then school staff must learn to write reports that can be understood by the child's parents. Chapter 12 will provide specific suggestions to help with this.

Nothing Comes of Nothing

Working with parents will mean changing your present routines. However, as I hope I have shown you in this chapter, there are many different ways of bringing these about; some are major changes but most are minor. To my mind, there is no good or bad way of working with parents; only a right or wrong attitude toward it. Hence my emphasis on teachers and therapists having a shared outlook with parents. In your striving for this, your partnership with parents will have begun. It's by doing nothing, that you ensure that nothing changes.

6

I Never Knew He Could do That

For several years I have done battle for an idea concerning the instruction and education of man, which appeared the more just and useful the more deeply I thought about it. My idea was that, in order to establish natural rational methods, it was essential that we make numerous, exact and rational observations of man as an individual, principally during infancy, which is the age at which the foundations of education and culture must be laid.

(Maria Montessori)

The title of this chapter is a comment that could equally well be spoken by a parent, teacher or therapist and said, incidentally, with either a tone of surprised pleasure or annoyance, depending on the personalities involved. It embodies, too, the predominant concern of teachers and therapists, namely the development of the child's competence. As educators (in the broadest sense), they are concerned with what children can do because that is the starting point for leading them on to new skills and abilities.

This emphasis on abilities runs counter to the public's perspectives of handicap and, dare I say it, some other professionals' views. For instance, here is one mother's recollections of her thoughts after being told that her newborn daughter had Down's syndrome:

I thought that I'd never be able to feed her or she'll never be able to walk or anything. And then the nurses told me that when I would get her home that . . . I'd never be able to feed her properly — it would take me an awful long time.

Not surprisingly, when parents are faced with the prospect of having their child 'assessed', they inevitably see it as showing up their child's weaknesses. At least that's what tests and examinations did for them during their school days! But I hope parents will come to see teachers and therapists as educators, rather than as examiners.

The philosophy of focusing on abilities is one that you will need to work at sharing with parents. You cannot assume that it is one parents will necessarily espouse.

Hence, I have chosen to begin by describing in detail how parents and professionals can focus on what children do and, although this accentuation of the positive will not eliminate the negatives, it should at least put them into perspective.

At this point I am not particularly concerned with *where* professionals and parents meet, it could be in the family home, your classroom or consulting room. Nor will I be able to cover all the challenges you will face when dealing with the diversity of children labelled handicapped. Rather I can give you a core approach that you will need to augment and adapt according to your clients.

First, though, we had better get clear our notions of 'development'.

Conceptualisation of Development

If we contrast our understanding of child development with the knowledge that man has acquired under the rubric of 'theoretical physics', then I guess we are all at the stage when the proverbial apple fell to the ground in Newton's garden. Consequently, our knowledge about how children grow up is characterised more by faith than facts. We believe that certain factors are influential and our faith may be bolstered by 'respectable' data but we cannot present definitive proof.

Misplaced faith is not without its dangers. Freddie Brimblecombe[108] gives but one example from the world of medicine:

> paediatricians were persuaded by a Finnish professor called Ylppo that the lining of the stomach of newborn infants had the magical property of absorbing oxygen. For this reason, 20 years ago paediatricians like me wasted valuable time bubbling oxygen into the stomachs of newborn infants who had failed to start breathing rather than direct our efforts to initiate respiration. (p.89)

Fortunately in the world of education and therapy, we don't live with life-or-death consequences but we are not without our untested assumptions and possibly misguided treatments, which social historians of the future might kindly describe as 'eccentric'.

It is against this background that I hesitatingly present a conceptualisation of child development. Should this prove unwarranted, my discomfort will be shared by many others because the tenets I outline are implicit in many intervention schemes with developmentally delayed or 'at risk' children.

Development is neither Unitary nor Uniform

As Figure 6.1 illustrates, it is best to view development as occurring within discrete, albeit overlapping, areas. Moreover, this subdivision can occur at various levels. For instance, at the most global level distinctions might be made between the child's physical, cognitive, social and emotional development. Or, as the figure shows, I have found it useful to subdivide children's play into four types. Likewise, early language acquisition can be conceived as proceeding within five domains, i.e. communication, verbal expression, verbal understanding, imitation and non-verbal understanding.

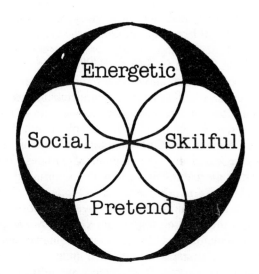

Figure 6.1: Areas of Development in Play

These subdivisions of development are one way of coping with its complexity. It draws attention to the diversity of behaviour subsumed under the global statement: the developing child. Moreover, it also takes account of a very obvious fact: that children's development may be more advanced or retarded in some areas rather than others. Such differential growth is normal, if inexplicable.

With handicapped children, the prospect of uneven development is even greater. Some disabilities may produce a global dampening of development. More likely, though, retardation will be specific to certain areas. The physically handicapped infant may be socially and cognitively unimpaired, whereas the mentally handicapped toddler can be physically normal but delayed in her language acquisition.

People who ignore these differences run the risk of making one of two mistakes; one I'll call 'optimistic', the other 'pessimistic'. The optimists focus on the child's best area and explain his or her poor performance in other areas as 'laziness' . . . 'lack of concentration or attention'. They are convinced the child could do it if he or she tried. By contrast, the pessimists see the child as uniformly poor and have few expectations for better performance, even in the areas unaffected by the disability. In each instance, one way of correcting this misconception is by taking a more analytical view of development. In so doing, the child's strengths will become apparent.

Children Differ in their Rate of Development

Following on from the above point, even if you average out children's developmental progress, there remain wide differences among them. If anything, these 'normal' variations are even more marked with disabled children. For example, Figure 6.2 illustrates the results obtained by Cliff Cunningham and his colleagues[65] when they assessed the developmental progress of some 60 Down's syndrome babies at various times during their first two years.

The 'shaded' area indicates their 'average' scores, defined as 66 per cent of the children falling between the two lines. Hence a further one-sixth of the infants scored above average, i.e. approaching the 'average' for ordinary infants and another one sixth were below average for Down's syndrome infants. Cliff Cunningham[25] comments:

we emphasise [to parents] that mentally handicapped babies are born with great innate variations in ability and personality. Thus not all parents can have the brightest Down's syndrome baby. I find that parents, though disappointed, are comforted by this. Unfortunately, many early intervention programmes have published results in high euphoria which, when diluted through various disseminations and media channels, have

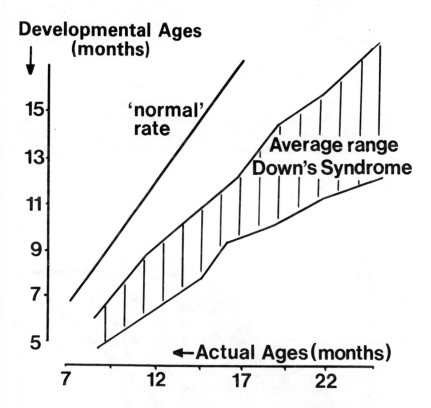

Figure 6.2: The Development of Down's Syndrome Infants.
Note: the shaded area shows the scores attained by 66% of the Down's syndrome infants; a further one-sixth had scores which were above average, i.e. toward the 'normal' range, and a further one-sixth had below average scores

Source: Adapted with permission from data presented by C.C. Cunningham.[65]

proclaimed that great benefits for potentially severely mentally handicapped infants will result from early structured stimulation . . . Whilst this is true for a small minority, our results strongly indicate a tremendous range of ability, regardless of the early intervention provided. (p.107)

We can neither explain why this variation occurs nor accurately predict the children who are going to be speedy or slow developers. We, and the parents, have to live and cope with this variation that is common to all children, whether they are handicapped or not.

As Cunningham[25] concludes,

we must not lose sight of the nature of the handicap in our desire to help. There are limits to what can be achieved and, whilst we must continually test these limits, we must, at the same time, maintain a realistic picture for parents. (p.107)

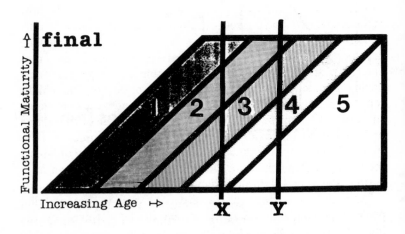

Figure 6.3: A Model of Developmental Stages

Source: Adapted with permission from figure presented by J.H. Flavell[66]

Development Occurs in Stages and Within Stages

The notion of stages in children's development has a venerable history. 'He who would learn to fly one day,' wrote Nietzsche, a nineteenth-century German philosopher, 'must first learn to stand and walk and run and climb and dance: one cannot fly into flying'. Likewise, the acquisition of language, of thinking, of moral understanding (to name but a few) have all been sectionalised into stages. The chief value of representing development in stages, is that it brings an order to what might otherwise seem like random and purposeless behaviours. More-over, it enables one to predict likely future behaviours in the short and long term. Remember, though, that stages *per se* are not an explanation of *why* children develop, rather they provide a description of the process.

There is, however, one very large drawback to stage theories of development. We are blinkered into believing that progress only comes from the acquisition of 'new' stages. Not so. Figure 6.3 depicts what I believe is a more plausible concept of stages. As you can see, when time passes, development occurs both within a stage as well as in the accretion of new stages. For example, at point X in this child's development one could expect to observe behaviours from four stages: stage 1 is nearly fully mature, stages 2 and 3 are developing, whereas stage 4 is only just emerging. In the period up to point Y, the following developments have occurred. Stage 5 behaviours are now emerging, stages 2, 3 and 4 are maturing but stage 1 actions, having attained functional maturity, drop out of the child's repertoire, although the potential for performing these behaviours still exists. Examples would be crawling as a precursor to walking or babbling to talking. I find this idea, first proposed by John Flavell [66] both sensible and serviceable. It makes sense of what I see when watching children. Often their behaviour is drawn from various stages and they shift fluently from one stage to the next.

And this idea provides a great service to parents and professionals alike in its reminder not to be deceived by the highest stage of which a child is capable. Rather you also need to ascertain what are the child's 'typical' behaviours, to arrive at a clearer picture of the child's developmental status. Moreover, you need to continue encouraging 'old', but functionally im-mature, stages as well as fostering the emergence of new ones.

Development Results from the Transactions Between the Individual and the People and Experiences in his or her Environment

That is the closest I will venture to giving an explanation of why children develop. I believe that children's future development is determined mostly by their present level of development because it is this which determines the extent to which they can contribute to, as well as benefit from, the experiences around them. Development is not something that happens to a passive recipient; rather children fuel and to some extent channel their own social, emotional and cognitive growth.

Secondly, development is nurtured by *current* experiences. There is a great temptation to look back into the past and search for explanations but more often the answer lies in the present. We known that human development once started is robust and vibrant and that it can overcome many traumatic deprivations.

Thirdly, development is, of course, influenced by the physical make-up of the person, the nervous system, genes, hormones and sensory receptors, but this influence decreases over time as it is overlaid by the acquisition of skills and behaviour patterns. Yet I suspect that the common man, not to say some professionals, would still cite these as the pre-eminent influences on an individual's development or they will use them to account for immaturity. With handicapped children, for example, they see only the disability, the deafness, the blindness or brain damage, none of which can be cured and so they despair.

They are wrong. Our notion of development puts disability into perspective; it is of decreasing importance as the person matures. Thus a deaf child fails to keep up in school with ordinary children, not because of his hearing loss but because he cannot communicate fluently or because he is too pig-headed. These are the true handicapping conditions and they can be 'cured'. Hence we have every right to be hopeful that we can influence handicapped children's development for the better.

Explain Development to Parents

So now to business: how to share these ideas with parents. By and large, most will have given little thought to why or how children develop. Their other children apparently grew up with little or no effort on their part. Now faced with a handicapped child, the questions begin to arise. With some parents, straight answers or explanations from you will suffice; for instance, telling them about the four points I made before.

However, I suspect that most, if not all, will have to discover the truth of this information for themselves. Mere words will not get the message, or its implications, across. Fortunately, you have a number of well-proven techniques to draw upon.

Developmental charts. So popular have these become that any teacher or therapist can be spoilt for choice. Sometimes known as activity checklists or progress assessments, the basic idea remains the same in all of them. They are listings of children's behaviours ordered in developmental sequence and grouped within the major domains of development. Figure 6.4 is an example of a chart which we devised and used on our Parental Involvemental Project at the University of Manchester. These P.I.P. charts[67] cover five major areas (physical, social, eye–hand, play and language development) and the skills included within each are those normally acquired by children up to four years of age. There are many other similar charts, both British and American, the *Portage Checklist*,[59] *HELP Profile*,[68] *Early Intervention Development Profile*[69] to name but a few.

For slightly older children, the *National Children's Bureau Development Guides*[70] could prove useful as they cover many 'of the usual' preschool activities. These guides were designed with non-handicapped but 'at risk' children in mind.

During the school years, the nature of development charts changes because children's behaviours are now determined by the experiences they have and by adult expectations. The type of chart which has proved most successful is that describing the stages in the acquisition of basic life-skills such as in self-care, personal and social skills.

Figure 6.5 is an example of one chart taken from *Pathways to Independence*, compiled by Dorothy Jeffree and Sally Cheseldine[71] during their Parents and Teenager Project. Once again, there are many other possibilities including the famous *Progress Assessment Charts*[72] and the *Behaviour Characteristics Profile*[73] developed in the USA.

Use of the Charts with Parents

The points you need to emphasise when working through the charts with parents are:

● *The stages children go through in each area* Because the

Section 17 : Spoken language

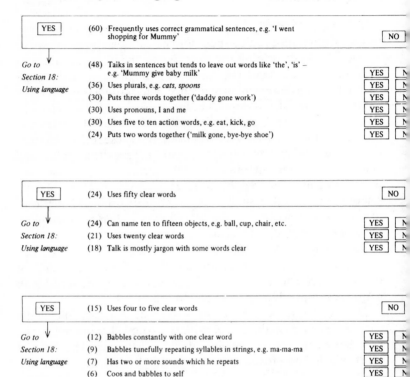

| YES | (60) | Frequently uses correct grammatical sentences, e.g. 'I went shopping for Mummy' | NO |

Go to
Section 18:
Using language

(48)	Taiks in sentences but tends to leave out words like 'the', 'is' – e.g. 'Mummy give baby milk'	YES	N
(36)	Uses plurals, e.g. *cats, spoons*	YES	N
(30)	Puts three words together ('daddy gone work')	YES	N
(30)	Uses pronouns, I and me	YES	N
(30)	Uses five to ten action words, e.g. eat, kick, go	YES	N
(24)	Puts two words together ('milk gone, bye-bye shoe')	YES	N

| YES | (24) | Uses fifty clear words | NO |

Go to
Section 18:
Using language

(24)	Can name ten to fifteen objects, e.g. ball, cup, chair, etc.	YES	N
(21)	Uses twenty clear words	YES	N
(18)	Talk is mostly jargon with some words clear	YES	N

| YES | (15) | Uses four to five clear words | NO |

Go to
Section 18:
Using language

(12)	Babbles constantly with one clear word	YES	N
(9)	Babbles tunefully repeating syllables in strings, e.g. ma-ma-ma	YES	N
(7)	Has two or more sounds which he repeats	YES	N
(6)	Coos and babbles to self	YES	N
(2)	Makes small throaty noises	YES	N

Go to Section 18: Using langu

Figure 6.4: An Example of a Developmental Chart

Source: Jeffree and McConkey,[67] by kind permission of Hodder and Stoughton

Giving Information

Section 24: Spoken information

Tick or colour in box   Date

		Tick or colour in box	Date
24.9	Can be clearly understood by others and uses appropriate language in all day to day situations both at home and in unfamiliar surroundings. Able to give and receive information and remember it		....
24.8	Uses appropriate language in day to day situations and responds to others both at home and in unfamiliar surroundings. Cannot always be clearly understood (i.e. articulation difficulty)		....
24.7	Expressive language good but not always appropriate. Response to others and to the situation limited		....
24.6	Can give specific information on request (e.g. name and address)		....
24.5	Good understanding and expressive language at a simple level — i.e. single words or short sentences. Will respond both at home and in unfamiliar surroundings		....
24.4	Good understanding at simple level. Expressive language at single word or short sentence level. Can be understood by family and friends — not always by strangers		....
24.3	Uses mainly gestures to make wants known, both at home and in unfamiliar surroundings. A few words. Quite good at being understood and understanding at simple level		....
24.2	Uses a few gestures and some idiosyncratic articulations to make wants known. Can only be understood by family and friends		....
24.1	Responds to cuddling and attention		....

Section 25: Written information

25.12	Writes and addresses letters (business or personal), keeps diary		....
25.11	Can write short personal letter		....
25.10	Can write short notes (shopping list, reminders)		....
25.9	Can write own name and address		....
25.8	Can write own telephone number without help		....
25.7	Writes first and second names without help		....
25.6	Writes first name without help		....
25.5	Writes own first name from copy		....
25.4	Can copy single letters and numbers		....
25.3	Can copy a circle		....
25.2	Scribbles purposefully with pencil or crayon		....
25.1	Holds pencil or crayon; attempts to scribble		....

Figure 6.5: An Example of a Skills Checklist

Source: Jeffree and Cheseldine,[71] by kind permission of the authors and Hodder and Stoughton.

different behaviours are in order, parents can spot skills that their child might soon learn and they come to realise that earlier behaviours, which they thought were of little significance, are the starting point for the major skills they want their child to acquire (walking, talking, etc.).

● *The chart will help them to observe their child in more detail* There will be skills listed that they have never tried before with their child. Urge them to have a go and not to take anything for granted; the child might surprise them.

● *The charts can be used to record the child's progress* Beside each item they can tick YES or NO. If they go through the chart at regular intervals, say every six months using a different coloured pen, they will be able to chart the child's gains.

● *Finally, comparisons can be made across the different areas, to identify the child's strengths and weaknesses.*

It's best to talk through the charts with parents on a one-to-one basis, after spending some time either watching the child at play or playing with the child yourself or observing the parent and child at play. This means that you will have seen the child exhibit some of the behaviours listed on the charts and these can be immediately ticked off as you read them with the parents. Don't rush through the charts; there's a lot of information for the parents to absorb. In fact some therapists and teachers prefer to use only one section of the charts at a time.

Give the parents a week or so to complete the chart at home. Arrange a second meeting during which you can discuss their findings with them and explore any difficulties encountered, such as management/compliance problems.

If you as a teacher or therapist are already familiar with the child, you may spot some discrepancies between your ratings and those of the parents. These are well worth probing. It could be that the child genuinely behaves differently in some situations: for instance, talks more at home than in school or attempts to feed himself at school but not at home. Alternatively, one or other of you may have adopted more lenient criteria in your interpretation of the item and there is really no disagreement. However, remember in future to spell out agreed criteria.

At the end of this phase, you and the parents will have a fuller and *shared* understanding of what the child can do. Of course, there is yet more information to be collected but, before going on to that, I think we should explore two formidable obstacles which might prevent you using developmental charts: the illiterate parent and the atypical child.

Illiterate Parents. You will not always know this in advance, so beware. Among the ideas I have come across are the following:
● *Interview* the parents about their child using the charts as your guide. Identify the main areas you want them to observe at home and then go through the charts again with them a week or so later.
● *Cartoons* Present the chart in cartoon form, e.g. 'stick-men' doing various actions, lying, rolling, sitting with support, then alone, standing, etc.
● *Video* Compile a video-record of children at different developmental stages and, as you play this back to the parents, elicit whether or not their children do these sorts of activities and/or whether they have tried them (there are some ready-made films in this area).
With immigrant families, you may also need the help of an interpreter (older son or daughter, community worker, etc.).

Very Atypical Children. By these, I mean children whose behavioural repertoire is very limited: for instance, multiply handicapped children, extremely hyperactive or disturbed children or very young babies. In all these instances, parents will have very few items which they can tick YES. It is likely that you could quickly ascertain these through talking with them. What will be more helpful to you and them is much more detail about precisely what the child can do. In fact, this is a necessary step with all children. Hence you might skip the charts altogether and move to the collecting of more detailed information.

Build on the Charts

Developmental charts are but a foundation. They have severe drawbacks if treated as complete assessments. First, they are not sufficiently detailed; the gap between one item and the next may be very large or the items do not get down to the specifics, e.g. 'knows four to five words' but which words does the child know? Secondly, the items are scored on an all-or-none basis, with no indication of how often or in what circumstances the child performs that particular behaviour. We need to overcome both these drawbacks if we are to progress toward effectively helping

ANALYSIS OF VOCABULARY

People			Objects			Social			Actions			Modifiers		
	Spon	Imit		Spon	Imit		Spon	Imit		Spon	Imit		Spon	Imit
Mummy			Ball			Bye			Brush/Comb ..			Big		
Daddy			Book			Hello ⎤			Down			Bold		
child's name			Car			Hiya ⎦			Drink			Clean		
Other names			Chair			Here			Eat			Dirty		
			Comb			Look			Fall (down) ..			Hot		
			Cup			Nite-nite ...			Gimme/Want ...			Little/Small ..		
			Dinner ...			No			Go			More		
			Doll			There			Gone/Allgone .			My		
			Milk			What			In			Nice		
			Shoe			Where			Kiss			Sick		
			Spoon			(Toilet)			Off			That		
PRONOUNS			Sweet						On			This		
Me			Teddy						Sit (down) ...			Your		
Mine									Sleep					
I									Stop					
You									Throw					
It									Up					
									Wash					

© *ST. MICHAEL'S HOUSE RESEARCH*

Figure 6.6: A More Detailed Assessment Chart

the child's development.

Here are some examples of how you might do this in the area of language development. The same principles can be applied to other areas, as we will see in a later section of the chapter.

More Detail

It may be stating the obvious but you will want more detail only in those areas which are of primary concern to you *and* the parents. In short, information to take action on, not to file away. Figure 6.6 is the Analysis of Vocabulary form which we give to parents concerned to further their child's language learning.

The words written on the form were chosen because (1) they are words children usually learn first, or (2) they are words that refer to objects and events that frequently occur in young children's environment, or (3) these words are useful for children to know; with them they can communicate their needs and wants.

The words are intended to form a '*core vocabulary*' in that, by knowing all these words, the children will be able to use language to refer to many different things and they can link the words into a wide range of sentences. However, there are many blank lines on the form for parents and staff to add in other words.

As you can see, the words have been grouped in categories to highlight the ways children combine words into sentences using rules such as Person + Action: Social Word + Person. It also serves the very useful function of highlighting those categories in which the child has an over-abundance of words and those with relatively few, if any, words.

Completion of the Form. The form records the words children use in *expressive* language. Only those words that the child has been heard to use are actually ticked on the form as follows:
● If the child thinks of the word by himself, i.e. uses the word spontaneously, the tick goes in the 'Spon' (Spontaneous) column.
● If the child copies the adult, i.e. the adult has said the word immediately before the child, the tick goes in the 'Imit' (Imitation) column.
We encourage parents to pin up the chart in a convenient location at home and tick off the words they hear their child use during the week. Or to have special play sessions when they could try eliciting words, e.g. making a doll do particular actions and see if the child labels them.

It is also useful to know the words which the child clearly understands when spoken by an adult, even though the child never says them, e.g. give teddy a kiss. If the child does so, the parent circles the words 'teddy' and 'kiss' on the form.

The 'completed' form invariably elicits comments along the lines of 'I didn't know she knew so many words'. Moreover, comparisons of the parent's form with the teacher's compilation of words the child uses in school or playgroup, can generate much interest and discussion, from both parties.

Arguably, though, the main value of the form is in the gaps it highlights: common words or whole categories of words which are absent from the child's vocabulary. From here, it is a small step to identifying new words that you might help the child to learn. (Incidentally, this form, or one like it, can be used with children using non-verbal signs.)

Typical Behaviours

We need to complement our knowledge of what the child *can* do, with information about what the child typically does. The most useful way we have found of doing this in the context of early language acquisition, is by having the parents tape-record and transcribe all that their child says during a free-play session with them.

There are various ways you can analyse the transcription, depending on the points you want to make. For example,

● the balance between words or sentences spoken spontaneously and those which are imitations of an adult

● the frequency with which the child uses words from various categories, e.g. may use more names of people and objects than action words

● the relative frequency of single words, two word or multi-word utterances.

The general reaction we get to this type of activity is one of disappointment: the parents were under the impression that their child was doing better than the transcript shows up. This is a useful opening for a discussion on how development occurs within stages as well as over stages and that the 'highest level' is rarely the most typical level for any child, or indeed adult.

Once again, comparisons of transcripts made in different settings and with different people, can also provide a lot of questions and discussion.

There is a second important type of 'frequency' records: that which describes undesirable or problem behaviours. For example, Figure 6.7 is a form devised by Elizabeth Newson and Tony Hipgrave[34] for parents to record when and why a child, Caroline, had temper tantrums. This sort of record begins to establish the patterns which underly the child's behaviour, in this case when her mother is busy and around meal times. They go on to add:

> people often feel put off by the idea of keeping records — we felt that way too! When you get used to it you'll find it easier than it looks — and it does work in getting our ideas clear and therefore in helping us to plan the best possible programme and carry it out. (p.40)

Frequency charts completed daily or at regular intervals are an excellent way of charting changes in the children's behaviour.

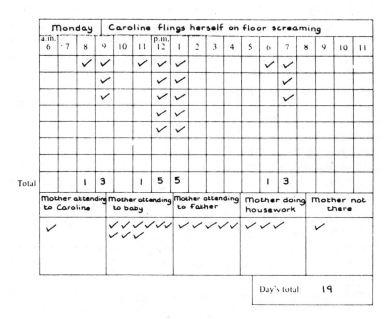

Figure 6.7: A Chart for Recording Frequency of Behaviours

Common Strands in Detailed Observations

From these specific examples, I want now to extract some of the principles to be borne in mind when seeking further information about what the child can do.

Devising your own Recording Forms. Often you will have to invent your own observation and recording forms, especially if you are working with children of widely differing ability levels. Each form will have to be tailored to the child's needs, identified in discussion with the parents or by the information obtained with the development charts and your own knowledge and observations of the child. As I have stressed before, beware of rushing into intervention too soon. Obtaining as much information as you can about the child, will enable you to devise a more focused teaching strategy. The books and curriculum guides listed in Chapter 12 will help you devise suitable forms.

Specific Behaviours. I hope you also noted that the sample forms were very specific. Everything was spelt out in detail; the words spoken or the time when the behaviour occurred. This not only provides essential information, but it actually makes the whole exercise so much easier for parents, in that the ambiguity and vagueness has been eliminated.

Easily Recorded. The forms serve two purposes: (1) a listing of specific behaviours and (2) a method for quickly and easily recording what the child did. Usually this involves merely placing ticks. What could be simpler? However, it's best to draw up the form with these two points in mind and leave copies with the parents. Some might devise their own, most will not.

In those activities which require more than 'ticks', such as writing out all that a child says, try to make it easier for parents. For instance, we suggest they audio-tape the session so that they can play it back at their leisure. And if they don't own a recorder, we lend them one.

Discourage parents from relying on their memory.

Practise in Advance. This is the secret of success in helping parents make their own accurate records. Not only should you spend time explaining the chart to parents, you should practise using it with them. For instance, you might observe the child together or watch a video-replay of the child or even the video of another child. In each case you should be able to clarify in advance any of the parents' misunderstandings or uncertainties. And, because they are more confident that they know what to do, then they are more likely to go away and do it.

Analysis of the Information. Arguably the best forms are those that clearly illustrate the significance of the information recorded: for instance, the blank spaces in the Analysis of Vocabulary chart. You and the parent know straight away what you might do next. Sadly, it is not always as clear-cut. In these instances, try to provide some guidelines for parents on how to extract useful information, such as counting the number of single-word utterances and compare with the number of two-word utterances. But keep this simple. My early efforts in analysing transcripts had parents calculating percentages and mean length of utterances. Talk about creating unnecessary confusion! In fact you do run the risk of overloading the parents if they have to master both *how* to record and what to do afterwards. If necessary, you can spend a subsequent session going over their records and helping them extract the relevant information.

Adapt to Differences among Parents. Needless to add, some parents will not be able to cope with these activities due to language or educational difficulties. They are, however, in the minority and, even with them, some modified or adapted form of recording could be possible, e.g. by placing ticks against cartoon representations. Alternatively, you could spend more time observing the child together or watching a video-recording, so that you can highlight the significant actions which their child performs.

Issues Raised by the Parents

Focusing on what the child can do through developmental charts and observation activities is an approach which will be welcomed by most mothers and fathers. There will be some, though, who have reservations and you'll cope best if you are forearmed. Among those that I have come across are the following:

'What's all this got to do with my child's problem?' Perhaps you did not spend enough time explaining how the information would

be of use or, if you did, the message did not sink in! Sometimes you may have to ask the parents to trust you because the value of the exercise may only become clear when they have done it. Or the parents may well have a genuine grievance. Could you be ignoring their priorities in favour of yours?

'*He's more delayed than I thought.*' Parents can come back more disheartened about their child's progress, such as when they realise that their two-and-a-half year old is just about managing to do the same things as a twelve-month-old baby. You have a number of options in restoring their morale. Emphasise the child's strengths: he or she may well be stronger in some areas than others. Secondly, remind them of the variations among all children. Thirdly, stress that your concern is, in Chris Kiernan's[52] words, 'to measure the child against himself and not against other children.' Fourthly, press on with devising learning goals because, when they experience success, their disappointments will quickly fade.

Interestingly, the corollary of this scenario, 'he's better or doing more than I thought', rarely causes a problem.

'*He can do it but he won't.*' Here you will have to probe deeper to discover the significance of this remark. It may indeed reflect a management problem; the child won't sit still long enough to complete the task. Alternatively, the parents may need to consider other possible explanations for their child's failure to perform, among them a lack of competence. You could point out how children create all sorts of diversions when they are aware that their lack of competence could be shown up. We have a lovely example on video-tape of a little boy who is supposed to be sorting objects by size but he tries to deflect me by pointing to things in the room, talking about his shoes and, when I ignore all these, he finally throws the object! The fact that he correctly sorted two or three objects could easily lead you to believe that he is capable of the task but he won't concentrate.

'*I didn't have time to fill in the charts.*' Actually, I rarely hear this type of comment, perhaps I have been lucky. When I do, I wonder first of all if the parents are able to cope with the written material, have they a literacy problem? It's worth discreetly checking this out, possibly through other professionals who know the family or by your own observations during a joint recording session. If they do have a problem, you can then take steps to help them.

For those parents who were unable to make time, you may need to review the value of the activity and explain why their contribution is so important. In some schemes professionals have negotiated a 'contract' with the parents at the outset. This briefly outlined both what they were prepared to do and what the parents would be expected to do. Those unwilling or unable to find the time would presumably excuse themselves at the outset and, if parents did opt in, it was in the full knowledge of what they had let themselves in for.

Lastly, there will be some families whose other needs are so pressing that the handicapped child could be the least of their worries. In these circumstances, teachers and therapists may need to back-off from making yet more demands on the parents and instead try to ensure that the family receives help from other social or health services, as appropriate.

Issues Raised by Teachers and Therapists

The involvement of parents in assessing their child's ability raises issues for professionals.

'You can't depend on parents' assessments.' Generally, the complaint is that they overestimate the child's competence. If this is so, then it is up to teachers and therapists to spell out the criteria they have in mind, as to whether or not a child should be credited with a skill or ability. It's worth spending time ensuring that the parent's observations are reliable because this will enable you to have access to much greater detail about the child than you would ever obtain in, say, a half-hour assessment session. Remember too, it's also quite conceivable that the child does perform better at home than in the school or clinic, so don't dismiss the parent's ratings as wrong.

'You don't know how far behind the child is.' That's true. My concern here has not been with normative assessments. If you feel it is necessary to have an accurate measure of the child's developmental status in relation to normal children's perform-ance, you could use one of the many standardised tests available : Bayley scales, McCarthy, etc. The trouble is, these rarely lead into educational or therapeutic action unlike the assessments I have focused on here.

'I can't find suitable charts for use with my children.' If you are waiting for the 'ideal' developmental chart or checklist, you will wait a long time. Each has its advantages and drawbacks. My

advice is not to ponder overlong on which is best, but rather to make the best of whatever is readily available to you. And, if need be, you can concoct your own. That's how most of us started.

'*I don't have time to go into such detail with parents.*' Or put more bluntly, 'isn't there a quicker way?' Yes, there is; you could work solely from charts or observations which you as a teacher or therapist have already completed and bring the parents in on the teaching programme. That would be better than nothing but it does run the risk of imposing your decisions on the parents and prevents them understanding the rationale for them. We want to share *knowledge* with them, not just information. As regards the more general issue of finding the time to work with parents at all, we'll come to that in Chapter 13.

Practical Hints

Finally, some practical tips I hope you will keep in mind.

Get the Feel of the Child Yourself. You need some direct personal contact with the child so that you have a reference point when parents talk about their assessments of the child's abilities. Teachers, of course, will have this knowledge but it is not always so with therapists or home visitors. They need to spend some time getting to know children, playing with them or 'testing' how they react to various events, activities, etc.

Many parents both enjoy and learn from watching another adult interact with their child. I hope spectators don't put you off! If their presence distracts the child, you could let the parents see a video-recording or watch through a one-way screen.

It is particularly beneficial if you can complete the same developmental charts or observation activities as the parents. Comparison of your assessments and theirs can be highly informative. Teachers and assistants are in the best position for doing this.

Visit the Home. This is not essential but it is surprising the new insights you can get into the child's behaviour. So even, if most of your contacts have to take place in schools or clinic, a visit to the family home in the beginning stages is well worthwhile. (See Chapter 5 for more details.)

Keep Copies of the Parent's Charts. This is so obvious it is easily overlooked. You will be able to refer to them when it comes to planning learning objectives; it will double or treble the information you have about the child on file and this could be most useful should you need to write reports for other services or professionals; it will tell parents that you value their work and encourage them to complete the charts.

We usually supply parents with two or more copies of each chart, so that they give us a spare one.

Review. From time-to-time, perhaps every six months, it is worth reviewing the developmental charts with parents and/or having them repeat some of the more detailed recordings. This should highlight the areas in which the child has progressed and identify others where little or no advance has been made. This information may help you to decide on future priorities. Needless to say, this can encourage you and the parents, not least because of the boost it gives to their morale; they know they *can* influence their child's development.

I told you before of the discouraging words spoken to a mother of a Down's syndrome baby girl: 'She'll never be able to walk . . .' Here's how her father continues the story . . .

We had her home about a week when I started trying to get her to take notice . . . lifting her up . . . the usual . . . keeping her more or less alert.

When she came to . . . 9 months, less than that even, we done our best. First of all started crawling; putting her down on her back and pulling her forward. And we did work very hard to get her to walk. We never gave her an idle minute — we were at her continuously — thought it was good to keep her on the move, instead of letting her lie around. And I was very pleased to see her walking in 17 months.

7

You Learn Something Every Day

Parents are teachers. Whether they are good teachers is no more relevant than whether they are good parents. Parents are parents because they are present at conception, birth and development of the child. They are also teachers because they are present at the most teachable moments: eating, walking, talking and interacting. (Jane Schulz)

Everyday learning; that's what this chapter is about. Not the sort that focuses on exceptional and specialised skills, but rather the basic everyday skills that all children have to master. Nor will this learning require special facilities or equipment. Instead it can take place in unsophisticated everyday surroundings. And although people with training and qualifications can do the teaching, the job is equally well done by ordinary everyday people such as parents. In short, we will be dealing with the type of learning that goes on in households the world over, every day.

As the opening quotation reminds us (written incidentally by a parent who is also a professional teacher) the people directing and stimulating this learning are parents. *Parents are teachers.* I hope these three words stay with you throughout all your work with parents. Your job is not to make parents *into* teachers; they are teachers already. Nor should you try to have them teach in the same way you do. Every teacher has his or her own style and we must respect the parent's style, just as we tolerate the differences among our colleagues.

There is one service you can provide to parents (in fact, it's one we could all do with), you can help them become *better* teachers. It's not easy to teach a child who is handicapped; your natural 'style' might be insufficient or even inappropriate. But, even if it isn't, you might not have the confidence to do what comes naturally. There are four areas in which parents could do with help: selecting precise learning objectives; suggestions for possible teaching contexts; acquiring more techniques to aid the child's learning; adapting their teaching in the light of the child's progress.

I shall deal with each one of these areas in the course of this chapter, outlining some of the principles you might follow and illustrating them mainly with reference to language learning.

Some of you may be familiar with these topics as you apply them regularly in the course of your work. Others, I suspect, may wish to have more detail than space permits me to give here. Many of the books and curriculum guides referenced in other parts of the book (see pp.292 and 308) will give additional information. My priority has been to focus on ways of getting the message across to parents. None the less, I trust that you, as well as parents and children, will be able to say at the end of the chapter, 'you learn something every day'.

Selection of Learning Objectives

- 'I'd love you to do something about his concentration'
- 'I want him to talk'
- 'Could we stop him running around so much?'

Three parents' views on how they would like their child to change for the better. The problem is, they are expressed as wishes, rather than a plan of action. Take the first one, concentration. If we are to do anything about this, we will need to define in more detail what we mean by that term. How will we recognise when the child is concentrating and when he is not? Learning objectives should describe the *behaviours* we want to see the child doing, i.e. the child will concentrate on matching picture cards for one minute.

The second parent's wish, to have the child talking, meets the requirement of describing a desired behaviour but still it is unsatisfactory. This time the problem is the breadth of skills involved in talking. With so many things to learn, the only feasible way of proceeding is to start with a more precise target in mind. For example, that the child will learn the words 'give me' and 'bye-bye'. Hence the second feature of learning objectives is that they should state *specific* behaviours.

Our third parent wishes to stop the child from running around. That sounds specific enough until you examine it more closely. Do they really want their child to stop running for ever? I guess not, especially as they were the very people who encouraged him to walk in the first place. Rather they want to stop their son running in certain circumstances. It is best to spell these out, picking the conditions when they are more likely to succeed and then move on to tackle the harder ones. For example, 'to stop him running around during meal times' and then later, 'stop him running around when he goes up to bed'.

The main advantages of stating your learning objectives in this precise manner are:

● *The objective will be attainable in a short time*, in days rather than months. This is good for parents' morale and helps convince them that they can influence their child's behaviour for the better

● *The objective helps to focus the teaching*; the parents will not need to spend an inordinate amount of time with their child. The teaching should be easily incorporated into their everyday routines.

● *The child's progress is easy to monitor*, admittedly the gains might be small (two new words learnt with thousands more still to master), yet we are aware that learning has occurred. Moreover, it is progress that can be noted by everyone; no special tests or procedures are necessary.

● *Other people can be told about the objective* When the goal is precisely stated, it is so much easier for parents to share it with other members of the family, even quite young children will learn what it means, or with relatives, neighbours and friends.

Given all these benefits, it is hardly surprising that all intervention schemes with handicapped or 'at risk' children invariably advise (or insist) that parents express their objectives as precise behaviours that the child will learn. Sean Cameron's[40] phrase sums up the reasoning: this approach is 'doomed to success'.

Convince the Parents

Some parents, perhaps most, will be initially sceptical, even disappointed, that you are not tackling the big problems with which they have to contend. If they are not committed to working with precise objectives, then it is unlikely that any of you will see progress.

From the outset, you must listen to the parents' concerns, helping them to define in more detail what they mean and their desires for improvements in the child. At this stage it is worth talking in terms of 'goals' for their child. For example, in the Wessex Portage Project,[58] the home visitor and the parents plan their overall goals for a six-month period. At the end of that period, they review their progress and that in turn helps them plan the goals for the next six months.

Once parents are assured that you are taking their goals seriously, they can then more readily work on a plan for attaining them. They could well discover for themselves, that this is best done through a series of subgoals or precise objectives. It is worth mapping these out for parents to show how one specific objective can be followed by another, then another, until the overall goal is attained. Of course you must warn them that this plan might need changing as you go along. The child might find some steps harder than others, hence you cannot be sure how long it will take. None the less, these reservations do not detract from the essential purpose of the exercise: to show parents the stages in attaining the desired end result.

If the parents are still unconvinced, and it's only a very small minority in my experience, your final hope is to persuade them to begin with one precise objective (almost as a favour for you) and, if it doesn't work out, you will try something else. The experience of success should sway the doubters.

Appropriate Objectives

The crucial element in selecting objectives is ensuring that they are appropriate to the child's needs. This is a complex matching task, for which you need detailed information on the child. Hence the information collected via the developmental charts, or during more detailed observations of the child's actions (see Chapter 6), is your main reference source. In fact, you should try to tailor this collection of information in such a way that the selection of precise objectives becomes obvious to the parents. For example, the Analysis of Vocabulary form which the parents complete by ticking the words they have heard the child use (see p.116), simultaneously shows all the words the child does *not* use. It is from this that the parents can select new words.

Table 7.1: Guidelines for Selection of Vocabulary Objectives

1. Concentrate on one or, at the most, two new words at a time

2. Pick a word that the child has already got the idea of and demonstrates it by action, e.g. uses gestures in play, or else a word which he appears to understand when you say it

3. Select a word that the child has been heard to imitate but not to use spontaneously

4. To widen the child's vocabulary, pick a word from the category which has relatively few words, e.g. if the child knows 15 names of objects, but only one action word, then it would be better to select another action word for him to learn rather than a sixteenth name of an object!

5. However, choose the words according to their developmental order. In general these tend to be
   - First: Names of people
   - Second: Objects or Social words
   - Third: Actions
   - Fourth: Modifiers

   Therefore, action words are best taught before modifiers; social words before action words, etc.

6. With modifying words; at first pick only one of the two contrasts, e.g. 'dirty' or 'clean' but not both. Only when the child really understands one, should the opposite be taught

7. Although the Analysis of Vocabulary form lists words which are useful for all children to learn, there may be other words which would be more suitable for your child to learn either because they reflect the child's interests or refer to significant objects or events within the child's environment. *Therefore, always be guided by your child's interests and needs*

Table 7.1 lists the advice we give parents on how best to select new words. We do not tell them the words we think the child should learn, we encourage *them* to make the selection. If they have overlooked one of the guidelines, we will draw their attention to this, but if they have good reasons for their choice, then we defer to them. Later when the child starts to use the new words, the chart can be updated and new learning objectives chosen. We have prepared similar charts covering early sentence usage and the 'meanings' inherent in children's early communicative acts, be they verbal or non-verbal.

Many of the curriculum packages available commercially incorporate checklists which aid the selection of goals. For example, in the Portage Guide to Early Education,[59] the checklist is divided into five developmental areas and, within each, the items are arranged in developmental sequence. Also provided is a card file, one for each item in the checklist. These cards describe the skill, e.g. 'Draws a square in imitation', and goes on to suggest materials and curriculum ideas to teach the behaviour concerned. These skills could be further broken down into even more precise objectives. Once again it is the items on the checklist that are *not* ticked that give parents the clue as to the appropriate learning objective for their child.

If you do not have any suitable ready-made guidelines or checklists for parents, you may have to devise your own. For example, Jill Garner[89] suggests it would be a great benefit to parents and teachers to special schools to draw up a structured curriculum, in which their teaching targets are spelt out and, if need be, broken down step-by-step. This can be given to the parents who will then be able to identify readily the skills the child uses at home as well as at school and to share with the teacher their ideas about future goals. Table 7.2 is an example taken from one such curriculum that is used at the Rectory Paddock School,[62] London.

Table 7.2: A Section from One School's Curriculum

SWIMMING

Stage 3: *With arm bands in deep water*

1. Child supported by adult can lie on his back — kick his legs
2. Child supported by adult can lie on his front — hold float, kick legs
3. Child can tread water holding one hand of adult
4. Child can tread water on his own
5. Child can tread water and paddle with his arms
6. Child has one chamber of arm band blown up, will tread water and paddle with arms
7. Child wears arm bands with no air in — will dog paddle to side

---

Source: Reproduced from *In Search of a Curriculum* by the staff of Rectory Paddock School.[62]

Skills Analysis

It is also worth introducing parents to the concept of task and skills analysis. For example, every task, even the so-called simple ones, are made up of a whole series of substeps. You might give the parents a demonstration of this:

The steps involved in building a tower of bricks are
(1) Looking at and focusing on one of the blocks
(2) Reaching out accurately for the block
(3) Grasping the block, typically between finger(s) and thumb
(4) Picking up the block
(5) Placing the block on top of another block with the sides correctly aligned
(6) Letting go of the block without disturbing the 'tower'
(7) Looking for another block and repeating all the previous steps.

Once they have grasped what you mean, let them try to break down a task they had in mind for their child. This is much easier to do with 'gross motor' or 'fine motor' activities and self-care skills than with more cognitive skills such as language. None the less, it is still possible and will bring home to parents the many new things their child has to learn. They should then appreciate the need to focus only on one or two steps at a time, knowing that ultimately these skills will come together in complete tasks.

Knowing Why

The point I have emphasised in this section is that parents should fully appreciate the *rationale* for the selection of objectives. It is all too easy for teachers and therapists to prescribe the objectives they think are best but as Peter and Helle Mittler[15] remind us, 'it is not partnership when parents are shown how to carry out certain physical exercises without being given any intelligible explanation about the reasons why these particular exercises are necessary. (p.17) You need to make explicit to the parents the decision-making process you use in selecting objectives, so that they can understand what you are getting at but, more importantly, so that they have a chance of learning to do it for themselves.

Teaching Contexts

For too long, teachers and therapists have been preoccupied with what to teach and how to teach it that they have ignored the 'where' of teaching. By that, I don't just mean the surroundings or location, although they can be important, but also the materials, equipment or activities through which the child can perform the new behaviour. Take, for example, an activity like 'drawing a circle'. One teaching context, the obvious one, is to give the child paper and pencil. But is that the only one?

Certainly not! There are many possible variants; for a start it might be better to use chalk, crayons, paint brushes or even finger paints rather than pencils. Instead of paper, it could be card, white board (for paint) or a blackboard. Does the child always need to sit at a table, when he could be using an easel or a wall (covered with paper) or the floor?

Why confine yourself to only one medium? The child can draw circles in sand, mud or soft dough. He could make circles out of string, lengths of Plasticine or by arranging small shells. And, of course, some of these activities can be done during car journeys or on a day's outing to the seaside, just as well as in the family kitchen.

The permutations for learning contexts may not be endless, but they are certainly many and usually much more than those listed in the currently available curriculum packages or books. Sad to say, our powers of imagination have rarely been stretched in education. We have been content to take the obvious, and easiest, approach for us and if the children are not interested then we insist and if they are not able to do it we continue repeating the activity until they master it. I hope this scenario is somewhat exaggerated but we certainly need to ensure that it is not a philosophy which parents adopt. I take comfort from Somerset Maugham's words, 'Imagination grows by exercise and, contrary to common belief, is more powerful in the mature than in the young.'

What then are good learning contexts for children?

● *Variety* Try to think of a number of different contexts that parents can use (three is the minimum I aim for). This gives the parents alternatives should one prove totally uninteresting to the child, while at the same time it encourages the children to realise that the skill can be applied in other contexts or, in professional jargon, they generalise their learning.

We encourage parents to use materials that are readily available around the home and to improvise if they haven't got the proper equipment. For instance, making doll's furniture out of shoe boxes or targets for throwing games from cardboard boxes and the 'balls' from crumpled paper stuffed into the toes of old tights.

'Play dough' can be made from flour, water and salt and picture cards from cereal boxes with photographs from magazines or catalogues stuck on to them. Have samples of these 'homemade' toys to show to the parents.

● *Child's interests* If you can tie in the activity to the child's interests, so much the better. Very often a favourite game can be adapted to your learning objective. For instance, Paul, a handicapped boy, spent most of his time at school rocking backwards and forwards and moaning. One day, his teacher discovered that he liked sitting on her knee and being rocked until his head touched the ground. From time-to-time, she stopped doing this and only recommenced when he made a sound. Soon he started to 'ask' to be rocked by making a grunt and gradually he learned to say 'more' when he wanted to be rocked.

It is worth drawing up with parents a listing of the child's favourite things: toys, games, specific activities, events (e.g. going to the park), people he or she likes to be with or foodstuffs, etc. Equally, any outstanding dislikes should be noted, so that these can be avoided. Update this listing regularly because children's preferences can change quite rapidly.

● *Novelty* Of course, you want to widen the child's interests, particularly if your listing of 'likes' is rather small. Encourage the parents to experiment with activities they may not have tried before. For example, Table 7.3 lists *early* social play games (suitable with children whose developmental age is twelve months or less) that we suggest to parents taking our *'Let's Play'* course.[75] We encourage parents to try some 'new' activities from the listing and to 'invent' their own. When we see the group of parents a week later, often they tell us how pleasantly surprised they were by the child's reactions.

It can be helpful to loan parents 'toys' or 'equipment'. If their child isn't 'turned on' by the new toy, then they have not lost their money. Moreover, they can get started straight away, rather than expending energy on discovering where they can buy the equipment and then finding the time to go and get it. With 'reluctant' parents, the toy may actually stimulate them into playing with the child. It's the excuse they needed.

Occasionally, some special equipment can be needed to capture a child's interest. For instance, we have added lights or bells to post-boxes to encourage children to insert and sort the shapes. Similarly, we devised a model playground (with swings, slides, paddling pool) for 'Playpeople' characters that could be used to encourage sentence structuring: 'girl down the slide', 'boy splashing water'. Few parents will have the time or inclination to make these special 'toys', although don't discourage those who do.

Table 7.3: Early Social Play Activities

- Following your face as you move from side to side
- Copies tongue movements
- You imitate the child's smiles
- Dancing with child in arms
- Cuddles and squeezes, changing tone of voice and facial expressions
- Swinging child in blanket; stop until he makes response then continue
- Finger rhymes: round and round the garden, etc.
- Play in front of large mirror: kissing, patting, etc.
  (can make from cooking foil stretched on stiff card or hardboard)
- Peek-a-bo games: cloth over head, going behind child's back, disappearing behind a screen, e.g. chair
- Mother and father take turns to call child from side to side
- Looking at picture books, photos
- Make funny noises: 'moo', sneezes etc.
- Wear hats and sunglasses to encourage child to explore your face
- Tickling games: blow raspberries on tummy
- Copying simple actions with toys: rattling, hitting, etc.
- Blow bubbles for child to burst
- Mask on face (beware of frightening child)

Toy libraries are a great boon to parents and professionals alike. They are common in Britain and most European countries. In the United States, toy libraries are most often associated with support for family day care providers. Availability to parents, as individuals or members of parent groups, is not widespread, although it is evolving. Interested parents and professionals should contact local traditional libraries and child care organisations in order to identify existing toy libraries and determine guidelines for setting up their own. Toy libraries may also be glad to hear of suggestions for toys or equipment they could stock.

● *Everyday household activities* By contrast, there will be occasions when the new learning could be easily incorporated into an everyday activity, such as washing dishes or bath time.

The advantages to busy parents are obvious: they don't need to find a special time or use unfamiliar equipment. The child gets a chance to participate in an activity which is repeated regularly. Some will delight in joining in with what mummy and daddy do.

For example, parents have used washing dishes to encourage their children's use of two-word sentences of the type 'wash fork', 'wash cup', 'wash spoon'; loading the washing machine for sentences like 'sock in, shirt in, pants in'; dusting the furniture for 'dirty chair, dirty T.V., dirty table'. With a bit of ingenuity, most household chores can become language-learning contexts.[74] Likewise, with less able children, feeding, bathing and dressing times might be used as contexts for other learning.

● *Involve other family members* If you can think of activities that other brothers and sisters would enjoy joining in, all the better. This will bring the family closer together and share the work load for the parents. It is worth getting to know the family's interests and hearing about the sort of things they do already with the handicapped child. It could be that some of these would be easily adapted to suit new learning objectives.

Let me stress, though, that the brothers and sisters should neither be forced nor expected to play with the child. That approach can be counter-productive. Rather you need to build up an interest that already exists and this is more readily nurtured if the parent spends time playing with them, as well as with the handicapped child, or when all the family, parents included, play together.

Points to Remember

There are several points that you will need to advise and reassure parents about.

● *Routine* Children need opportunities to practise new skills; they rarely master them straight away. We aim for *daily* 'teaching' sessions and, depending on the learning contexts we are using, recommend that parents try to establish a routine of the same time each day. For example, having a session every morning before the child leaves for school. This ensures the child a slot in the family timetable.

● *Short sessions* Teaching sessions don't need to be long to be effective. A good rule-of-thumb is always to stop *before* the child wants to. Making the child persist at an uninteresting task, is likely to be a remnant of their own school days. Reassure parents that two to three minutes can be quite adequate, provided that it occurs every day.

● *Free from distractions* It can be helpful to have the child on his own, in a spare room such as a bedroom. Remove distracting toys or objects *before* the child comes into the room.

● *Pick your time* Don't embark on a teaching session when the child is fretful or tired. It's better to wait until he or she is alert. This advice applies equally to parents. If they are feeling hassled, annoyed or exhausted, it's probably better to skip the session for that day.

● *Be an opportunist* Encourage parents to take advantage of opportunities as they arise rather than sticking rigidly to their planned activities. In fact, when parents give you instances of having done this, you can be sure they have got the message. One parent, when he saw his daughter throwing toys into the paddling pool to create splashes, joined her and modelled the sentences he was working on: 'Ball in, bucket in,' etc. I leave you to guess what he said when he accidentally fell in!

● *Over-learning* Even when children have mastered the activity, it's good policy to give them yet more practice. This will consolidate their learning and the joy of succeeding will help to compensate for the times during new activities when they find the going more difficult. Encourage parents to mix 'old' and 'new' objectives in their activities with children.

Teaching Styles

'Children should be led into the right paths, not by severity but by persuasion.' The words of the Roman playwright Terence, written over 2,000 years ago, are as true now as they were then. The trick is to master the art of persuading. In this section I shall focus on the adults' behaviour, looking at the ways by which they can help or hinder the child's learning.

Although comparatively little research has been done into parent–child interactions, one unanimous conclusion has emerged: there are wide differences among parents' styles, even though the children are of comparable abilities. Interestingly, husbands and wives are more like each other than they are like others of their sex. Sally Beveridge[32] summarises the differences in this way:

Some parents are naturally more directive than others in their approach and prefer to intervene actively and to prompt their child's activities. Others are less directive and prefer to set up activities and then sit back and see what their child will do. (p.120)

Hence there is no absolutely 'good' or 'bad' way of interacting with handicapped children. The only valid criterion for judging is whether or not the children learn during the teaching sessions. If they do not, you might suggest some changes the parents could make in their teaching style.

These lessons were brought home to me in a study I carried out with Sally Cheseldine.[76] We monitored the children's expressive language in free play with parents over a four-week period. Then, in consultation with the parents, we selected specific learning objectives for each child, involving some type of two-word sentence. We loaned the family suitable teaching materials (picture blocks or doll play toys) but gave them no instructions as to how they should use them to achieve the learning objective. Parents audio-taped their teaching sessions, so that we were able to monitor their progress. Half the parents were successful, the remainder were not. When we analysed the successful parents' teaching style, it incorporated most of the techniques recommended by professionals: talk in short utterances, mainly in response to the child's actions or vocalisations and give lots of models. By contrast, the unsuccessful parents had used verbal questioning or demand strategies.

My first piece of advice to you then is to

OBSERVE THE PARENTS' NATURAL STYLE OF INTERACTING WITH THEIR CHILD

It really should not come as a surprise that parents can intuitively adopt 'good' teaching styles. They have a great deal more expertise at handling their child than anyone else and, long before we came along, they had successfully taught their son or daughter many things. It is rather presumptuous of us to prescribe a teaching method without giving parents the chance to try their own way. Your way may not be any better; indeed, you could be making it unnecessarily harder for the parents. But worse still, the parents are denied the credit for having taught the child: it's your method that worked, even though theirs might have been just as effective. The parents are then made to feel even more dependent on you.

It is important therefore that you take time to observe the parents interacting with their child, either at home or in the clinic, both during 'free play' activities as well as in teaching sessions. A video-recording will help you, and the parents, to make a more detailed analysis (see p.255).

Based on this knowledge, you might then suggest teaching contexts that are more in accord with the parents' preferred style. For instance, turn-taking games, in which the child has to follow the mother's commands and then she does what the child says (e.g. sit on the chair; sit on the table; sit on the floor) might suit the more directive parent, whereas activities based around pretend play with dolls could be a better choice for parents who prefer to follow their child's lead. Yet, in each instance, the objective can be the same: such as encouraging two-word sentences of the type verb–object.

Barbara Tizard[9] takes this point further in her advice to teachers when allocating jobs to parent-helpers in the classroom.

A more forceful parent may be better organising groups for games where the children need to learn and adhere to a set of rules (like ball games, cards or games like 'follow my leader'), rather than working with a particular child who is likely to feel overwhelmed. (p.184)

The second guideline I commend to you is

GIVE PARENTS THE OPPORTUNITY TO SEE OTHERS TEACHING

When you think of it, parents usually have few opportunities of seeing 'good' teachers at work. The closest they will have come are the recollections from their school days or watching relatives or friends dealing with their children. Neither of these is particularly apposite when faced with a handicapped child.

Observing other teachers can occur quite informally. For instance, they could watch you interacting with the child either at home, in the clinic or classroom. Alternatively, they could spend some time generally observing what goes on in their child's classroom or they could view video-recordings of their child or watch video-programmes about children like theirs. These experiences will let parents pick up 'tips' or even a whole new style of interaction. They may assimilate these without being aware of doing so. I am not implying at this point that parents should imitate the teachers they see, quite the oppposite. I believe we need to let parents pick and choose for themselves but first they must have the experiences to draw upon. Often it is our lack of confidence which prevents parents from seeing us at work with their child.

But observation alone is not always sufficient: explanation can double or triple the benefits. This is especially so when it comes to specific techniques, such as the giving of reinforcement or physical prompts, when the nuances of the teacher's behaviour are not readily apparent or the rationale for them. It helps if you can go over these with parents, preferably as they observe the techniques being used, for instance, by a colleague or while watching a video-recording of you with their child. A third alternative is to show an extract from a ready-made programme or a past recording with another child.

Don't rush through the explanation. Much of it will be new to parents and they will need time for it all to sink in. It helps also to give lots of different examples of how these techniques can be applied. My preference is to avoid professional *jargon* and to make the techniques as much like 'common sense' as you can. Focusing on the child's point of view can help get across the rationale underlying them. For instance, the need for reinforcement to be *immediate* can be illustrated by the child who not only learnt to place a toy in a box, but also to follow this quickly with throwing the box and toy on to the floor. The father either gave no reinforcement for placing the toy in the box or else said 'Good girl' just as his daughter was about to throw it! She probably thought that her dad was as pleased as she was with the clatter of falling toys.

Finally, you could give parents the chance to practise these new techniques under your supervision. This could be with their own child or else through role-play, with you taking the child's part. The latter method is useful practice for coping with problem behaviours that arise periodically. A video-recording of their attempts will make your feedback to the parents more meaning-ful. Remember to focus mostly on the times they used the technique well: a point I will take up in more detail later (see p.144).

And, in case you have neither the inclination nor the confidence to get to this level of sophistication, let me reassure you. The crucial starting point that every teacher or therapist can manage is for parents to have opportunities of seeing them teach.

The third and final rule I want to propose, is that should you decide that the parents' teaching style is inappropriate, then

LINK YOUR RECOMMENDATIONS FOR CHANGING THE PARENTS' TEACHING STYLE WITH HELPING THEIR CHILD TO ACHIEVE THE LEARNING OBJECTIVE

My reasons are as follows:
● It forces you to be *specific* in the changes you recommend to parents.
● It confines your criticisms to one particular context and avoids over-generalisations. It is all too easy to destroy a parent's confidence by making global criticisms or labelling them as 'over-anxious' or 'too bossy'. You need to bolster parents' confidence and self-esteem, not weaken it.
● It acknowledges that, in other contexts, the parent's natural style of interacting could be perfectly satisfactory. The change you are suggesting applies to only one context. For example, we advise parents to talk mostly in three-word sentences during teaching sessions designed to help their child acquire sentence rules. But this does not mean they should talk pidgin-English all the time. Over and above whether it would benefit the child, such a change would be very hard for parents to maintain. Confining the 'new' behaviour to one context, makes it more manageable for parents. But sometimes the parents can discover, or be helped to discover, how they might change.

For example, Jilly's dad was a man who would put up with no nonsense. His attitude was that Jilly could do the things but she didn't try or didn't try hard enough. You had to push her all the time. Jilly had Down's syndrome but her development was not noticeably delayed — she had walked at 13 months — but she was nearly two years old and still wasn't talking. We video-recorded Jilly and her father playing freely with some toys and then a session when they were looking at a picture book. The first thing he said when the tape was replayed was 'Gosh, I never shut up.'

He felt 'under pressure', not relaxed and admitted that it wasn't just because of the video. He often felt like that when he was trying to get Jilly to do something. We then asked him to have another session with Jilly, only this time, the rule was that Jilly can do whatever she likes with the toys. On playback he noticed that he was talking less and that Jilly seemed more keen to show him toys or have him play with them, e.g. kissing the doll.

There are two points worth noting in this example. Video enabled that father to see himself as others see him. Secondly, we manipulated the session so that he could see the consequences of his changed behaviour on the child.

Video is an ideal way of confronting people with the truth of their behaviour (see p.261 for further details). It is not, however, the only way. With many parents your recommendation will, in itself, suffice. After all, most will see you as the 'expert'. Alternatively, audio-recordings or written records of your observations could be used: such as a count of the number of times they asked the child to do something.

It is worth encouraging parents to evaluate themselves. For instance, during language-learning games, we ask parents to audio-record a teaching session and keep a tally both of the number of 'model' sentences they give the child and the total number of times they speak overall. Our guidelines for a 'good' session, is when the number of models comes to more than half the total number of utterances. In this way, parents can keep tabs on themselves. It also ensures that you are explicit about your instructions. In fact, when advising parents to change, don't hedge it around with qualifications or 'maybes'. Give it to them straight. If you don't believe it will work or don't say it with conviction, then why should parents try another way?

It helps greatly if parents can quickly see a change for the better in their child. I well remember one mother telling me that she was very sceptical about talking less, not believing that this could result in her daughter talking more. She decided to give it a try, just to prove me wrong. Fortunately, the converse was the case! Louise's improved behaviour won me a convert.

However, I'm not always so lucky, nor will you be. You might need to warn the parents that the change in the child may not come quickly but it will come. Secondly, you could get them charting the child's behaviour in some detail so that even small improvements can be detected (see p.118).

Finally, it can at times be difficult for parents to maintain a new style of interaction: old habits die hard, as they say. This is particularly so when it comes to handling problem behaviours. The parents know what they should do but under pressure or strain they revert to their old ways of 'giving in'. The challenge for you is to evolve ways of encouraging parents to persevere. Husbands and wives can be a great support for one another, each 'checking' the other. Likewise, I know of teachers and therapists who have gone to the family home to coach parents through the 'problem times' when the undesirable behaviour occurs, e.g. bed times or meal times. Indeed one colleague even stayed overnight to help the family cope with the new routine of ignoring the wandering child who wakened the household every night around 3.00 a.m. That's dedication!

One solution, then, is more frequent contacts between you and the parents at these key times. Another is more novel and, to my knowledge, untried in the field of parental education. It's called *self-modelling*, which Peter Dowrick[77] defines as, 'the behavioural change that results from the observation of oneself on video-tapes that show only desired behaviours.' (p.106) What happens is this. Subjects are video-taped as they attempt to perform the desired new behaviours. All their bad attempts or mistakes are then edited out, leaving only a two- to five-minute sequence which shows them at their best. It has been shown that regular viewing of such perfect sequences, in and of themselves, has resulted in improvement in the subject's behaviour.

Peter Dowrick cites examples of physically handicapped children who have walked better or learnt to swim or to feed themselves; of athletes who have improved their running and of teachers who have taught better. He admits that we know little, as yet, about why these improvements should occur but he notes the demise of one assumption, namely that people learn best by having their errors pointed out to them. Personally, I incline to his 'confidence building' theory, 'I can do it because I've seen myself do it — and I know how to do it again.' That's exactly the reassurance some parents will need. Perhaps you will join with me in testing its application to parents who find it difficult to persist with new teaching styles.

Advancing the Teaching

Once you and the parents have selected your objectives, chosen your teaching contexts and possibly adapted your teaching styles, any further decisions regarding the teaching process will be based on one main consideration: an evaluation of the child's progress. If the child has improved, you can go on to work toward other objectives. But, if there is little or no progress, then you and the parents will need to review your teaching styles or the teaching contexts or the objectives you selected. In either case the trigger is the same, an assessment of the child's current behaviour in relation to previous behaviours. It goes without saying that you and the parents must agree on your assessment of progress. It is for this reason that I am wary of relying solely on subjective impressions. It's much better to have some evidence to back up your conclusions.

Measuring progress will probably be a novel concept for most parents. Hitherto, they have relied on their memories in assessing whether or not the child had changed and probably depended on major milestones in making their judgements, such as the child walks alone, says his first word or uses the potty. If the gains are not as obvious as these, parents could easily conclude that their child's behaviour is no different. For instance, after a year-long study of Down's syndrome infants playing with common toys, we asked their mothers if they felt their children's play was any different now than it had been twelve months previously. Most felt their child's play was little different and none could cite specific changes. Yet our records[78] showed marked changes in the children's play.

Moreover, the parents were no better judges of their own behaviour. All felt they played with their child in much the same way but again our records[79] told a very different story.

Many of the suggestions I have made already in this chapter, and the previous two, will encourage parents to take a more searching and fine-grained look at their child, making it more likely that they will detect even small changes. However, I also want to describe two ways whereby you can highlight progress, or the lack of it.

RECORD OF THE CHILD'S USE OF LANGUAGE IN TEACHING GAMES

CHILD'S NAME ..David.....   TEACHER ...Dad.........   OBJECTIVES ...."kick".; 'Object + On/Off'

	NEW WORDS				NEW SENTENCES		
DATE	GAME	IMITATIONS	SPONTANEOUS	DATE	GAME	IMITATIONS	SPONTANEOUS
2nd Oct	Football	✓✓✓ ③		2nd Oct.	Dressing teddy + dolls	✓✓✓✓✓✓ ⑦	
4th Oct.	Pretend kicks with pictures	✓ ①		4th Oct	Dressing up	✓✓✓✓✓✓✓ ⑧	✓ ①
				5th Oct	Dressing teddy + cut-out figure	✓✓✓✓✓✓ ✓✓✓ ⑪	✓✓✓ ③
6th Oct	Football - telling dad to kick	✓✓✓✓✓✓ ✓✓ ⑨	✓✓ ②	6th Oct	Dressing dolls	✓✓✓ ③	✓✓✓ ④
8th Oct	Football (as above)	✓✓✓ ③	✓✓✓✓✓✓ ✓ ⑨	8th Oct	Picture book	(Not interested)	
9th Oct	'kicks' with pictures	✓✓✓✓ ④	✓✓✓✓ ⑤				
				10th Oct	Dressing up - telling dad	✓✓✓✓ ⑤	✓✓✓✓✓ ✓✓✓✓✓✓ ⑪

Figure 7.1: Recording Progress by Using Frequency Counts

Frequency Counts

The most popular method by far, is to keep a count of the number of times the child attains the objective which you have set. For example, Figure 7.1 shows a chart completed by David's mother from audio-recordings she made of her teaching sessions. The chart shows an increase first in the number of imitations, followed nearly a week later by improvements in his spontaneous usage of the word and sentences. These charts are relatively easy to complete during the teaching sessions; they involve placing a tick in the appropriate column. However, for parents who are trying to cope with novel teaching games, this extra work can be avoided by the use of a tape-recorder. It has the added advantage of letting them reflect on their child's behaviour.

Charts of this type are also useful for monitoring *decreases* of children's undesirable behaviours. For instance, the number of temper tantrums or wet pants. This time, the parents need to note every incident during the day. We advise parents to pin up the chart in an easily accessible place, so that they, or other family members, can keep an ongoing tally.

I don't want to give the impression that it is easy to persuade parents to keep records of this type. In my experience most need to be convinced of the value *to them* of engaging in this 'extra paperwork'. So be sure to spell out your reasons. Many of the suggestions made in Chapter 6 about frequency charts apply here too (see p.118). Two further points can be added.

First, give the parents a *prepared* chart and go through a sample recording session with them. Secondly, when you see their completed chart, have them 'talk' you through it, filling in what went on in the sessions each day and draw out the implications of the pattern that has emerged. Do *not* presume they will have seen what is obvious to you. You might want to test out some of their ideas by having a teaching session with the child yourself or by watching the parents. This could help you decide whether or not changes are needed in teaching style or contexts. Alternatively, you may want to simplify your objectives. For example, instead of having the child say the names of objects, you might be content to have him play an active part in a fetching game, thereby consolidating his understanding of language. Over-ambition on our part is a frequent cause for a child's failure to show detectable progress.

Finally, you might also need to refine the record-keeping. The disadvantage of such specific records is that you can easily overlook other sorts of progress. I recall one mother who was trying to teach her son, Paul, a new word 'wash' in the context of him getting washed for bed. She reported that he was much more interested in turning the taps on and off than washing himself. In fact, he started to say 'on' and 'more' and even said a sentence for the first time without ever saying the one word the mother had chosen, wash. Was this progress or not?

Hence, encourage parents to be alert for other changes. In this instance, we asked the mother to keep a listing of all the new words or sentences they heard Paul use during the week. This was displayed on the kitchen wall and Paul's seven-year-old sister was charged with writing down the new words, much to her delight.

Diary Records

Detailed frequency counts may prove unnecessary after a time or may not even be required in the first place. You and the parents will be the best judges.

A useful alternative is to have the parents keep a daily diary of how their teaching endeavours worked out and their child's reactions. This might only amount to three or four sentences but even this can be sufficient to remind parents what their child was like a week or fortnight ago. Here's one mother's comment on the value of a diary to her:

> I think you're amazed at how much they do do . . . because you have got to remember what they've done for the diary and all that . . . and when you look back and see just how much they can absorb, I think it surprises you because you don't expect them to have absorbed so much in such a short time.

Incidentally, the diaries I have used are nothing fancy, a sheet of paper ruled into seven rows with the days of the week written down a left-hand column.

Diaries are a most useful method for teachers and therapists to keep each other informed about daily happenings at school and at home which are relevant to current teaching objectives (see p.282).

With illiterate parents, a telephone call or a personal visit are the best ways of encouraging them to monitor the child's progress because they then have to give you a regular update.

It's Not as Easy as it Sounds

If my past experiences are anything to go by, some reviewer is bound to say that I have made it all sound rather easy. Without getting too defensive, let me pre-empt that comment by assuring you that it will *not* always be easy.

I have tried to map out a broad outline of how teachers and therapists could work with parents face-to-face. Much of the detailed decision-making I have to leave to you, because so much of it depends on the personalities involved: the parent, the child and you. Some of these decisions will not be easy. Indeed, even the best of professionals at working with parents have found no ideal solutions for the thornier issues, such as how to avoid parents becoming overly dependent on you and ways of encouraging them to take over responsibility for decision-making and problem-solving; how best to help parents cope with multiply handicapped or severely disturbed children when their morale is low and their need for a complete break is great; how to establish and maintain working links with parents of young handicapped adults when conflicts of interest arise between their wishes and the rights of their son and daughter.

There may be times too when you feel at a loss for ideas or when you disagree with the parents and can't get your point of view across. There may even be occasions when a parent is ungrateful or is critical of you, and even complains to other parents or colleagues about you.

And so I could go on listing many other potential difficulties, but as I have no prescriptions to dispense that will cure any or all of these ills, that would be pessimism in the extreme. Rather each of us has to face up to the difficulties when, and if, they arise; reliant as always on our professional judgement, but having the will to find a way. That may be very optimistic, yet I believe we need to endue our services for handicapped children and their parents with an aura of optimism, at least in the sense Dietrich Bonhoeffer defines it:

> The essence of optimism is that it takes no account of the present but it is a source of inspiration, of vitality and hope.

That, too, is easier said than done.

PART THREE

Working with Parents in Groups

OVERVIEW

The emphasis shifts in this section of the book from working with individual parents or families to managing groups of parents. I choose the word 'manage' deliberately because it sums up the task which lies ahead of you. My dictionary defines it as: 'control, influence, guide the running of, direct; deal with and succeed despite difficulties.' The latter really appealed to me!

Meetings of parents come in all shapes and sizes. Among the more popular formats are:

School meetings When all the parents with a child attending the school are invited to come together now and again, usually to be given information of a general nature. The common experience is that only a minority of parents attend and teachers complain that the parents they would most like to see, are the very ones least likely to come. We shall examine how meetings can be made more attractive for parents.

Class meetings A variant is to hold a meeting for parents of one class, during which the teacher can talk informally with each parent. The chief advantage is the parents will have more in common and they will have the chance to discuss matters more freely and in more detail than larger groups allow.

Courses for parents Some schools and services have organised short courses for parents, consisting of a series of meetings over a defined period of time. These offer parents the opportunity to develop particular skills in handling their child.

Mother and baby groups As the name implies, these are an opportunity for 'new' parents to meet with others and share their experiences and feelings. Many parents speak highly of the value of such groups in coming to terms with their child's disability.

- *Let me see that I was not the only one.*
- *It was great to chat with other mothers and social workers, etc. about child. It gives mother confidence; she benefits from other mothers' experience.*
- *Could compare and get hints from other mothers. You feel*

153

> *better when you see kids worse off than your own.*
> ● *It was a relaxed morning, very friendly and you can air your problems with other parents.*

Such groups are usually facilitated by a professional worker, health visitor or social worker, but in some areas they are organised by a parents' association.

Opportunity groups Although the format may vary, the essential aim is to bring together preschool children with and without disabilities. Very often the mothers are involved in organising the playgroups and have the opportunity to share with and learn from other mothers.

Self-help groups Parents too have taken the initiative in forming support groups, perhaps wholly with the aim of lobbying for better services. The best developed example of a range of such groups are those organised in Southend-on-Sea, Essex (England) and described in Gillian Pugh's[40] book *Parents and Partners*.

This listing is not meant to be exhaustive but it does capture some of the diversity which inevitably results when two, three or more people come together.

Difficulties

> For many people, going out to a meeting, especially in the evening, is an effort. For those who have just returned home from work even greater effort is required to turn out again, especially in cold wet weather. The meeting has also to compete with favourite T.V. programmes and family routines. All of this adds up to the fact that a school is unlikely to get a majority of parents to its meetings unless they think it will be of value to them, interesting and enjoyable.

That is how Barbara Tizard[9] summarises the challenges you face.

However, she goes on to point out that in their demonstration research project, they achieved attendances from 75 to 95 per cent of families at meetings. Their strategy embodied many of the successful features used in other schemes and which, on reflection, could be described as common sense. However, as my friend, Dorothy Jeffree, loves to point out, that is a misnomer because on existing evidence, good sense is not at all common.

Consult the Parents

That's rule 1. You won't get a time or date which suits everyone but at least you will increase the likelihood of pleasing most of the people. Weekends may be preferable to week-nights, and repeating the meeting on a second occasion facilitates shift-workers and those unable to attend on the first occasion.

Discuss with parents the obstacles preventing their attendance. Among the more common reasons in our experience are:

● parents did not think it would benefit them or their child
● they did not have a baby-sitter
● they had difficulties with transport
● they were uneasy about going alone.

There are ways round these as we will see later.

Explore the topics that interest parents. For example, Barbara Smith's[38] survey of parents with mentally handicapped children, showed that over 80 per cent were interested in self-help skills, closely followed by language and communication. Independence came next, followed by inappropriate behaviours (both with ratings of over 60 per cent). This reinforces Barbara Tizard's[9] point that

> the topics parents were most interested in were those specifically related to their own child's education . . . Meetings with outside speakers and commercial films and talks on general subjects like, 'the importance of play', were less popular as they were not usually seen as directly relevant by the parents. (p.150)

Who Minds the Child?

It is rarely satisfactory for parents to meet with young children present; the distractions are too great for the parents to participate fully in the group. The only exceptions are possibly young babies; active preschoolers can get up to too much mischief. Finding alternative care-givers for one or other parent is not easy.

Some groups meet while the child is at playgroup or in school. But this doesn't suit fathers or working mothers. However, if teachers' aides are available to look after the class, it is a good opportunity for small group meetings of the children's parents.

Evening meetings can pose more of a problem if you are to get both mothers and fathers as well as single parents along. You either could arrange for child care (crèche) or have a panel of volunteer helpers willing to baby-sit. Such arrangements are easier to organise for occasional meetings and are appreciated very much by parents. For instance, half the parents in Barbara Tizard's project made use of child care arrangements that catered for babies and children up to 13 years of age. This was staffed by teachers, students and secondary-school pupils.

Where to Meet?

Choose a location that involves the least amount of travelling for participants. Well-known locations are preferable. Among the possibilities are colleges and schools, community or church halls, clubhouses, recreational centres or hotels. If the location provides a chance for socialising after the meeting, such as indoor sports or a bar, all the better. Generally these locations provide more comfortable surroundings than school rooms (not least in having adult-sized chairs) and avoid some of the unfortunate connotations which parents may have of schools and clinics.

Make sure the general meeting room is of appropriate size for your group, not too big or too small. For larger groups, a semicircular arrangement of chairs is preferable to rows, whereas circles of chairs should facilitate small-group discussion.

Bring a Friend. Some people are uneasy about attending a meeting on their own. Assure them that they are welcome to bring a friend along. Usually this is an elder daughter, their sister or the child's grandmother.

Transport. Special schools have to contend with the extra difficulty of parents living throughout a wider geographical area. Those without cars can find travelling difficult, especially if public transport is not available or unreliable. You can help in a number of ways: arranging lifts with neighbouring parents or staff, sharing taxis, providing a mini-bus pick-up service or, if regulations permit, using school transport for meetings held in school time.

Ensure the Parents Know. The best method by far is a personal invitation, conveyed via a telephone call or home visit, during which you tell the parents what the meeting is about and why you are keen for them to attend.

Leave with them a leaflet or card, stating clearly the starting time, location and travelling directions, if necessary. A summary of the programme, likely finishing time and child-minding arrangements should be included.

A note can be sent during the week of the meeting via the school transport or you could phone.

Minority Groups. Families whose command of English is poor are unlikely to attend your meetings unless you surmount the language barrier. Barbara Tizard[9] and her colleagues give many suggestions on this topic, including the use of interpreters and translating invitations into the language of the home.

Reluctant Parents. Lastly, there will be some parents who would prefer not to mix with others and the thought of regularly attending a mother and baby group, for instance, would not be at all appealing. Here is one mother's comments:

> My baby is Down's syndrome, no group will change that, so it is all a waste of time. You need to do your own thing with your baby. If you accept your child you do not need people to make you feel better. I love my child; I do not think of her as being Down's syndrome. I do not have to go there [group] to get reassured about her.

Successful Meetings

Put bluntly, chance has little part to play in determining whether or not a meeting is successful. You can plan to make it so. Yet I detect a great reluctance to expend energy and effort in planning meetings. Usually they are conceived as an 'extra' or 'chore' or, worst of all, a 'time-saver' and the consequences are predictable: both you and parents grow to dislike and hence avoid meetings. Yet the potential value to parents of coming together in groups is very great. Do not ignore it because of your inexperience nor squander it because of your ineptitude.

There are six potential advantages to be derived from parents coming together as a group and although they may be present in single meetings they are more likely to be realised during a series of get-togethers.

(1) *Learning from other parents* Group meetings provide

parents with the opportunity to learn from others. This can occur at a number of levels: the encouragement of knowing that other people have experienced or are experiencing similar problems as yourself; the support of fellow learners which can encourage you to keep going when morale is low; and, perhaps, specific advice from those who have proved the success of certain methods.

Time and again, parents have spoken of the value of sharing experiences with others.

It is helpful to meet parents with handicapped children younger and older than one's own and discuss different stages of development, etc.

I got moral support from the group and suggestions from other parents on how to deal with any problems one might have with the child.

(2) *Broader base of knowledge.* In face-to-face contacts the pre-eminent concern is with the individual child and his or her needs. At group meetings, parents have a chance to take a wider perspective and possibly acquire a broader understanding of how children learn and why their behaviour can be atypical. From this broader base of knowledge, they can go on to make their own deductions about the implications for their child. They become less dependent on professionals for advice and may begin to take the initiative in devising new learning games for their child. All of this could occur in individual professional–parent contacts, but here the social pressures on both are such that it is all too easy for the 'expert' to dispense short-term prescriptions. Group meetings are a complementary antedote, particularly when the parents have the chance to discuss among themselves.

(3) *Good discussion can facilitate change.* There is plenty of evidence to suggest that groups are more effective at inducing people to change their actions than are lectures or talks. Kurt Lewin[80] explains it in terms of discussion minimising the resistance to change. In the group each person exchanges views and considers the merits and advantages of various courses of action. Hence they realise that other behaviours are acceptable and worthy of consideration. Moreover, when a consensus emerges, the new behaviour becomes the decision of the group, a conscious and willing choice on the part of every participant to

accept the advocated behaviour, not the half-hearted acquiescence to an imposed change.

(4) *Development of friendships.* The social isolation of parents with a handicapped child has been frequently documented.[33,42] Groups give parents the chance to meet with other mothers and fathers who know exactly how they feel for most have lived through the same experiences. Mutual help, such as baby-sitting circles, weekend or holiday breaks, become possible. Moreover, the old adage of 'united we stand' can forge parents into a powerful lobby for improved services or new ventures.

(5) *Involvement of fathers.* With so many parent–professional contacts occurring during working hours, a more honest description would be maternal-involvement schemes. Meetings held on weekday evenings or at weekends can enable fathers to become more involved. Moreover, it gives them the chance of meeting other fathers, an experience which some men have found particularly valuable in coming to terms with their child's disability. At the risk of perpetuating stereotypes, men don't generally talk to their friends or workmates about their children, whether handicapped or not. Hence they lose one way of checking out whether their reactions are typical or not.

Of course, some fathers may not want to be involved and some mothers may actually prefer if they didn't. Our task is to set up an opportunity for parental involvement, rather than the expectation that all must be involved.

(6) *Involvement of working mothers, single parents.* As the social structures change in our society, so too must work habits. More face-to-face contacts may occur at weekends or evenings and, while professionals may begrudge working such 'unsociable hours', parents' meetings held at these times could help us to make the transformation. It is certainly a mistaken, even dangerous, assumption that these parents are any less interested or that they are not capable of working in partnerships.

The foregoing points must be seen as potential benefits of parents meeting together. Some may never be realised, no matter how hard you try. Others may provide a supreme test of your skill and ingenuity before you succeed. In this part of the book I want to share with you some of the factors that make for successful meetings.

I begin with 'Brightening up a talk', a common way of instructing groups of people; a task that falls to every professional sooner or later, but one for which they receive little or no preparation. Here I shall look at the use of visual aids and audience-participation activities and effective ways of ensuring your message gets across.

By contrast, the next chapter focuses on 'Handling groups' with an emphasis on learning through discussion. Leading groups toward a productive outcome is a skilled and yet highly rewarding task, albeit beset with many traps for the unwary and unskilled.

The final chapter deals with 'Organising a course' and examines the steps involved preparing, serving and improving your offerings. The challenge is to produce learning experiences tailored to parents who perforce have differing needs. This ethos, of course, is fundamentally opposed to that prevailing in most courses of professional training. Hence parent courses should *not* be modelled on those you have experienced, or endured!

You will discover, I think, that much of the content of these three chapters is applicable beyond working with parents. When I came to reflect on what was unique about parent groups as distinct from meetings of colleagues or other professionals, or the public in general, I could think of very few justifiable differences. After all, parents come from all strata of society and hence it is impossible to make generalisations solely on the basis of their parenthood. If anything, the uniqueness of most parent groups lies in the diversity of personalities they embrace. If you can cope with this, then it is likely that you will manage to give better talks, handle group discussions more efficiently and organise effective courses for many other groups as well as parents.

The tradition of meeting, a time-honoured one in human society, is very much under threat today. Neighbourhoods where everyone grew up together are rarer and extended family networks have been broken. People have to travel to work or to shop or for entertainment and the choice is such that they can head off in many directions. Regular opportunities for congregating, such as in churches, are available but seldom used. The home has become even more self-contained, with its modern appliances and home-delivery services. When people do venture forth, it's often in insulated capsules, known as 'cars'!

Perhaps all this change is for the better and we will learn not to hanker after old ways. But I cannot help but feel that our desires for companionship, for sharing, for helping and for being helped, are more than folk memories. They are human needs.

8

Brightening up a Talk

Sooner or later, you will receive an invitation to give a 'talk'. This time-honoured way of communicating knowledge may be on the wane but I doubt if it will ever die away. A talk has certain advantages.

(1) *Efficient* Your message can be conveyed simultaneously to a group, a crowd, maybe even a mass of people. Hence a talk is a very time-efficient way of communicating basic information relevant to your listeners.

(2) *Responsive* The message can be tailored to the audience needs; just like the comedian's choice of jokes. Moreover, your listeners have a chance to *ask* you for further information or clarification. Books, films, television programmes can never match the 'live' event.

(3) *Personal* The message becomes embedded into an experience. It is somewhat akin to paying to see entertainers on stage rather than investing the money in buying their record. The event is all the more memorable and meaningful.

A successful talk is a mixture of information, entertainment and inspiration. The proportion of each will vary according to your audience (parents, colleagues or students), but I believe these basic ingredients must feature. Exclude one and you reduce the potency of your presentation.

This chapter sets out some basic principles to bear in mind when standing in front of an audience. It is not, however, a treatise in elocution. An ordered mind precedes an ordered tongue. Hence my suggestions are intended to help you communicate your message in a clear, entertaining and inspirational way.

I begin with *preparation*, the selection of what you will say and the methods you will use to do it, then I examine ways of making the *delivery* of the talk more effective, including taking a look at

161

visual aids: what's available and how to use them efficiently. But the main emphasis in the chapter will be on *audience partici-pation*, giving your listeners the chance to become involved in discovering the meaning of your message for themselves.

When you have practised all these skills, then that is the time to brush up your pronunciation and articulation. These arguments should sound familiar; think of children learning to communicate. They have to know what they are saying, before we worry about how they say it.

Preparation

The gap between idealism and realism is all too apparent when it comes to people's motives for attending your talk, lecture or seminar, or whatever you choose to call it. Ideally, the audience has come to learn but that's a half-truth at best. There are far more effective and reliable ways of learning than sitting in a draughty hall on uncomfortable seats listening to a speaker prattling on about a subject which bears no relation to its advertised title.

The reality is that the audience will have many diverse, even intermingled, reasons for attending; for some it's a break in routine: a night out, time off work, a new experience. Others will welcome the chance of meeting people, renewing old acquaintances or making new friends. A few, but maybe even all, have come because it was expected of them: staff sent by their boss or parents 'blackmailed' by professionals; curiosity will arouse others: what's the venue like, who else will be there and what will the speaker look like?

Any audience represents an amalgam of differing motivations to say nothing of diverse backgrounds and life experiences. You are going to have your work cut out if you are to live up to Abraham Lincoln's adage of pleasing all of the people, some of the time. Incidentally, his preceding statement is surely reassuring to every speaker: you can please some of the people, all of the time.

But back to your amalgam: sorry audience. I have two pieces of advice to offer. First, obtain as much information about them as you can: who they are, their backgrounds, what is the purpose of the group, the age/ability range of their children, the type of questions they are likely to ask, etc., etc. A good organiser will volunteer much of this information without being asked, potential organisers please note, but if they do not, it's up to you to check it; preferably via a personal conversation.

Appeal to the lowest common denominator is my second recommendation. I presume that everyone (well nearly everyone, now that I think of some of the speakers I have endured) prefers a talk which is *easy to follow* rather than a learned exposition which hurts your brain; that is *entertaining* in the best sense of the word, i.e. 'performance intended to interest'; and one which leaves the audience with a sense of *well-being* rather than of inadequacy. Keep these three precepts in mind and you will avoid delivering a sermon.

What will you Talk About?

Three factors will decide this for you: the time you have available, the audience you are addressing and your knowledge and experience.

Time. Sometimes the length of time you have available to talk is set by the organisers. *Keep to this.* Professional speakers will fit their message accordingly. Running over time is a sign of sloppy preparation and/or poor decision-making; everything gets put in because you can't decide what to leave out.

It is especially necessary to keep to your allotted time when you are one of a number of speakers, each of whom has been given, say 15 minutes. Over-running your time is not merely an imposition on the audience, it verges on rudeness to your fellow speakers. If no time limit is given to you, then set one for yourself and share it with your audience: 'I'm going to talk for around . . . minutes, after which . . .'

There is no ideal length for a talk. It will vary with the audience and their expectations. For example, if you are the only speaker at a special meeting that people have driven miles to attend, a ten-minute presentation will leave them short-changed to say the least. Equally, this might be the ideal length when you are one of five speakers at the open night of a local school.

My advice to speakers giving the main address is to limit yourself to 25 minutes if you are giving a straight talk; 40 minutes if you are using visual aids during the talk and to 60 minutes if you are involving the audience in participation activities. I hasten to add that these are approximate guidelines. Gifted speakers can hold an audience's attention for 60 minutes with their oratory, whereas a 20-minute talk, poorly presented and ill-thought out, will not be redeemed by visual aids or activities. But in general these guidelines express the average audience's tolerance for an average speaker; statistically speaking, that's likely to include you.

Paradoxically, the worry of inexperienced speakers, how on earth will I fill the time?, is short-lived. The bigger worry is knowing what to exclude.

Audience. The second constraint on the content of your talk is the people with whom you are communicating. A presentation to parents on language disorders in children should differ from that given to experienced speech therapists. Why? Their prior knowledge of the subject is vastly different. Failure to take that disparity into account and you run the risk of bewildering parents and/or talking down to your colleagues. Sadly, the former is more common. Too often we are more concerned that our presentation is well thought of by any colleagues who may be present or a fear that our work might appear less special if we simplify. The judgement you have to make, and it's not easy for the inexperienced I admit, *is to gauge what those in the audience already know, what you feel they need to learn and/or what they are interested in learning.* Personal contact with the group before your presentation is very helpful, for example, attending a previous meeting. In particular, you will be able to observe the audience reaction during the talk and hear the type of questions the members ask afterwards. Failing this, you might have a chat to the organiser or other representatives of the group or indeed with someone who has previously addressed them. And don't just ask how many people are likely to be there! I wonder why that is such a popular piece of preparatory information?

You will, of course, learn more about your audience *during* the presentation. You will have opportunities to gauge their interest and knowledge. That is one reason why I strongly advise audience participation; a theme to be developed later (p.179).

Do not be afraid to check out points with the group: 'Have you heard about impedance methods of testing children's hearing?' Don't explain if you get a quick positive response from nearly all the group. And if there is a sullen silence, it may tell you something about their level of interest in the topic. An audience of live people is constantly sending out unsolicited non-verbal feedback to you. (The time to worry is when it becomes verbal.) Skilled speakers will try to tune into this, and just as in a conversation, they will modify their flow accordingly. That skill can be nurtured and I will come back to it when describing ways of practising (p.167). Rapport between speaker and audience transforms a monologue into a shared experience. The key is for you to come with a reasonably flexible rather than rigid plan for your talk.

Your Knowledge. Lastly, the talk will be limited by your knowledge. You have been invited because of what you know. Only the foolhardy, or politicians, accept invitations to talk about a subject on which they know little or nothing.

● If you haven't been given a topic, then set one for yourself. Share it with the audience, preferably as a title in the pre-meeting publicity or, failing that, during the introduction to your talk.

● Next, you will have to select the main points or messages you wish to get across. At this stage, focus on the *meaning* rather than on the method.

● Prioritise these points; which ones could be omitted if necessary?

● Place them in order. Are there any which must come early so that later ones are understandable?

As a rough rule of thumb, I reckon you can communicate one major point every ten minutes. Hence in a half-hour presentation three main points are sufficient.

The most common mistake is *information-overload*. Your audience needs time to take in and assimilate your message. You must give the members time to digest one point before moving on. Fortunately, there are many aids to digestion at your disposal. Hence your next decisions are concerned with how you will get each point across. Will it be:

Verbally An explanation, an analogy, a description of a past client, a humorous story or even having the points written out on a slide or blackboard, viz. 'Speech and language are different'.

Visually Demonstrating equipment or teaching materials, presenting the results from a survey or experiment in graphs or figures, showing slides of children or extracts from a film or replaying a video-recording.

Enactively Can those in the audience discover the meaning via an activity in which some or all of them participate?

Later I shall look at this in more detail and especially the last two, as they are the most effective ways of communicating, but, at this point, I want to impress on you the variety of ways you have at your disposal. Make full use of them.

The Beginning and End

At the end of this decision-making phase, you will have a fairly detailed outline of the content of your talk. It only remains to be topped and tailed. You need a beginning and an end.

In the Beginning. Start confidently and intriguingly. The worst mistake is to begin by apologising for yourself: 'I'm not sure why I was asked . . .' or 'I don't know very much about this topic but I'll do my best'. Rarely will these win the sympathy of those in the audience. If you really believe what you say, you shouldn't be wasting their time by agreeing to talk. On the other hand, if it's an attempt at self-abasement, it could well backfire. Why should they believe the rest of what you will say? There's little to be gained from making public your anxiety and lack of confidence.

Good openings can be as varied as a creative imagination will allow. Among the front runners are:

● *controversial statements* 'if a child doesn't talk by seven, he'll never talk'
● *a quotation* 'the things we know best are the things we haven't been taught'
● *a personal anecdote* 'when I was growing up . . .'
● *the description of a child you have treated* 'Jimmy was only eleven months old when he first came to my clinic . . .'
● or merely a *joke*, preferably one with a message that can be linked with the rest of your talk.

Best avoided are opening sentences that present a complicated definition, full of embedded clauses; those that have names of experts or a run of sentences with more than twenty words in them. The time spent thinking of a novel opening will prove well worthwhile.

The End. I hate talks that peter out. 'I think I'll leave it there . . . that's all I can say . . . I think' (awkward pause — sporadic applause). We would never dream of doing it when conversing or when writing, so why end your talk on such a downer? Rather your closing remarks should be the climax of your talk. They are a chance to make an impact because they are the last thing the audience will hear and therefore the most likely to be remembered. Hence, at the very least, you should end with a summary of your main points. Even better is a memorable catch-phrase or quote that encompasses the essence of your message. In short, plan to go out with a bang, not a whimper.

Practice

Your preparation has to continue beyond *what* you will communicate and encompass also *how* you will do it. The next three sections will examine the presenting of a talk, the use of visual aids and audience participation, but at this point I want to enter a plea for rehearsals preceding the performance. The analogy with entertainers is wholly deliberate. Your professionalism demands that your presentation is as effective as you can make it. The inexperienced should practise in private.

Colleagues. Give the talk to a group of colleagues and afterwards, possibly even during, listen to their reactions. Ask them to focus on the *way* you are presenting the information. If they are tuned in to some of the pitfalls I have outlined, so much the better.

If you agree with their criticisms and accept their suggestions for improvement, then *repeat that part of the talk there and then.* You're practising a different act for the first time.

Admittedly, this exercise can prove embarrassing and some people will find it very threatening. They would much prefer to avoid such an ordeal: goodness, isn't giving a talk bad enough without having your faults pointed out! In reply, my argument is that the practice session with colleagues is a learning experience not an assessment.

Secondly, I don't believe you, or anyone else, has given their best ever talk. You certainly could do better. Thirdly, you can all learn together, each person takes it in turn to make a short presentation and receive feedback. In that way, you are all in the same boat. Comments from your audience in this context are much more likely to be frank and informative than those given after a public talk, which invariably tend to be complimentary.

Video-tape. This has the power to let you see yourself as others see you. And what an eye-opener that can be. Used in conjunction with feedback from your colleagues, it is a powerful tool for improving your presentation. Politicians, government officials, businessmen, even the clergy, have undergone video-based training with specialists in communications. You too will learn a great deal from seeing yourself 'perform'. The most informative is a recording of a talk you have given to a 'real' audience. Next best is a presentation to colleagues and of some value is a recording of yourself with no one present.

The most striking thing you will discover are the mannerisms you never knew you had: the rubbing of your nose, waving of your hands, rocking back and forth on your ankles and so on. We all have our 'tension-reducers', but some can annoy your listeners.

More importantly, look for impediments to communication. The bowed head for ever reading notes, the illegible slide, the over-hasty introduction of the next point and so on.

Audio-taping. Although not as informative as video, it can highlight poor delivery: speaking too fast, over-use of jargon, heavy reliance on fillers, 'um' . . . 'aah', and mispronunciations. It is best used to supplement comments from other people.

Practise alone. If people and equipment are not available, then at least practise alone. It needn't be at a special time, you can rehearse as you drive, while in front of the television or even on the toilet. There's another of my secrets given away!

You might rehearse some segments more than others. For example, the opening sentences or the results of an experiment or the functions of a new piece of equipment. However, you must be confident that you can say it all in the time allotted without rushing or cramming. Indeed, the real thing invariably takes more time, so leave five minutes spare. If you are running over, cut down on your contents beforehand. I'm amazed that so many speakers still stand up so ill-prepared. They end up poaching other speaker's time or being cut off in mid-flow or boring the audience. The 'best' of them do all three!

Getting it Right on the Night

The big moment has come and you're on, well almost. A few

preparatory checks remain.

● Get there early and *personally* check out that the machinery you need, videos, overhead projectors, is working.

● Ensure that screens, television sets and blackboards can be seen by the audience. Does the hall need to be darkened? Who will do it?

● If using a microphone, check the sound level and on/off switches. Do you need a roving microphone, e.g. clip-on rather than a static, podium type?

● Is water on hand to counteract your dry throat?

● Is there a better way of arranging the audience's seating? For example, small groups are better arranged in a circle rather than rows; semicircles of chairs are preferable to the middle-aisle arrangement.

● Where will you stand when talking? Choose your own spot.
   You're on: good luck!

Delivery

Your personality comes through, at least in part, in the way you communicate with others. Thus the way people present a talk varies greatly. Indeed that is one of the refreshing and intriguing aspects of hearing a speaker for the first time. So the best advice is to be yourself. That said, there are some tips that are guaranteed to help get your message across.

(1) *The audience must hear you talking*

● If you are softly spoken, practise projecting your voice. Monitor your level during the talk: some people start off OK and then drop away. Worst of all are those who shout, 'Can you hear me at the back?' 'Yes', we reply, and then they resort to an inaudible whisper.

● Use a microphone: the inconvenience to you is more than outweighed by removing the strain on your listeners.

● Monitor your speed of delivery: a common nervous reaction is for people to talk too quickly.

● Keep your voice level constant: some speakers are tempted to drop their voices as they make an aside, such as a 'funny' remark they have second thoughts about. This creates an unnecessary tension among the listeners. Those who heard, wonder if they were meant to and those who didn't, wonder what was said.

(2) *The audience must see you talking*

● Do not read your talk. You end up looking at your script more than at the audience. Moreover, the style of language we use when writing, differs markedly from that used in conversation, not least in repetition and redundancy. Hence it is much harder for listeners to follow.

Instead: (a) have your points written out on cards, these will remind you what you want to say (note: number these in case they get dropped); (b) do not be afraid to pause while you look at the card, it may be a welcome breather for the audience; (c) practise the talk beforehand, then you will have mentally prepared sentences for conveying each point.

● Stand when speaking. It gives you a presence and is an easy focal point for the listeners.

● Get close to the audience. Among the obstacles that prevent you doing this are: standing on a raised platform; a table in front of the speaker; the audience's tendency to sit at the back. It intrigues me why this should be.

(3) *Watch your language*

● Avoid jargon. But it's much easier to identify other people's jargon than to recognise your own. We all have common phrases or expressions that are meaningful to our profession or service but perhaps convey a different meaning to others. A parent who had heard me talk of Down's syndrome, rather shyly asked me if there was such a thing as an Up's syndrome. Note the dictionary definition of 'jargon': '. . . too technical to be intelligible to the ordinary public; pompous language full of clichés; gibberish'.

● Speak simply and directly. For example, use active rather than passive verbs; avoid double negatives and use everyday words rather than abstract words or complicated phrases. Use the language of conversation rather than discourse.

These points only become real when you hear yourself. Hence the importance of practising with a video- or audio-recorder.

(4) *Watch your audience* Communication should be two-way. Learn to 'read' your audience's reactions. An increase in shuffling, coughing, yawning or people looking down or around them, are sure signs that you are losing their interest. Puzzled looks on some faces, blank stares on others, may indicate the need for you to clarify a point.

Some people are better reactors than others: keep a look out for the smilers and head nodders. They are a great reassurance.

However, one of the best arguments for involving the audience in your presentation, is that it makes explicit the two-way flow of information that turns a talk into a conversation.

(5) *Check the time* Finally, keep a check on how many minutes you have left. The ideal is a clock behind, or to the side of the audience; the next best your own wristwatch or, failing that, an unobtrusive reminder from the chairman or a colleague.

The crucial check period is when you have five to seven minutes remaining. It's at this point that you have to decide to omit some of your material if you are to finish in time. Prepare for this contingency in advance; earmark a section toward the end of the talk that could be omitted or mentioned only briefly. This presumes of course that you have got your priorities right and the important points have been made at the beginning.

By all means let the audience know what they have missed; 'I was going to say something about . . . but I'll have to skip that.' If your listeners are really interested in that topic they can bring it up during the question time.

Handling of Questions

A talk without questions is like a dinner without dessert. Question time can be the sweetest part for the audience, if not for the speaker. This is the chance for them to have their personal query aired, if not answered. But, even so, it's the speaker's (and/or chairperson's) responsibility to ensure that the question time is of value to everyone. Dialogues on idiosyncratic issues are best conducted in private. So how do you make question times valuable and less of an endurance test for the speaker?

● *Getting questions* You need a ready flow of pertinent questions. These are more likely to come if:

   ● you wait for questioners to summon up the courage to speak

   ● your talk has been relevant to the audience's needs

   ● you have invited questions during it, e.g. 'If you want to know more about this, I'll gladly give you further information during question time'

   ● you mention related topics during the talk, so that those who may be interested are made aware that you know something, e.g. 'This same approach can be used with sleep problems, although I haven't time to go into that now'

- you have involved the audience *during* the talk; if they have sat silently for 60 minutes, a habit has formed that is hard to break
- you handle questions in an informative and welcoming way, e.g. 'That's a very good point' rather than 'What a strange thing to ask'.

And if you have done all this, and still there are few questions, then marvel at the way you held them spellbound.

- *I don't know* Nobody but yourself expects you to have answers for every question. The analogy in many a speaker's mind is the cross-examination of the interview or court room. Not so for the audience. Either they are genuine seekers of information, who like as not have been disappointed before and so are prepared to be again, or else they are content to have aired the problem. 'I've tried everything to stop him swearing', may be an attempt to justify themselves, rather than a challenge to your ingenuity.

If you don't have an answer, then say so. Audiences recognise waffle when they see it and it may put people off asking other questions. You can invite other people in the audience to comment on the question. They might be dying to give their opinion!

- *The persistent questioner* (may the chairperson protect you). Best handled by inviting other people to ask a question; hence the importance of eliciting plenty of questions. Or you can invite the questioner to talk with you afterwards and make a quick getaway. Or with long-winded questions, you can interrupt them in mid-flow, either verbally 'I think I've got your point' or non-verbally by looking away.
- *The unintelligible questioner* If you do not understand the question, get it clarified before you begin to answer. If you're still not sure, state your interpretation and check if it agrees with the questioner.
- *The critical questioner* Occasionally, very occasionally, a questioner may voice a complaint against you or local services or will directly disagree with something you have said or take objection to you personally. Keep cool. Check there has been no misunderstandings. Restate your position. Avoid a heated public debate. Invite the person to see you afterwards or agree to differ. A joke or light-hearted comment might help to reduce the tension: You're bigger than me, so I had better shut up.'
- *The irrelevant questioner* If you judge the topic irrelevant to

the theme you have been talking about, then give a very succinct reply and suggest other sources of information. On the other hand, if the audience seem very interested and a related question quickly follows, it might be worth pursuing it there and then, provided that you feel competent to do so.

● *The final questioner* All good things have to come to an end and it's best to stop before the questions dry up. I'm wary of announcing 'we'll take two more questions' when there's been little or no indication of anyone wanting to speak. The embarrassing silence is a poor end to an evening.

It's better to declare the last question once it's been asked, 'I think this is the last question we'll have time for.' Also, try to finish your answer by a restatement of your main message. It's your prerogative to have the last word.

The Reluctant Speaker

Throughout this section, I have made one assumption: namely, you are willing to give a talk. Unlike some other aspects of your work, this can be an option and some will choose never to do it. I realise that some people are understandably nervous and anxious about speaking in front of others. But I do believe that it helps you to confront these fears. You will feel better about yourself. If you are a reluctant speaker, just think, *what is the worst thing that could happen to you when you are giving a talk*? Then ask yourself, *is that a justifiable fear*? Has it ever happened to anyone else? If not, why should you be the first? Are there precautions you could take to avoid it? I think that you will discover that most of your fears are irrational.

Accept the challenge of public speaking. The self-confidence gained will stand by you when dealing with individual parents and on getting your views across in case conferences or in debating the need for new services. It is an excellent foundation too for those wishing to make video-programmes.

Visual Aids

A sure way to brighten up any talk is to include some visual aids. At the very least, it introduces variety; at best, it crystallises your message into an unforgettable image which no amount of words will ever do.

Visual aids can take many forms:
- video extracts
- slides
- overhead projector
- blackboard/whiteboard
- flip charts (large sheets of paper)
- demonstration of equipment
- examples of toys, teaching materials, etc.
- a 'live' teaching/assessment session.

Admittedly, you can get by without any of them, they cut down on your preparation time and there are fewer things to go wrong, but such selfishness doesn't help the audience. Here are some instances when I feel it is obligatory for speakers to provide a visual aid.

Statistics. People's number-phobia often makes them blank out at the mention of a number greater than ten; worse still are relational concepts like one in ten or 20 per cent. It certainly helps to see data written down and even better if they are presented pictorially, as a graph or diagram.

Lists. People's capacity to remember a listing of points is limited to four out of five at the most and that assumes they are attending fully. A visual listing gives them more time to digest the points. Again, a pictogram such as a cartoon is more memorable than a straight listing of points.

Novelty. If you are describing a new experiment, teaching method or special equipment, it is so much easier to get the message across if you can give a demonstration or show a video-recording or at least still photographs or diagrams. Otherwise the audience has to build up its own visual images from your words and that's not easy.

Effective Aids

Your choice of visual aids is likely to be a compromise between what's best and what's available. The two front-runners, because of their versatility and increasing availability, are undoubtedly video and the overhead projector. Chapter 11 is devoted entirely to the use of video, hence the main focus in this part of the chapter will be on the overhead projector. However, many of the points I will make about the effective use of the overhead projector, apply equally to the other visual aids which can replace or complement it, such as *colour slides*, when you want to show people and places, or *flip charts* and the good old *blackboard*, for lists, diagrams and data.

First, though, two fundamental points that apply when any kind of visual aid is used.

The visuals must be clearly seen by everyone in the audience This truism is the one most frequently abused: the illegible writing on the blackboard or flip chart, the over-exposed slide, the mass of writing on the overhead transparency or a small television set for a large audience. I'm sure you could add to this list from your experience of attending talks.

The visuals should appear when you want them to Too often the opposite occurs. The projector or the recorder fails to work; a slide or transparency is missing or appears out of sequence or upside down. Whatever the 'disaster' it will mar your presentation and get you unnecessarily flustered. *Personally* check the equipment and your aids before you begin.

Overhead Projector

The advantage of this projector is that the room does not have to be darkened; it allows you to stand facing your audience while showing or pointing to the illustration so that eye contact can be maintained and their questions or discussion can be easily slotted into the presentation.

For those unfamiliar with this projector it is basically a box with a strong bulb in the bottom of it, magnifying glass across the top of it and a mirror held at an angle over the box to reflect the light on to a screen or white wall. The box also houses an electric fan to keep both the bulb and glass surface from overheating. To focus the 'picture' you raise or lower the mirror by twisting a knob on the supporting arm. To raise or lower the picture on the screen you tilt the mirror. The screen should be set tilting forward to ensure the picture is square and not wedge-shaped. This can happen if the projector is too low down.

Transparencies

The illustrations you want to project have to be copied on to transparent material rather like tough Cellophane, referred to as transparencies or acetates. This is available in three forms: as a roll that is wound across the top of the projector; as single sheets square; as special transparencies for use with photocopying machines. The single sheets of acetate are also sold in various colours.

Making your own Transparencies

Although it is possible to have transparencies commercially made, it is easier and cheaper to make your own. All you need is acetate and special felt-tipped pens (ordinary markers do not work). Projector pens come in either permanent or water-based inks and there is a wide range of colours. Only those colours that contrast strongly with a white screen are most effective: black, blue, red or green. Yellow should only be used for shading.

With the pens you can write or draw whatever you want. But a more professional finish can be obtained by using the following.

Rub-off Lettering. For example, Letraset, to give a printed text. There are also sheets of press-on shading and shapes (dots, arrows, lines) for making diagrams.

Stick-on Paper Shapes. Packets of these are sold in most stationers. They come in a variety of shapes and sizes and stick well to acetate. They appear on the screen as strong black shapes, very useful when drawing graphs.

Tracing. With acetate, tracing a cartoon or diagram is very simple: just place it over the illustration and mark out what you want to highlight. Different colours of ink can be used to emphasise different aspects.

Coloured Acetate. Can be cut to shape and stuck on to the illustration to give a solid colouring effect. It is particularly effective for drawing attention to particular features: headlines, bar graphs, etc.

Photocopier. The marvels of science now mean that you can produce black and white transparencies with a photocopier. Special acetate sheets (labelled 'for photocopying') are loaded instead of paper into the machine and the original (photograph, cartoon, diagram or table) is transferred on to it. Ordinary typescript or news print is much too small for photocopying; this should be *enlarged at least four times* before putting it on to acetate.

With the help of a photocopier and some of the other suggestions made above, you should be able to produce transparencies of quality and clarity. The latter is probably the more important. Make sure the print is large and any handwriting is clear and bold. Don't cram too many words on to the transparency: use headings, key words. Avoid large empty spaces but don't go too near the edge otherwise it will not be projected. A touch of colour in text or illustrations can work wonders.

Presentation of Transparencies

There are a variety of techniques to choose from when using this projector.

On the Spot Writing. The projector is used instead of a blackboard or whiteboard with the advantage that you can continue to face the audience. Used in this way, it can project the points emerging from group discussion or for recording decisions.

You can also add details to a prepared transparency. This can be done repeatedly if the outline is drawn in permanent marker and the additions are made with water-based pens.

Reveal by Stages. The prepared transparency is covered with a piece of paper or card which can be gradually moved to reveal the section to which the speaker is referring.

Add/Overlay Further Details. The first transparency may show the broad outline; then a second transparency is placed on top of the first adding further detail and several more may be added to complete the picture.

Use of an Indicator. To draw attention to a particular part of the transparency, place your pen on the glass, with the nib indicating the point in question. Do not hold the pen in your hand as any shaking on the screen will be magnified. Alternatively, you may cut out a small arrow from card to place on the transparency.

Remember *there is no need to point at the actual screen and hence turn your back on the audience.*

Common Faults in Presentation of Transparencies

(1) *The writing or print is too small* You must take into account the size of your audience, how far from the screen they will be, and the amount of magnification (i.e. how far is the overhead projector from the screen). Better err on the large side as it is very frustrating to listen to someone referring at length to something you can't see.

(2) *The transparency is continually trembling* This will happen if you continue to hold the transparency after putting it on the overhead projector, or of you insist on continually readjusting it, or use your finger to indicate points on it. Remember you cannot see the screen and it is very easy to develop nervous habits which will be magnified by the overhead projector and distract your audience. You should also avoid waving your hand over the transparency as you might over a wall chart: you will only blot out the whole screen!

(3) *The projector distracts* Switch it off when it is not in use. A brightly lit screen is a distraction and it is confusing to leave a transparency on when a different point is being discussed. If the fan of the projector is too noisy, try oiling it or tighten the screw which holds it in place.

Preparation of other Aids

Much of the foregoing is equally applicable to preparing other aids, such as slides, or when using a blackboard or flip chart. Do experiment.

We live in an age when there are more and more aids to communication being developed. Yet people's irrational fear of machinery often forces them to stay with traditional methods of voice and pen.

Our methods of communication will be compared inevitably with the advances that the public experience in daily life, most frequently on television news, current affairs and documentary programmes. Isn't it time we caught up?

Audience Participation

This is by far the most effective way I have discovered of communicating with an audience. If it sounds daunting, let me reassure you. You will quickly discover that it makes your job easier rather than harder.

It aids communication because:
● it gives you feedback about their knowledge and expectations and some insights into their personality
● it gives the audience a chance to discover through doing, the meaning of what you are saying
● it breaks up the need for constant concentration, you and they can take a breather
● it can bolster their self-esteem and feeling of well-being
● it relaxes the audience and makes it more likely that they will ask questions.

An Example to Analyse

When I'm asked to talk about *play*, I often begin by asking those in the audience to tell me their favourite *play activity when they were around five years of age*. These I list on a blackboard, flip chart or overhead projector. Depending on the size of the audience, I get an instance from everyone or else I continue until upwards of 30 examples are listed. You try it now: what were some of your favourite activities?

This activity has proved successful with parents, teachers, therapists, even eminent medical consultants! So what does it achieve? Note down your answer.

Here's the value I see in it.

Most obviously, it vividly illustrates the quantity and diversity of activities we call play. The audience members have defined for themselves what they take play to be. There have been other pay-offs as well:
● *humour*, the incongruity of the overweight lady pretending to be a ballet dancer
● *recollection*, in some small way the audience may relive the feelings of what it was like to play as a child
● *learning from others*, they hear of new play activities or discover things in common with people that they never thought possible.

My guess is that the answer you put down focused mainly on

the end product: the variety in play. It's a common failing of educators to ignore the *process* of learning and focus solely on the products. And that is the real value of audience participation. It ensures they are a part of the learning process.

Styles of Audience Involvement

There are many ways you can involve an audience, depending on its size and the topic you are addressing. I shall focus on activities designed to help them see things from the child's viewpoint. But first some other possibilities.

Ask them questions. This works best if the questions are straightforward. It's an obvious way of getting some information about them: 'How many have a child under five years', 'Have you heard of "hypotonic"?' You can ask questions to draw out their existing knowledge, such as the skills children have usually mastered by twelve months of age, alternative names for the condition 'mental handicap' or ways of communicating with other people. All of these are good openers: I leave you to guess the theme of the talk they precede.

You can also use questions to get the audience to see the value of the information you are giving them. For example, before presenting the results of a survey or experiment, have them guess what they think the outcome was. Like as not, you will get a range of replies and everyone will be much more attentive to the actual results when you announce them.

Needless to say, beware of asking questions which are too obtuse, difficult and beyond their ken. Silence doesn't always mean ignorance.

Observations. This is a useful way of alerting your audience to the complexity of everyday events or so-called simple tasks. For example, in another part of a talk on play, I have volunteer helpers skipping or trying to throw paper darts into a plastic bag. I then invite the audience to list the skills needed to do these tasks successfully.

Video-replays offer great scope for observation activities. For example, the number of imitative compared with spontaneous utterances the child produced. Or counting the questions that the teacher asked the child.

Occasionally you can invent an activity that everyone can

participate in there and then. For instance, they can discover how speech sounds are produced in the following exercise.

> I want you all to say the word '*basketball*'. OK, after two; one, two . . .
>
> This time as you say it, think of the movements you are making with your mouth and tongue. Now say it . . . and again . . . and again. I want you to press the top of your tongue against the back of your front teeth, those of you with false teeth be careful, and now say 'basketball'.
>
> Let your tongue move freely but this time don't move your lips, keep them shut.
>
> Finally, tell me this, were you breathing out or in when speaking the word?

(Inevitably you'll have to demonstrate what it sounds like to talk when breathing in. We always speak on an out-breath.)

This experience will surely have impressed on them the need for fluent and flexible movements of the lips and tongue for clarity of speech and what it feels like to know the sound you want to make but being unable to produce it (i.e. saying basketball with your lips closed).

Brain-storming

Any audience is full of knowledgeable people. I say that not to add to your worries and trepidations, rather to encourage you to harness their expertise and ingenuity. Here's an example of what I mean.

> Children do not need toys to play (a self-evident truism easily forgotten in times of financial rectitude). Therefore, in talking about play, I will invite the audience, or groups of them, to list all the different games and activities they could play with three cardboard boxes of varying sizes, a motorcar tyre and a length of rope. The explicit aim is pretty obvious: a wide variety of games that would be fun for children and adults to play. Listing these on a blackboard, etc., gives the less imaginative participants a handy bank of ideas.
>
> But, if anything, the implicit message is even more valuable: 'what clever people we are to think of so many uses for junk'.

Brain-storming sessions can be fruitfully used with many other topics. Inventing games to illustrate the meaning of sentences such as 'mummy kick', 'daddy kick', etc., or exploring possible explanations for 'problem' behaviour, such as the child who wakens the household in the middle of the night, or identifying improvements in services, or increasing contacts between handicapped and non-handicapped children in the neighbourhood.

Anytime you are faced with a 'problem' and a list of possible solutions, harness the audience's brain-power.

Taking the Child's Viewpoint

I believe that most of the mistakes, which parents and professionals make in their handling of children, stem from a failure to see the child's viewpoint. For instance, a fundamental error is to treat speech and language as one and the same thing. Giving a definition of each will make little difference. Rather you have to let them discover the truth of it for themselves. Recall Israel Schiffler's words: 'New *information* can be intelligently conveyed by statements; new *knowledge* cannot.'

An Example: Discovering the Difference between Speech and Language

I tell those in the audience I'm going to teach them a sentence from a little-known African language called Ndirande. I write it for all to see: MOMO DEJA WAMPADU KUM. I then produce a large poster, my favourite is Paddington Bear sitting on a suitcase. This is my visual aid to which I point when saying the sentence. I then have them repeat it after me a number of times. Then I ask, 'what is it?: It's . . .' and the loud reply comes back. Lastly, I ask one member of the audience to point out to me 'Momo deja wampadu kum', and invariably they do. 'Well done' says I, 'you've learnt that very quickly'. Fain surprise when they say they haven't and invite some people to tell you what it means. Declare all guesses to be wrong.

Point out how they were all speaking a language without having the faintest idea what they were talking about. They could have been the worst swear words conceivable. But not only were they *imitating*, they also were able to answer my question, 'what is it?', and point out what I was talking about. This is exactly what can happen to children. Produce a Ladybird picture book and pretend to be talking with a child — using a higher pitched voice:

Adult Oh look, Daddy's kicking the ball.
Child Daddy's kicking the ball.
Adult That's right. What's happening?
Child Daddy's kicking the ball.
Adult Very good. Show me Daddy kicking the ball . . . Very good.
Adult Let's turn over. Oh look, the girl's having a bath.
Child The girl's having a bath.

And so on . . .

The child *appears to know* the language but it's just like you saying 'momo deja wampadu kum'.

You can then go on to illustrate the problem-solving that's involved in deciding the meaning of words, such as 'momo'. I point to the picture of Paddington Bear, then to an actual teddy-bear as well as to a picture of one. Each time I say 'momo' and the audience has to guess what I mean. The answer may be obvious to you but, none the less, you do get a range of responses, including 'Mummy', said incidentally in all seriousness because 'momo' sounds like it.

Now take a second word, 'wampadu'; it's to mean 'sitting'. Again I point to Paddington, the teddy-bear and its picture. There are fewer guesses this time. A few other clues might help: a cup on a chair, a picture of a dog, a poster of a monkey sitting on the loo. Bewilderment is rampant. Highlight the range of meanings, that have been proposed, some of which could be right. Children too have to cope with our ambiguities. We point to a picture of a teddy-bear and say 'It's *teddy*; there's his *fur*: it's *brown*, *soft*'.

Finally, ask those who didn't puzzle out the meaning, whose fault was it, yours or theirs. Invariably they blame you; if children fail to learn the meaning of words, who's to blame then . . . Touché!

From here, they can begin to identify ways in which adults can make clear the meaning of words, namely

● *repetition*, as they discovered, it's very hard to understand the meaning of a new word straight away; you need lots of examples in a variety of contexts

● *linking* the word to a single referent: actual objects/events are

more meaningful than cluttered pictures
● *saying* only one or two words at a time, 'teddy's sitting' is much easier than 'look at the teddy-bear sitting on the case'
● *the child has to be attentive and interested*; therefore it's best to talk about what the children are doing, looking at or talking about, rather than what you think they should know.

I have yet to find an audience of parents or staff who fail to make those four suggestions. They are precisely the same conclusions to which the language experts have come after expending millions of dollars on research.

Lessons Learnt

I have presented this lengthy example on the distinction between speech and language, not just because of the centrality in understanding the principles which must underpin language intervention, but it also illustrates the key elements in a successful audience-participation activity. What makes it work?

READ AGAIN THE DESCRIPTION OF THE ACTIVITY AND NOTE DOWN THE KEY ELEMENTS YOU PER-CEIVED

If you've begun to read this without doing the above activity, you are more interested in information than knowledge, at least that's how Israel Schiffler might comment. As for me, I think you're inclined to be lazy. If you have answered the question, compare your notes with these.
Everyone was involved, or at least had the opportunity to be involved.
Realistic learning experience for adults The activity wasn't role-playing. It was for real. However, this meant some plausible invention to ensure that it was new to them. (The sentence was my creation)
They experienced failure The message hit home when they failed to grasp the meaning of the sentence or of the words. Not only did they know of their failure, but in varying degrees they experienced some of the emotional reactions which accompany it: frustration, bewilderment, annoyance, impetuous guessing and so on. Indeed, I invariably have people asking me, 'But what does momo deja wampadu kum really mean?' They can't live with failure!

They saw themselves as children see them My behaviour as 'teacher' was intended to mirror themselves. For this reason, it's worth throwing in some of the clichés that arise between parent and child . . . 'Would you please pay attention' (sound somewhat cross after a wrong guess), 'Oh, you're very clever' (after imitating the nonsense sentence) and so on. The self-deprecating laughter from the audience tells you when you've made your point.

They discovered the solution Once the audience members were given the insight into the child's difficulties, the solutions became obvious to them: repetition, linking, etc. My function was to list these and reinforce the truth of each.

Humorous The modicum of anxiety induced, makes it easy to elicit some nervous laughter. On good nights, the whole proceedings can border on the hilarious. I had one mother who insisted that the sentence meant, 'Mama, did ya' want the door to come?' Admittedly my Belfast accent added to her confusion.

You may have noted other successful features; I'd be delighted if you did. The challenge, though, is to translate these principles, or as many of them as we can, into other audience-participation activities that will illustrate more facets of children's development. Of course, the first rule must always be to tailor the activity to convey your message. Or, put more simply, you'll have to think of your own!

Obstacles to Audience Participation

Your fear that things might go wrong is likely to be the biggest argument against trying for audience participation in your next talk. My words alone will not dissuade you: it will require some bravado on your part, allied to a spirit of adventure. However, I can reassure you on some points.

What if the audience doesn't answer the question. This is an irrational fear when you think more about it. Nearly every audience assembles freely to hear you; the people are not there against their will. Secondly, those in the audience feel uncomfortable if they do not play their part; a feeling you will have experienced no doubt during the silences between questions to the speaker. Thirdly, you are the one controlling the proceedings; in the 'power' position. If things do go wrong it's likely to be your fault.

The first 'activity' must be one that everyone can participate in freely and easily. You have to warm them up. Hence I would opt for a question like, 'tell me your favourite play activity when you were five years old', rather than 'what does play mean to you?' The latter is abstract, unclear and irrelevant. Such questions are likely to stifle all but the bravest of respondents.

What if nobody volunteers? Bringing people out to perform in front of their peers can present difficulties. You are working against the normal convention of audiences remaining seated and it is risky for your volunteers, in that they don't know what they are letting themselves in for. Against that, you will have warmed them up with an easy activity and shown them a different style of talk. Moreover, there are invariably people in the audience who secretly like to be in the public eye but whose natural modesty prevents them from volunteering straight away.

Therefore, be prepared to wait a minute or so for your volunteers. You could fill in the awkward silence with some comment like 'I've never seen so many people interested in their shoes before'. A second tactic is to make eye contact with some likely people. If they sustain it, they will probably accede to a personal request: 'would you help me?' You are on to a winner if somebody volunteers another person. Insist that the proposer comes out. If they are brave enough to break the silence by talking, they are brave enough to volunteer. In fact, it's another way of signalling willingness. If all of these tactics fail, the last resort is to dragoon the people you know into helping: the chairperson or a colleague. I have never been left without a 'volunteer'.

What if it doesn't go the way I intended? This is where I eat my words about you being in control. Things can go differently, I admit. It doesn't happen often if your activity is well thought out but, if it does, you have to make the best of it. Some quick thinking is called for.

One activity I use involves one participant throwing paper darts into a small plastic shopping bag held by another. This is so difficult that no one has succeeded in getting more than one out of five in. I then have those in the audience suggest ways of making the game easier: stand nearer, use balls instead of darts or have a bigger bag. It's the last one I'm prepared for. I produce a bigger shopping bag and we re-enact the game with it. It went sadly wrong when an over-anxious Scotsman managed to do worse and not one of his darts went in. So what would you have done? Give him a second go? . . . have the person holding the bag throw the darts? . . . get somebody else from the audience? In fact, none of these was necessary. The place had dissolved in laughter and it became a running joke through the night. The moral is that you and an audience see disasters differently.

I haven't the right personality. Perhaps you are right. A certain bravado is required to give the appearance of confident control. Any uncertainty or embarrassment on your part is quickly transmitted to your audience. But while I will listen sympathetically to your difficulties, I can't help but feel you may be underselling yourself, all the more so if you haven't tried it. A practice session with supportive colleagues may give better grounds for making a decision regarding the suitability of your personality.

Conclusion

For interest, I once had an audience of 25 teachers list the main points they recalled from a talk in which participation activities featured liberally. Without exception, all of them recalled every point. When I asked how they remembered it so well, their answer was equally unanimous. They recalled first the activity they had participated in or watched and this helped them to remember the point being made. A vivid illustration of the truth of an ancient Chinese proverb, '*I hear and I forget; I see and I remember; I do and I understand.*'

9

Handling Groups

In this chapter the scene shifts from large meetings to small groups; a much better forum for parents to learn from each other. Among the more common types of groups I have in mind are:

● class teachers meeting the children's parents once a term to discuss current activities and the child's progress

● a group of parents taking a course organised by teachers or therapists, for instance, a parents' workshop (the whole course could be based around small discussion cum 'work' groups led by a tutor or these could feature alongside talks or video-programmes)

● on-going 'support' groups meeting fortnightly or monthly, organised by professionals or parents themselves, for instance, mother and toddler groups, luncheon clubs, toy library get-togethers.

Many other types of groups can and do exist, their format being as diverse as their participants. Their value to parents has been attested to over and over: the most obvious indication being their willingness to continue attending. However, it can be a daunting prospect for a young professional to organise and lead a parents' group. The reason?: *groups have a mind of their own*. The same people are individually reasonable, gentle and understanding, but put them together in a group to discuss a contentious issue and they can transform quicker than Jekyll into Hyde.

Other times the effect is quite the opposite: deafening silence. As two mothers commented, 'I thought I'd let other people do all the talking. I felt too ignorant to open my mouth' and 'I knew I'd blush if I spoke, so I never spoke.' In either case, the group leader may wish the floor would open and swallow either them or the others but not everyone, that would be hell!

Jennifer Rogers[81] astutely noted the extra difficulties faced by newly trained teachers and therapists:

> Many young people come straight into some occasional teaching of adults from having recently completed their own university education . . . Simple inexperience and uncertainty may lead these young teachers into attempting to simulate with the adult class the kind of teaching with which they themselves have been most familiar. Many of them find themselves in the odd situation of being the youngest in the classroom, yet being the person who is expected to take the lead . . . [Some] may retreat through panic into lofty formality rather than face the hazardous excitements of a more relaxed approach. (p.91)

The skills required in handling groups may come easier to some people than to others. I doubt if your training as a teacher or therapist gave you the opportunity to acquire or practise them. Nor, I must admit, will this chapter. You may read about the skills necessary for leading groups of adults, but you will have to discover their value for yourself.

The techniques of group management described here are applicable to single meetings of parents, group work carried out during a course or with parents who meet regularly as a group.

My focus will be on the use of groups to share knowledge with parents; on helping them to decide on a course of action in relation to their child and on encouraging parents to learn from one another. I will *not* be covering what has become known as '*group therapy*' in which the emotional and personal problems of the participants are dealt with. There is, of course, some overlap but group therapy is a more specialised area in which novices should only venture in the company of brethren who are experienced in therapeutic techniques.

Group Games?

If, as they say, the game of life is played in groups, then our introduction through the games of childhood is probably the best model to carry forward with adults. Think back to a memorable game you played as a child. For me, it was a day-long game we called 'Rally-O', a team version of hide-and-seek in which the captives could be freed from 'jail' by their team mates. The mutual

when the course has ended. Written materials can be particularly useful when only one parent is able to take the course and to help absentees recap on what they had missed. Further details on the preparation of course hand-outs and manuals for parents are given in Chapter 12.

Each of these topics is covered more fully in other parts of the book. My concern here is to tempt course organisers to experiment with a range of teaching methods and to add the spice of variety.

Homework. This is neither an optional extra nor a punishment. It is an essential ingredient to every parent course. If parents are to extend their learning from the course to the home, then you must plan for it to occur and help parents to do it. Some general points first.

● When advertising the course, warn parents that they will have to set aside some time to working at home with their child. Gaining their commitment in advance precludes excuses about lack of time.

● Supply parents with the necessary charts and forms to use during the activity and give them a *written summary* of what they have to do.

● Ensure that at the next course meeting every parent has the chance to report on their activity and to have their queries aired, maybe answered.

● Schedule at least one visit by a course tutor to the home, to observe parents implementing the practical activity. *This is highly recommended*, not only for the extra help it brings to parents, but for the insights it gives to the tutors.

● Identify parents who are finding it difficult to follow what they have to do. Go over the procedures individually with them.

The activities you get parents to do, will obviously vary according to the aims of the course. However, they can have some features in common. Among the more important I would put manageable, successful, graded and relevant.

● Parents are busy people with many other roles to fulfil, as well as educator for their handicapped child. Therefore, the activities you suggest must fit easily into family routines. A rough rule of thumb is ten minutes a day.

● As Philippa Russell[21] noted, 'any good intervention programme must teach parents to succeed'. Keep the activity simple and succinct.

● On our courses we grade the activity in terms of the demands which the parent has to make on the child. We begin with observations of the child, then parental modelling and, last of all, direct teaching. Parents need to be restrained from plunging into the last and the most difficult straight away. A structured plan of activities for the course will help.

● Throughout, the parents must see the relevance of the activity to their concerns. This is not always easy to achieve, especially when attempting to meet the foregoing criteria as well. With some thought and not a little ingenuity, often the *context* of the activity can be variable and the techniques remain constant.

The planning team will need to map out possible activities and build these into the overall course programme (see examples in the next section).

Practical Details. General points in arranging parents' meetings have been covered previously (p.154) but here are some specific suggestions in relation to courses.

Recruitment

● Prepare a brief information leaflet on the course, giving details of the course programme, what it involves, who it is for, the times and dates of meetings and the names of people to contact for further information.

● An invitation to come on the course is best conveyed personally or by a letter addressed to parents by name, rather than 'Dear Parent'.

● A feature or news item in the local paper or a spot on local radio will help alert other interested parents but even with parents who have received a personal invitation the publicity will endue the course with extra worth.

● If you are eager to get fathers as well as mothers along, then: make this clear when issuing invitations (put it in the leaflet); try to speak personally with the fathers, rather than via the mother; ensure the time of the meetings is convenient for fathers; can you offer to help with genuine baby-sitting problems?

Timetabling

● This is negotiable between the organisers, the helpers and the parents. In our experience the most popular format for courses has been six meetings, once a week, on a weekday evening, commencing at 8.15p.m. However, some fathers have expressed a preference for meeting at the weekend.

● It is important to leave time between sessions for the parents to try out new techniques, etc., at home. Sometimes parents (and staff) prefer a two-week interval.

● Once your timetable is worked out, circulate it to all participants, listing the days and the dates of meetings. Beware of public holidays falling within the course.

Venue

Among the possibilities are colleges offering evening classes, community halls, local clinics or schools. Send written directions with your letter of invitation.

Equipment

● Ensure that the necessary visual aids (video, overhead projector) are available and working. Make contingency plans in the event of breakdowns.

● If you are unfamiliar with the equipment, practise *before* the meeting.

● Organise in advance the typing and reproduction of written materials: hand-outs, observation checklists, etc. Ensure sufficient copies are available for every participant. Note: husbands and wives should have their own copies.

Brief the speaker and course tutors

● The planning team must give invited speakers detailed instructions on the topics they are to cover, the time available to them and how their session fits into the overall course programme; for example, what has gone before and what follows. The twin dangers to avoid are unnecessary repetition by speakers and irrelevance.

● Leaders of groups also need instructions about the group-work in each session and what they should aim to achieve in the time available. It is advisable to have the same tutor with each group throughout the course.

During the Course

The actual running of a course paradoxically requires less effort on your part, assuming of course that your preparation has been thorough.

First-night nerves. These can beset organisers and participants alike. Right from the start you should try to convey an aura of confidence and involvement. Your role is very much that of the good host putting your guests at ease.

● Use first names and make a point of introducing people to each other. Name badges (adhesive labels) can be helpful.

● Serve tea or coffee at the beginning to overcome the initial unease.

● Have a display of booklets, toys, etc., for people to look at in case conversation flags.

● Alternatively, you could distribute hand-outs or written material for people to peruse before you begin.

Course Outline. At the first meeting it is worth spending a little time reviewing the course programme and, in general terms, how you intend going about it. Make time also for participants to share their fears or anxieties, probably best done in smaller groups.

Sense of Achievement. If possible, try to have parents leave the first meeting with a sense that *they* have achieved something. Participation activities, group discussions, even making simple toys are all possibilities. These can also be useful 'ice-breakers', giving people an excuse to laugh and relax. We pack a lot into the first meeting on the premise that the parents' motivation, and our own, is likely to be highest at this time.

Times. Start at the time you stated and keep to the advertised format. Finish at the agreed time. Over-running on the first night is excusable; therafter, it is bad planning. Draw up a time schedule for each session and ensure that all tutors have a copy.

Advance Notice. Give advance notice of any programme changes. In particular, try to avoid changing the date of a session. If you must do so, ensure any absentees are told. Even then, you run the risk of some participants turning up on the original date and they don't like it!

Reviews. The planning team needs to meet between sessions to review how the course is going and to plan ways of responding to the needs expressed by parents during the course. This is covered in more detail later (p.238).

After the Course

There is general agreement that the value of courses for parents are maximised when follow-up arrangements are clearly thought out and planned. As Gillian Pugh[40] stated, 'to whet the appetite and then withdraw . . . would surely be irresponsible and counter-productive'.

● Individual contacts with parents, albeit at less frequent intervals, is one approach that appeals mainly to therapists and psychologists.

● By contrast, the groups formed on a course could continue to meet regularly. For example, at the Manor Park Special School in Worcester, there are now five groups of five or six mothers who meet with the head teacher, at least one psychologist, a health visitor or public health nurse and social worker. Each group originated with a parents' workshop.

● Home/school diaries, telephone contacts, end-of-term meetings are some of the other ways of keeping in touch.

You will have to be prepared. John Hattersley and Laurence Tennant[44] note, 'In our experience, the time-limited courses can produce some benefits to families but more often underlines the longer term need for support.' (p.81)

Repetition of the Course

The final act of the planning team is to review the course, revise it in the light of experience and prepare for another run of the course.

The repeat need not occur straight away; indeed, the rest will be very welcome, but it is certainly much easier to re-run a course if: (1) you document your experiences so that you can be reminded of all you did and so that others can learn from them, e.g. a brief report outlining the course, how it was received and suggested changes; (2) you 'package' the course; filing all the necessary resource materials (videos, publicity leaflets, etc.) so that they can be easily found and re-used.

Moreover, it is worth sharing details about the course with those in similar settings throughout the country. Articles in professional magazines or talking at conferences are among the possibilities. Your work can then benefit other planning teams.

Sample Courses

In this part three different styles of courses for parents will be described. First, *workshops* based around talks and discussion groups; secondly, *video-courses* that involve specially made television programmes with supporting written materials; thirdly, *Open University packages* consisting mainly of specially commissioned texts with linked television and radio programmes.

Workshops

Parent workshops have been used in both Britain and the US to help parents learn more about working with their handicapped children. In Britain, they were pioneered by Cliff Cunningham and Dorothy Jeffree at the Hester Adrian Research Centre, University of Manchester, and they have since been based mainly in special schools for handicapped children.

In the US, many types of social agencies provide such workshops — Headstart; service agencies for handicapped people; parent associations such as the Association for Retarded Citizens; family service agencies; schools or the adult education programme of school district or community colleges and so forth. As community practices vary so widely within the US, parents and professionals should contact local provider agencies and educational institutions to identify workshops held in their area.

Briefly, the workshops usually consist of a series of weekly meetings, usually ten in all, held on a weekday evening, each lasting about two hours. No children are present at any of the meetings. The first half of the evening is given over to talks on specific topics related to teaching. For example, assessment, observation, teaching techniques and so on. After this the workshop divides into small groups of about eight to ten parents each with a tutor. These are the core of the workshops and it is from there that the name derives. The emphasis is on *work*, in that parents (1) discuss the evening's lecture and relate the content to their child, (2) plan activities they will carry out with their child and (3) report on the past week's homework and discuss any difficulties encountered.

The primary aim of the workshops is to provide parents with a model that will help them identify their child's particular developmental needs and ways in which they can be taught in everyday situations. Cunningham and Jeffree[87] state:

our goal was that parents would internalise a teaching model for approaching their child's behaviour and learning. By internalise, we mean that the parent has achieved a skill in applying the principles and concepts such that she need not overtly articulate each step on each occasion but can intuitively react to the child and learning situation.

However, they go on to note that this process requires time, in that the parent 'must apply it, then re-apply and re-evaluate so it is demonstrable to them that this model can work in their homes and with their own children.' (p.11)

The main teaching was done in small groups, led by a tutor, usually a class teacher in school-based workshops.

Gillian Pugh[40] succinctly summarises the characteristics of an ideal tutor.

The tutor must be well versed in not immediately providing direct answers but in turning questions back to the parents. The parents within the group can provide a wealth of alternatives and new solutions to old problems and the tutor must take care not to intimidate parents with 'expert' answers. Cunningham and Jeffree's reference to being positive and confident has already been mentioned. Attwood speaks too of the need for honesty and for the tutor, where necesary, to admit ignorance over some problems. He stresses also how important it is for tutors to be concerned about the health and welfare of the family as a whole and not just the handicapped child. (p.74)

In the main, workshops have been instigated by psychologists, usually those attached to the special education or child guidance services, with help from teachers, therapists, health visitors and social workers. They have been organised for parents whose children are of preschool age, attending school (the most popular) and for those in adult training programmes or centres.

Tony Attwood[88] advises a rather different emphasis for each.

The parents of young preschool children need support in adjusting to the psychological effect of having a handicapped child, reassurance that the child will continue the process of normal development, although at a slower rate, and preparation for and discussion of future problems. The specific remedial programmes should be accented towards promoting early developmental processes and basic self-care skills. The school-age children, as another potential group, often require more help with regard to communication and education skills, while the parents of older children and adolescents may require more support in adjusting to behaviour and personality problems. These parents are often the most difficult to help as abnormal patterns of development and behaviour have already been established in the early years with the inevitable development of secondary handicaps. (pp.71–2)

The difficulties of evaluating the effectiveness of workshops are well described by Jill Gardner.[89] In particular, the difficulty of knowing what is actually happening at home as a result of the workshop.

However, recent reports give evidence of parents attaining the learning goals they selected for their child and of improvement in their teaching skills, especially if the tutor makes a visit to the home and gives the parents constructive feedback on their teaching approach.

Parents are invariably enthusiastic about the workshops. As Hattersley and Tennant[44] note:

The workshops had helped them to approach their handi-capped children in a more positive calm way. Many of them commented on their ability to be more objective and constructive in dealing with particular problems which in turn had helped to reduce their feelings of hopelessness and despair. They felt that they were more able to set their expectations for their child at an appropriate level and to move a little towards accepting that the whole family needed a certain degree of independence. (p.80)

Further details about workshops are given in the following articles.

Attwood, T. 'The Croydon workshop for the parents of severely handicapped, school-age children', *Child: Care, Health and Development*, vol. 5, no. 3 (1979), pp.177–88.

Cunningham, C.C. and Jeffree, D.M. 'The organisation and structure of workshops for parents of mentally handicapped children', *Bulletin of British Psychological Society*, vol. 28 (1971), pp.405–11.

Gardner, J. 'School-based parent involvement: a psychologist's viewpoint' in P. Mittler and H. McConachie (eds), *Parents, professionals and mentally handicapped people: approaches to partnership* (Croom Helm, London, 1983).

Hattersley, J. and Tennant, L. 'Parent workshops in Worcestershire' in G. Pugh, *Parents as partners* (National Children's Bureau, London, 1981).

McCall, C. and Thacker, J. 'Working together — a progress report on parental workshops', *Apex*, vol. 5, no. 3 (1977), pp.7–8.

Pugh, G. 'Parent workshops: an overview' in *Parents as partners* (National Children's Bureau, London, 1981).

Video-courses

Basing a course for parents around video-programmes was the novel concept introduced by St Michael's House in Ireland as part of their research programme,[90] and one that has been taken up in other countries as well.

Video has benefits to parents and organisers alike. For the parents it is an excellent teaching medium in that it easily integrates several potent teaching techniques. Parents can *see* new ways of interacting with children who are similar to their own; the presenters *explain* why certain approaches are recommended and during the programmes the parents can take part in an activity, e.g. rating a child's language as imitated or spontaneous. Hence, video can ensure that new information is presented in an easily understood way, especially to parents who may be less verbally proficient.

It has advantages of another kind for course organisers. The amount of time spent preparing and planning the course is minimal; that's already taken care of. The course does not depend on having 'knowledgeable' people available to give talks or lead groups. The programmes can be repeated easily for absentees.

Another feature of the video-courses is that they focus on a specific topic in children's development. The course produced by St Michael's House, 'Putting Two Words Together', as its name suggests, focuses on the formation of two-word sentences and the associated widening of vocabulary which occurs at this time.

During the course, parents are introduced to methods of:
- assessing their child's present linguistic skills
- selecting new learning objectives
- devising teaching games that embody the communicative functions of language
- generalising learning to novel contexts
- monitoring their own use of language.

Each of the five video-programmes lasts between 25 and 34 minutes and is designed to be viewed one programme per week. They are styled on television documentary/instructional programmes (c.f. Open University programmes in Britain) with two presenters giving voice-over explanations to captions or shots of adults working with a child.

Practical Activities. After viewing each programme the parents are expected to carry out a set practical activity at home (e.g. transcribing their conversation with the child); evaluate for themselves how well it went using the guidelines listed in the handbook and report back on it at the next course meeting.

These activities are considered an essential element of the course. They prompt parents to break away from existing routines and experiment with the new ways of interacting with their child which they have seen on video. But the activities have effects beyond these behavioural changes. The parents are left to make their own decisions regarding the specific objectives or techniques they feel are most suited to their child. The course guides their selection but it does not dispense prescriptions. Hence the course respects and tries to nurture the parents as decision-makers for their child; a feature that can be easily excluded within structured intervention packages such as Portage but one which is now being stressed within the literature.[17]

Procedures in Use of the Video-course. Groups of parents, on average twelve mothers and fathers (approximately eight families), take the course over a series of six evening meetings held weekly in the nursery, preschool or clinic which the child attends. Two tutors are present at the meetings: most often psychologists, speech therapists or teachers.

To date, the course has been used with parents in some 15 centres throughout Ireland. Invitations are issued to parents solely on the basis of the appropriateness of the course to the child's present level of language development. The percentage of parents accepting the invitation usually exceeds 90 per cent and over 80 per cent complete the course.

Detailed analysis of audio-recordings from a sample of 33 parents and children interacting at home, before and after the course, showed significant improvements in the children's expressive language and marked differences in the way parents talked to their child.[91]

Weakness. The specific focus of the video-course is at once its strength and a weakness. The detail it provides parents has proved most valuable, particularly when expert advice, such as from speech therapists, is not readily available to them.

However, the course is obviously *not* appropriate for parents whose children are beyond the two-word stage or who have not yet reached it. What sort of course can we offer them? An ideal solution would be more courses for parents, dealing with these and other topics.

This possibility will become ever more real as video-equipment becomes common. However, the main requirement is availability of staff with the necessary skills and time to devote to the production of courses. It may not be too far in the future before parents have a choice of courses, so that they can select those most suited to their needs at that point in time. Video-courses are a step in that direction.

Further information about video-courses are contained in the following articles.

McConkey, R. 'Videocourses for parents: an example of systematic dissemination', *NEWS: Association of Child Psychology and Psychiatry*, no. 16 (1983), pp.7–11.

McConkey, R. and O'Connor, M. 'A new approach to parental involvement in language intervention programmes', *Child: Care, Health and Development*, vol. 8, no. 3 (1982), pp. 163–76.

McConkey, R. and O'Connor, M. 'Videocourses for training staff in social services', *Journal of Education for Teaching*, vol. 9, no. 1 (1983), pp.46–54.

McConkey, R., McEvoy, J. and Gallagher, F. 'Learning through play; the evaluation of a videocourse for parents of mentally handicapped children', *Child: Care, Health and Development*, vol. 8, no. 6 (1982), pp.345–59.

Enquiries about the video-courses produced by St Michael's House should be addressed to:

Research and Training Department
St Michael's House
Upper Kilmacud Road
Stillorgan
Co. Dublin
Ireland

Open University Packages

Since 1977, the Open University in Britain has been developing a range of short courses aimed at parents, based around attractively produced written units, with linked television and radio programmes.

The focus is on non-handicapped children at different stages; for instance, existing courses include 'The First Year of Life', 'The Preschool Child', 'Childhood 5 – 10' and 'Parents and Teenagers'.

Parts of these courses could prove suitable for parents with handicapped children, although to my knowledge they have yet to be used in this way. But my chief reason for featuring them in this book, is as a model of another type of course which could be offered to parents; namely, one based around written manuals.

Like all Open University courses, these parent courses are designed primarily for independent study at home. Enrolled students can submit optional assignments and if they are completed satisfactorily, they receive a statement of course participation. But as Jane Wolfson[92] points out, the courses eschew an academic approach.

> The course may be defined as functional education, i.e. intended to encourage the direct application of learning in everyday life . . . The overall aim was indeed to develop courses with a flexible format which would allow students to follow their own interests and which, to quote an early planning paper, 'would equip students with the knowledge and skills to assess their own and their children's needs and take appropriate action, thus maximising opportunities for the personal development of both parents and children'. (p.177)

The Preschool Child course consists of eight colour-illustrated books, containing ten to twelve topics in each (88 in all), with two to four pages to each topic. The book titles include *Through the Day* (with topics like 'Dressing', 'Food, glorious food', 'Stories'); *Work and Play* (including topics on 'What's naughty?', 'Talking while you work and paint') and *Going Out* (sample topics are 'Shopping', 'Your child's own books', and 'What happens when you die?').

The course books deliberately use a magazine format and style with integrated text, illustrations and activities for participants to carry out at home, such as a diary of children's television viewing, making picture books, analysing children's drawings.

Television, radio and audio-tapes are used in the course when these are deemed more appropriate media than print. For example, television has been heavily used for the analysis of natural interactions in playgroups, clinics and homes; whereas radio and tapes are used to explore language development. These programmes are broadcast on the national radio and television networks but they are also available on pre-recorded cassettes. In general, though, participants tend to view these as 'extra support' materials rather than integral parts of the course. A postcourse survey found that over 90 per cent of participants gave 'very helpful' ratings to the books, whereas it was around 35 per cent for television programmes and 15 per cent for radio broadcasts.

Course participants are encouraged to join a self-help group and the university publishes a listing of voluntary community education co-ordinators who can put enquirers in touch with other students. Some even take the initiative in setting up study groups.

Another development has been the use of the course by professionals such as health visitors or public health nurses, social workers and nursery school heads, with parents in their area. To facilitate groups of this type, the university has recently produced two 'packs' under the general title 'Parents Talking'. One deals with *The Developing Child* and the second with *Family Relationships*. Both are produced with parent discussion groups in mind, including self-help groups meeting in their own homes, playgroups, parent and toddler groups, local clinics, community centres, hospitals, child care centres, family centres and group meetings in nursery schools. Each pack consists of 20 topic leaflets, usually reprints from existing courses, each two to four pages in length. Among the leaflets in the *Family Relationships*[93] pack are those on 'Learning to Love', 'House Rules', 'Wills of their Own' and 'Feeling Low'. As the introductory leaflet makes clear:

> The topic leaflets are all written for you to read at home. They ask you to look at your own situation and experiences and give you information and guidance to enable you to make your own decisions. They contain quizzes and activities which ask you to record your ideas and feelings. They let you look at problems and come up with new ways of tackling them.
>
> Learning on your own can be lonely. At some point we all need someone else to talk things over with. Meeting in a group allows you to do this. You can share ideas and swop experiences. You can learn from each other and go on to tackle problems together. Use the leaflets on your own at home and come to your group meetings to discuss what you find.

As you might guess, these Open University courses are expensive to initiate: over £250,000 at 1977 prices for the first two courses, the 'First Year of Life' and the 'Preschool Child'. However, the income from student fees meant that nearly half of these costs were recouped after only two presentations and, as more people take the course, the development cost per student becomes smaller, making this a highly cost-effective method of sharing knowledge with parents.

In the future, similar courses for parents of handicapped children might evolve. At the time of writing, the university, in association with Mencap, has plans for a course entitled 'Mental Handicap: Patterns for Living', aimed at improving the understanding between families and the range of workers in the field and to increase their awareness of the needs and wishes of mentally handicapped children and adults.

Other organisations (local education authorities and agencies, national parents' groups, universities, polytechnics, community colleges) could be interested in producing courses too. Increasingly, the technology and expertise is available. The Open University packages are hopefully only the first of their kind. In the US, departments of continuing education, universities, community colleges and local school systems often provide courses through their adult education programmes.

Finally, it is possible for teachers or therapists to base a workshop course around one of several books written especially for parents. Elizabeth Newson and Tony Hipgrave[34] designed their book *Getting Through to your Handicapped Child* as a handbook to be used by groups of parents or professionals. They include an appendix describing its use within workshops.

Another possibility is the book edited by David Mitchell[94] entitled *Your Child is Different*. In fact, this is an adaptation of a handbook which accompanied a series of radio programmes produced by the Continuing Education Unit of Radio New Zealand, one of the first distance-learning packages for parents with a handicapped child.

Bruce Baker[95] and his colleagues at the University of California (Los Angeles, USA) have developed a series of manuals specially for parents of mentally handicapped children under the title *Steps to Independence*. These were originally designed to augment parent courses and subsequent research has shown that they are most effective when used in this way, rather than studied privately at home.[96] Nearly 100,000 copies of these manuals are now in circulation, probably the 'market-leaders' in North America.

Likewise the John Tracy Clinic[97] in Los Angeles, California, for parents of young deaf children in the United States, has published a manual-based, one-year correspondence course that has been translated into 17 languages and taken by close on 50,000 families in 129 countries.

Further information about:
(1) the Open University courses can be obtained from:
Community Education Office
The Open University
PO Box 76
Milton Keynes MK7 6AA
(2) the John Tracy Clinic can be obtained from:
206 West Adam Boulevard
Los Angeles
California 90007

(3) *Steps to Independence* can be obtained from:
Research Press
PO Box 31779
Champaign
Illinois 61821

Parents' Reactions to Courses

Every course is a compromise. The people enrolled all have peculiar needs; yet, by its nature, a course has to focus on common concerns. We have already examined some ways of ensuring that individual needs are accommodated, but the only sure way of knowing how close or not you have managed to do this, is by checking with the people who know best: the parents.

Unfortunately, we have little tradition of seeking consumer reactions in education, a relic of compulsory schooling and the 'like it or lump it' philosophy. But listening to and observing parents during and after a course can give you fresh insight into improving your course.

Parental feedback can be obtained informally and entails little extra work on your part, or you can do a more thorough job via questionnaires and structured interviews. In either case, the result is the same, to make your course ever more complete and less of a compromise.

Informal Feedback

Here are some specific suggestions for obtaining feedback from parents directly and indirectly, during the course.

Staff Reviews. The team involved in planning and running the course should meet after each session of the course to share their personal reactions as to how it went and to pool the information they obtained, through observing the parents' reactions (e.g. during question time or discussion) or talking with them at coffee breaks, etc. Suggestions for modifications or new plans can be discussed and decided upon.

These meetings should be timetabled in advance but preferably *not* immediately after the course meeting when the euphoria of a job done dampens one's critical faculties. Equally, there is a temptation to be more concerned with getting things ready for the next meeting if the review occurs too close to it. Perhaps the-morning-after-the-night-before is the best solution.

Parent Review. About half-way through the course, it is worth scheduling a short review session, in which parents can give their reactions about (1) what they have got out of the course so far and (2) what they hope to get out of the remaining meetings. This is best done within small groups of, say, six to eight parents, so as to ensure that every parent gets a chance to respond. Note too the positive approach of the questions used. Parents, in my experience, are reluctant to criticise, so a direct 'Tell us what's wrong and we'll try to fix it' will get little response.

I find it invaluable to write the parents' replies on flip charts or a blackboard, so that the information is available to the whole group should you want to discuss it further and you also have a written record to bring back to the staff review meeting.

Attendance. This is a less direct but, none the less, highly informative source of feedback. Keep a record of attendances and watch out for regular absentees. At your review meeting, you might discuss the likely reasons and take some action, e.g. a telephone call or home visit. Parents who apologise for their absences, or warn you in advance that they cannot attend, are of less concern because they have signalled their interest in the course.

Activities at Home. The parents' completion of suggested activities at home can also be an indication of their involvement and interest in the course. It's a warning sign when parents make excuses for not carrying out the activity. You may need to spend more time ensuring the activity is relevant to their needs.

Home Visit. During the course, a visit to the parents' homes is an opportunity to hear their individual reactions. They might well raise specific issues here that they would be reluctant to discuss in a group setting. Some of them you may be able to deal with on the spot. Others may cause you to rethink elements of the course.

Formal Feedback

Thus far, the aim of your feedback has been to improve the

course you are currently running. However, it is equally important to review the whole course and try to establish its effectiveness, either immediately afterwards and/or after a period of time has elapsed. This will aid your planning of any further courses.

In this section, I shall outline some ways of doing this, particularly through the use of questionnaires and structured interviews. I should add that these formal methods could equally well be applied *during* a course. My preference though is to go for the more personal approach outlined above. Of course, these can also be used to complement questionnaires.

Parents' Reactions to the Course

On the final meeting of a course, we invite parents to complete, anonymously, a short questionnaire about the course (see Figure 10.1).

This approach has a number of advantages. It ensures that *everyone's* reaction is obtained. The replies are given *anonymously* so that parents can be more forthright than they might otherwise be face-to-face. The questionnaire ensures systematic coverage of a range of topics.

We find it useful to mix 'closed' questions, those which parents tick, with 'open' questions, where they write in their answers. Multi-choice questions are easier and quicker to complete but you must ensure that you have listed all the alternative answers, otherwise you will not have adequately sampled their opinions.

Open questions can be more informative, once you overcome people's natural hesitancy to commit their thoughts to paper. These questions give parents full scope to give a personal reaction: the answers range from the predictable 'very interesting' to the totally unexpected. Among the most fruitful questions for us have been 'What do you feel you got out of taking the course?', 'What aspect of the course did you like best?', 'Were there any parts you did not enjoy or you feel could be improved?'

Collating the information is a time-consuming task but one worth doing; you will discover the elements of the course which were universally appreciated and aspects which people would like to see changed. You may be able to identify some trends, such as younger parents being more critical of the course than older parents. The data can also be included in a report of the course for presentation to service administrators.

Figure 10.1: Questionnaire for Evaluation of Courses

Let's Play — Feedback Sheet

We would like to have your reactions to our course.
This information will enable us to improve the course for others.
You do not have to give your name. Thank you for your help.

1(a) *Give a mark out of 10 for the parts of the course you found MOST USEFUL*

Video-programmes	☐	Meeting other people	☐
Meeting course tutors	☐	New activities with child	☐
Handbook	☐	Group discussion	☐
Toy-making	☐	Play charts	☐

(b) *Which did you find most useful?* ....
(c) *Why was this?* ....
....

2. *The amount of work you had to do during the course; was it . . .*

   ☐ Too much   ☐ Just right   ☐ Too little

   (Tick or check one)

3. *Would you recommend the course to others?*

   ☐ Yes definitely   ☐ Yes   ☐ No

4. *Would you like to take other courses similar to this one?*

   ☐ Yes definitely   ☐ Yes   ☐ No

5. *What topics would you like courses on?*

....
....
....

Let's Play — Feedback Sheet (continued)

6. *We would like your suggestions for ways of improving the course*

Have you any suggestions on . . .	OK now?	Change I would suggest
Times of meetings		
Venue		
Numbers attending		
Discussion sessions		
Toy-making		
Practical activities		
Other (please specify)		

7. *Any other comments you would like to make:*

Could you please give us some details about yourself

MALE ☐   FEMALE ☐   If professional staff please state job title ....

AGE   Under   20 ☐   21-30 ☐   31-40 ☐   41-49 ☐   50+ ☐

Age at which you left full-time schooling ....

Changes for the Better?

There is, however, another dimension to evaluation of courses. Do they achieve their objective of making parents more informed and competent at handling their children and are there signs of the children progressing? These are deceptively simple questions. I have already touched on them in the context of face-to-face work with families (see Chapter 7) but they become even more complex when faced with *groups* of parents. Nevertheless, it is important that you justify the amount of labour put into the course by establishing the gains which ensue.

Increase in Parents' Knowledge. The most popular way of assessing courses has been to give parents some form of test covering the course content. These have come in various formats, including multiple-choice tests and the more adventurous replaying of short video-extracts which are stopped at decision-points and the parents are asked to record what they would do next.

It is worth noting Bruce Baker's[45] views on these assessments. He was a one-time proponent of this method of course evaluation. 'Measures of parents' behavioural knowledge, teaching skill and child behaviour may all show significant changes but these have been found to be uncorrelated.' (p.338) In short, parents may know more but act no differently and conversely some parents can bring about marked changes in their children but score no better on tests of knowledge.

Changes in Children. The simplest way to determine if there has been any change in the children, is to ask the parents. Admittedly, it will be their perceptions that you will obtain: the reality could be different. In our questionnaires we also include items on which you would expect to find *no* changes in the child's behaviour as a result of the course. These help to pick up any 'halo' effects in parents' responses.

Another approach is to ask other adults who are familiar with the child, to indicate the changes they have noted.

A more stringent form of evaluation is to collect data on the children's behaviour before and after the course. This could be done by interviewing the parents and teachers; by having them complete behavioural checklists or rating scales; by administering standardised tests or instruments or by making direct observations of the child, such as measuring the child's mean length of utterance in expressive language. These same assessments can then be repeated after the course. The risk of bias can be further reduced by having these assessments carried out by people who were not involved with the course and who are unaware as to whether or not the parents have completed the course.

These procedures entail quite a bit of work but they bring many extra benefits. For a start, it forces you to be more specific about the aims of your course and the changes you anticipate it will have on the children. Otherwise, you will not be able to select suitable measuring instruments. Also the data obtained before the course commences will provide you with valuable information that should help you tailor the content more toward the parents' needs.

Changes in Parents. This is a more difficult area to tackle mainly because most courses aim to bring about diffuse and diverse changes in parents. Different people could be expected to react differently and hence uniform changes are unlikely to be found across all parents.

The nearest I have come to obtaining satisfactory measures of changes in parents' behaviour was during the evaluation of a course for parents on language development.[91] We advised parents that during teaching sessions with their child, they should speak in utterances of three words or less, mainly in response to the child's action and vocalisations and to use declarative sentences rather than questions or demands.

We asked the parents to audio-tape two play sessions at home before and after the course. We were then able to chart significant changes on the above variables for mothers and on two out of the three for fathers (they did not change significantly in the percentage of their utterances in response to the child). Obviously the more precise your advice to parents, the easier it is for you to look for, and detect, changes in their behaviour. Very few studies to date have been able to do this successfully.

If behavioural measures are beyond your scope, an alternative is to ask parents to rate themselves on the changes they think they have made in the way they act with their child. Or other people who know them well could be asked to do this.

Finally, an area of change that has been much neglected is parents' *attitudes*, either toward their child or their perception of themselves as parents. It is reasonable to predict that courses

Figure 10.2: Parental Attitude Questionnaire

SITUATIONS INVENTORY

We would like you to indicate how you feel when you are with your child in particular situations or circumstances. Put a mark nearest the comment which best describes your feelings at the time. Do not spend too much time thinking about each comment. Just give your first reaction.

Situation   PLAYING WITH CHILD

*I have lots of fun with child	I don't have fun with child
Child acts on his//her own	Child needs lots of attention from me
I tell N. what he/she should do	I just talk about what's happening
I give child individual attention	This fits in with my doing other tasks
*I get harassed	A relaxing situation for me
Child always keen to do this	Child may resist doing this
I aim to teach something	I don't tend to teach things in this situation
*We do this often together	We hardly ever do this together
I don't allow child to mess about	We can mess about a bit
I expect child to be able to do things without help	I give child a great deal of help here
*I feel I am doing a good job as parent on these occasions	I don't feel I'm doing a good job as a parent on these occasions
*I try to create new experiences for the child	I go through a familiar routine with child

Figure 10.2: Parental Attitude Questionnaire (continued)

I control what happens	....	Child controls what happens
Child always does what I ask	....	Child doesn't do what I ask
I take more time (because of child's problems)	....	I take no more time than with an ordinary child

should also affect these attitudes for the better. Figure 10.2 is an example of a questionnaire we use. (This is adapted from one originally devised by Shirley Judson and Bob Burden[98] and ascertains parents' reactions in specific contexts, such as playing with or dressing their child.) A factor analysis of responses from 67 parents yielded one main factor which we labelled '*enthusiasm*'. The items loading highest on this are starred on the form. The questionnaire was administered through interviews in the home before and after parents came on a course to help them nurture their child's play. Afterwards mothers had significantly higher enthusiasm scores, not just in the context of play but also when dressing or shopping with their child.[99] This suggests an overall boosting of parental morale and confidence, confirming the comments many parents had made at the end of the course.

You might devise other ways of tapping parental attitudes, depending on the nature of your courses.

Evaluate: Then What?

The prime justification for expending energy on evaluation is to produce a better course. Hence the course team's job is not complete until the members have reviewed the data they obtained via formal and informal methods and examined the implications of their findings. These should be recorded in detail so that the lessons learnt will be retained. Do not trust your memory.

The final job of the course team should be to write a report on the course: its format, content and evaluation. Among the people it could be sent to, are the following: (1) colleagues with whom you work but who did not participate in the course (your report might encourage them to be involved in future courses);

(2) administrators of your service, for information and in support of your requests for extra resources!; (3) editors of journals or magazines with a view to publication (your report could help people in other parts of the country to plan their own courses); (4) parents who took the course or others who might be interested in taking a future one.

Second Best?

Finally, for those who may feel that courses are only second best to individual contacts, you might ponder on Bruce Baker's[45] conclusions at the end of his review of all the available research of parent participation in intervention programmes with young severely handicapped children whether clinic or home-based, done individually or through groups. He writes, 'the available research does leave us, however, with one caution — more is not always better. We neither find evidence that more costly individual training nor that time-consuming home visits enhance treatment outcome.' (p.37)

PART FOUR

Spreading the Word

OVERVIEW

Two related themes run throughout the three chapters in this section. One may sound rather familiar because there have been echoes of it previously. In the chapter on 'Learning through Video', for example, I have collated suggestions about how to set up video-equipment and use it effectively when working face-to-face with parents or in groups. For the novice, basic facts are given about the equipment, while, for readers with some experience of it, I hope the practical tips given on its use will help you and your parents get more value out of video.

Likewise the chapter on 'Writing for Parents' starts with the basic rules that will make your writings clear and succinct. A wide range of possibilities is then described and I hope some will be new ideas which you could apply to your work.

The final chapter, 'Telling Others', lists ways whereby parental involvement could become a reality for more parents, both within your service agency and schools. Once again, my aim is to open your eyes to new possibilities and initiatives which parents or professionals might take.

If all this smacks of 'left-overs', then let me reassure you: they are! It is true that you could work effectively with parents and not use any of the skills and techniques described in these chapters, but I believe that would be a loss to the parents you are in contact with and to yourself.

The second theme that runs through these pages has a refrain that urges you to look beyond your little niche to find ways of making available your expertise and knowledge to many more parents; more than you could ever deal with personally and even to those parents who have no ready access to professional help. Hence, in the chapter on video, I explain how you could make video-programmes which might be swopped, loaned or sold to other colleagues or parents. Or you could write articles, reports or even books from which others could learn about your experiences. Chapter 12 will give you further details about these, while in Chapter 13, among other things, I describe how you might organise training courses or workshops for teachers and therapists who have little or no prior experience of working with parents. I very much hope this theme will appeal to those therapists and teachers who are experienced in working with parents and to the lecturers and tutors whose responsibility it is to train young professionals. These two groups have a major role to play in spreading the word.

Service Evolution

Work with parents may make little difference to the existing job routines of teachers and therapists, at least in the early stages. However, a venture has begun that will have profound implications for the future structuring and organisation of our services to families and to children. Why? You will have given a foothold to a new philosophy of consumer involvement.

Service evolution is ever present: change is always around, albeit at such a slow rate that sometimes we find it hard to detect. For example, during the past 50 years, there have been major changes in services for handicapped people and their families.

The shift from institutional to community care has gained momentum; the dominance of the medical model is waning and the ethos of charitable endeavours has been replaced by a spirit of professionalism. Our colleagues of a generation ago could scarcely credit the changes and I doubt if many could have predicted them with any accuracy. None the less, the seeds of the transformation were around, albeit in the endeavours and beliefs of a few.

It would be foolhardy of me to claim that our predictive powers are any better today. Our services will surely continue to evolve but I am less confident as to the form they will take. There are many imponderables. But among the seeds of change which I hope we continue to sow for our descendants, is that of partnership between parents and professionals. As yet the seedlings are scattered erratically and their growth is, at best, sporadic. None the less, we have learnt enough about nurturing their growth to care for them better. It is up to today's labourers, you and me, to prepare the soil and plant the seeds, so that future generations can reap a richer harvest.

11

Learning through Video

Video is potentially the most effective teaching aid ever invented. We have barely begun to tap its power.

● If you have ever wanted to see again how a child reacted, or analyse the events in detail, perhaps in slow motion and keep a record for showing to colleagues, then video is the answer.

● If you have ever wished that you could compare a child's behaviour now with what it was like a week, a month or a year ago, only video will let you.

● If you have said in exasperation 'these parents need to see themselves and the effects they are having on the child', try using video.

● If you are all set to give a demonstration but the children fail to co-operate, or don't turn up, a video-recording will save your blushes.

● If you wonder how a child behaves at school or at home but you haven't the time to go and observe, watch a video-recording.

● If you are fed up repeating the same thing to every parent, spare yourself the boredom, record it once-and-for-all on video.

● If you want to enliven a meeting, hire a video-programme for the evening.

Video also brings benefits to the learner.

● *'I can see what you mean.'* Video is a particular boon to people who have difficulty with reading or who are not used to reading or find it hard to grasp the meaning of what they are told; for example, immigrant parents. Pictures are so much more informative than verbal explanations.

● *'Could I see that again?'* Easily arranged; the video-recording can be replayed as often as required and at whatever time or location suits the viewer.

● *'I saw things I never saw before.'* Video gives viewers the chance of seeing what goes on at times when visitors are not normally present; for example, in classrooms or on outings.

● *'I didn't realise so much went on.'* Video-recordings can be examined in detail so that viewers can extract much more information than they could when observing the same scene as it happens.

With so many benefits to 'teacher' and learners alike, one would have thought that video-dealers would have been inundated with orders and that the equipment would be in daily use within all clinics and schools. Not so. Video is variously viewed as a novelty, a mystery or a luxury. Some of the more common myths are as follows.

'It's too expensive' The prices have fallen dramatically in recent years. A basic video-system of recorder, camera and television can now be purchased for around £1,200. Ironically many centres have actually bought video-equipment, but fail to use it.

'It always breaks down' Modern video-equipment is much more reliable. If well cared for, the likelihood of breakdowns is greatly reduced. But all the people using it must know how to treat it properly. Most 'faults' tend to be the result of operator-error and can be easily rectified without a technician.

'It's too difficult to operate' The new cameras and recorders are more compact and portable; they dispense with the need for extra lighting and they can operate off batteries. The tapes are loaded in cassettes that run for up to four hours (Britain) or eight hours (US). One hour's practice is sufficient to master the basic operations of video-equipment.

'It's too time-consuming' Setting up the equipment, and playing back the recordings, does entail extra time; that's true. But this has to be off-set against the time likely to be saved in the longer-run through the effective use of video.

'It's too intrusive' For some people the presence of a camera and recorder can be off-putting and unsettling. But there are ways of minimising the disruption, such as the use of one-way screens. Moreover, familiarity reduces an awareness of the camera.

Underlying all these excuses, may be an unspoken but, none the less, real fear: 'I don't know how to use video'.

Hence this chapter is a beginner's guide in putting video to use for you. The first part details how it can be used when working with individual parents or staff, in schools or clinics or at home and the second part describes the making of video-programmes for showing to groups. Details are also given of how to obtain ready-made programmes that could be used on courses, parents' meetings, etc.

Alternatives to video

Other visual aids have now become second-best but, in case you have to make do, the possibilities are:

Cine films or home movies The 8 mm movie-camera is very much cheaper than video but the film is much more expensive than tapes. You also need a projector for playback. A friend may have a complete set that you could borrow.

Colour slides and tape commentary Although still-photographs do not capture the flow of action, they do allow viewers more time to examine each shot. Slides are best for diagrams and figures or for showing examples of toys and equipment.

16 mm films You might consider hiring a film for a parents' meeting, but only if you have a projector readily available. If you have to borrow or hire a projector you might as well get a video-recorder as colour films are usually available on video.

However, this chapter will concentrate only on the use of video and my aim is quite simple: to encourage you to discover the power of video in working with parents.

Use of Video

This part explores the use of video when working with individual families and their child. It is intended to be read in conjunction with Part Two: *Working with parents face-to-face*. Hence the emphasis will be on setting-up a video-equipment in home, clinic or school and suggestions on how it can be used to teach parents more about their child and themselves.

Setting up Video-equipment

The minimum set consists of a *video-recorder* (preferably a portable model), *camera* (preferably with a tripod so that it can be left unattended) and a *television set*. With this you can record in clinics, classrooms, homes and out-of-doors. Optional extras include a remote microphone and extra lights.

In the Home. A portable video-system can be used anywhere in the house, provided that there is sufficient light. Hence scenes of toileting and washing can be recorded in the bathroom. In general, though, most of our recordings are done in the family living room.

● The camera is best placed in a corner by the window (so that the light shines in from behind) and at a distance of at least four feet from the action.

● Link the T.V. set to the recorder during filming so that you can check the pictures. But make sure the screen cannot be seen by the child or parent: it will distract them.

● If you are using a remote microphone, position it close to the action, e.g. on a chair or settee or suspend it from a light fitting or fixture.

When filming toddlers or older children, have the equipment set up and checked *before* the child comes into the room.

In Clinics. The above points apply here too. However, if you use video-equipment regularly in the same room, the installation of a few extra fitments or fittings will make it more convenient. An omnidirectional microphone can be suspended from the ceiling (use two if the room is large and the children likely to wander); extra lighting could be installed, a wall-mounted bracket for the camera could be fitted along with a shelf at chest-height on which the recorder and television can be placed out of a child's reach.

For those lucky enough to have a *one-way screen facility*, video-recordings can be done even more unobtrusively.

● The recorder, T.V. monitor and camera can all be placed in the observation room, with a remote microphone in the 'playroom'. You may also need extra lighting in the playroom to counteract the dimming effects of the smoked glass through which you are filming.

● Alternatively, the camera could be wall-mounted in the playroom with its cable through to the observation room.

● Best of all, is a system of remotely controlled cameras, wall-mounted on two opposite corners of the playroom. From the observation room, they can be made to swivel and zoom in and out. Although such sophistication is advantageous, it is not a necessity.

On Location. Portable video-equipment that is battery-operated can be easily used in classrooms, playgroups, buses or on outings. For this type of filming the camera is best hand-held. The biggest difficulty comes in obtaining clear sound recordings, but the *uni*directional microphones attached to newer video-cameras do cut down on the extraneous sound.

Tips on the Use of Video-equipment

Practice. Ensure you know how to set up the equipment before visiting a family or meeting them in the clinic. A panicking operator does not inspire confidence.

Permissions. Tell the parents why you want to video-record and get their agreement. If you intend to show the recording to colleagues, state this clearly. We obtain parents' *written* permission if the recordings or extracts from it are to be shown to other parents or people outside our service.

Camera Focus. The most common fault is out-of-focus recordings. The camera should be focused on the centre of the action, e.g. a table top or a hearth-rug for floor play, by zooming in to the maximum extent, adjusting the focus control and then zooming out to a wide shot of the scene. The camera now remains in focus whenever you zoom in or out.

However, if the child moves away from or comes nearer to the camera, the focus will need to be adjusted. The brighter the room, the more the camera aperture is closed down, thereby allowing a wider range of in-focus shots.

Counter. Always set the recorder's digital counter to zero at the beginning of the recording. During the session, use the counter to note significant behaviours which you want to highlight during playback. This saves you replaying the whole session if time is limited.

Label the Tape. After a recording, write on the cassette the child's name, date of recording and a brief description of events recorded. A supply of adhesive labels is useful if the tapes are being reused.

Copy Extracts. If there are extracts from recordings which you want to keep, these are best copied on to a library tape, thereby letting you reuse the original tape. To do this, you will need a second video-recorder. Connect it up to the first via the video in/out and audio in/out sockets and record on the second machine while the first is playing.

Care of Tapes. Rewind the tapes, place in their cases and store upright in a dry room, never on top of one another, and keep away from magnetic fields.

When to use Video-equipment

The short answer is whenever it can help you. And while that may be everytime you visit a family at home or meet a parent in the clinic, the sheer accumulation of recordings will force you to be more selective. In my experience, there are certain key times in working with parents when video-recordings are particularly useful both to you and to them.

(1) *Getting to know the parent and child* A video-record made during your first or second contact with the child and parent that shows them interacting, will provide a basis for discussions with the parent and give you a feel for their patterns of interactions.

(2) *When you want to coach the parents in a new style of interaction* With video you can show them a model of how they should interact with the child and later it can be used to give them feedback on their attempts at first using the new approach.

(3) *When you want to review progress* A previous recording of the child can be replayed and contrasted with the child's current behaviour. This is particularly valuable with severely handicapped children who may appear to make little or no progress.

Of course, there will be other times when video can be valuable, such as giving fathers (or other family members) an update on what you have been working on. But the crunch question is not *when* you use video but rather *how* you use it. Just as people can read a book and learn nothing so, too, they may watch a video-recording and be none the wiser.

Teaching through Video

First some general principles, then specific instances of the use of video to help parents observe their child, observe themselves and acquire new techniques.

How do I Look? This is everyone's first response to video-playback; a carryover of our desire to look at our best when having a photograph taken. Consequently, parents need time to get accustomed to seeing their child, their home and, most of all, themselves on television. Use the first five minutes or so of playback as familiarisation. Replay the scene if there are teaching points you want to make.

Share Reactions. Video gives you a unique opportunity to share reactions to a joint event. Encourage parents to comment freely either through general comments like 'is this what he typically does with his toys?' or you can pick up on specific actions 'why do you think she did that?' It is also a chance for you to check out the parents' *feelings*: were they cross, anxious, pleased and so on. Many people find it easier to talk about their feelings after the event rather than during it.

Pause. Make full use of the pause control on the recorder so that your explanations and discussions need not be rushed.

Repeated Replay. A sequence can be replayed several times so that different aspects can be highlighted. For instance, the child's non-verbal signals, then her play behaviours and, finally, her speech sounds. This overcomes the human failing of concentrating on only one thing at a time.

Be Selective. There is a limit to what you can teach in any one session. Hence you must be selective in the topics you focus on. Unfortunately with video there is a temptation for the unexpected and unforeseen to distract from your intended aim.

Written Records. It helps to focus the parents' attention if some form of written record is kept during the playback. Initially, this might be undertaken jointly by you and the parents, but gradually make this their responsibility.

Who Looks after the Child? Ideally the parents need to view the video playback while someone else is looking after the child. Some children may be happy to play alone or with another child; a colleague or another member of the family might do it but if all else fails it's your job to look after the child once you have briefed the parents on what to look for in the replay.

Observe the Child

Invariably one of your first goals in working with parents, is to have them observe their child more closely. For example, John was a three-year-old boy who, according to his mother, never played with toys; he threw them away. While watching a replay of John with toys, she frequently pointed out all the instances of throwing: 'there he goes again', 'look at him', 'it's always the same you know'. However, what she failed to comment on, maybe even to notice, were the many other things John did with the toys. Hence on a second replay we started to make a listing of all the other things John did with the toys as well as throwing, i.e. turning them round in his hands, mouthing, banging one against another. We began by pointing these out, then we transferred the initiative to the mother, e.g. pausing the recorder but leaving it to her to describe the action. Having to write each action down forced the mother to look more closely and to re-evaluate her impression that these actions were important.

On the second visit, we took this activity a stage further by noting how *often* John did each action. The mother then discovered that John's throwing was not in fact his most frequent action.

Advantages of Video in Observation. Of course, these observations could have been done by the parent while watching the child at play, but working from a video-recording makes it easier to learn observation skills.

● It distances the parent from the action and there is an increased chance of viewing the scene more dispassionately than if they were physically present.
● If they are unsure what is expected of them, the playback can be started again.
● The observations can be taken at the parent's pace. The playback can be paused or re-run if they are getting overwhelmed.
● The parents can be given feedback and any disputes resolved before the action restarts.

In summary, video enables you to break down the complex task of observing into more manageable bits.

Generalise Learning. The next step is to have the parents carry out observations when they watch the child at home, say on two or three different occasions during the week. After the training with video, the parents' records are more likely to be reliable accounts of what happened at home and the whole exercise should be more meaningful to them.

Observing Oneself

Video really has no equal in letting you see yourself as others see you. Observers can tell you what they saw you do or you might be able to remember but only video can actually show you *all* that happened.

The advantages of video can be best summarised in one word: self-awareness. Discovering one's own shortcomings or mistakes, is the best way of understanding the need to change and of sustaining that change. Video gives greater self-awareness by letting adults:

● view themselves as though they were looking at another person

● focus on themselves and not the child which is their predominant concern in live interactions

● reflect on their feelings during the interaction and think of alternative ways of acting.

Less perceptive parents could be helped by your questions and probes or by having to keep some form of written records as they watch the recording, e.g. the number of times they commented negatively on what the child did.

Generalise this Learning. Once again, video is but a training tool for the parents. They need to be encouraged to continue this type of self-evaluation in everyday activities. Among the possible strategies for doing this are: encouraging the parents to give you a report on what they did as well as hearing about the child's progress; have them keep simple records of their behaviour at home; discussing with them the pro's and con's of other approaches and making them more aware of their feelings and the reasons for their actions.

Learning New Techniques

Video is a quick and effective way of mastering a new teaching technique for use with a child, such as giving reinforcements, using prompts, styles of questioning and so forth. With video, the learner can first see a *model* of the technique being used; and then from a replay of their attempts they can evaluate how well they used the techniques.

Models. You can of course give parents a model of a technique then-and-there with their child. You do not need to have video. However, video does widen your options.

● *Ready-made examples* You can overcome the possible danger of the child being unco-operative by showing the parents a previous recording of the technique in use. If need be, you can augment this with explanations, pausing or replaying the tape as necessary.

● *Replay your modelling* Even more effective is talking them through a replay of a modelling session you carried out with their child. This enables you to emphasise crucial elements, explain why you made certain decisions and show that you too are capable of making mistakes!

Evaluation of parents. Three options are available:

● *Self-evaluation* Merely showing the video sequence to some parents is sufficient for them to spot their mistakes and realise how to correct them. Sometimes it helps though if they are given a prepared checklist on which they can note whether each step was carried out or not.

● *Guided evaluation* Alternatively, you can view the playback with the parent. The most vital thing to remember is to point out all the things which *went well* as well as the *mistakes* and you should be as precise in your praise as you are specific in your criticism.

● *Re-teach* Finally, the parents might be asked to have a second attempt at using the technique. This, in my experience, is never very popular; partly because it puts the parents under even greater pressure to do it right this time and by now the child might be more than a little fractious. If you do opt for a re-teach session, keep it short. You might also dispense with the video playback; verbal feedback, hopefully all positive, should suffice.

Other Uses of Video

Finally, here are some other ways in which video can be used with individual families.

● *Parents borrow the video-equipment for home recordings* This will give an insight into home life when all the family is together and you might see whether or not the parents have extended their learning to times when you are not present. This can be a chance also for the parents to share their learning with other members of the family, e.g. using video-playback to point out to the siblings some effects of what they did.

● *Case conferences* Showing video extracts of the child and/or parents can personalise case discussions and facilitate members of the team in sharing their opinion and knowledge with each other.

● *Group work* Video extracts of individual families could be used with groups of parents as a trigger for discussion or as a method of learning about new techniques. This point will be taken up later (p.267).

● *Teaching aid* Parents could use video as a teaching aid with older and more able children; for example, recording their child and showing him or her the playback in an attempt to improve the clarity of speech. Likewise, it could be used in social skills training for mentally handicapped adolescents. The advent of home video-recorders has made this a more viable option today.

● *Training yourself* Of course, you can also use video to help you become a better communicator with parents. Watching a playback of yourself when working with parents will do for you all the things we noted it could do for parents. A taste of your own medicine as they say!

Making programmes

The ultimate advantage of video is that it gives you the chance to make your own television programmes. These do not need to be all that sophisticated to be effective. Among the home-made programmes that parents seem to enjoy most and find beneficial are:

Daily activities, what goes on in playgroups, day centres and schools at times when parents are not usually present; example programmes could be a 'typical day for the class' or 'our outing to the zoo'.

Information programmes that explain handicap and its effects or outline the services available locally and how to get in contact with them.

Guidance, the aim of these programmes is to give parents specific guidelines on activities they might carry out with their child, along with an explanation as to why they are important.

Programmes can be shown to illustrate a talk or with groups of parents to get discussion going or as the centre-piece for a parent meeting in school. Barbara Tizard, in her project on involving parents in ordinary nursery and infant schools, found that

> between 75 and 100 per cent of families would come to film meetings, provided that they were offered at least two different opportunities to attend. Not only did the parents come, but they were enthusiastic about the films. Fathers and working mothers, who rarely, if ever, have the chance to watch their children in school, were particularly appreciative. But all the parents enjoyed being able to watch the children without the feeling that their presence was a distraction. (p.156)

Video could make these experiences a reality for you too. Of course, your programmes will not have the same gloss and professionalism of those broadcast on national television, but what your programmes lack in technical perfection is more than compensated for by their content. For a start they will have *local appeal*, depicting people and places that the audience is familiar with. Moreover, the viewers can *identify* with the situations depicted. Often this does not happen with ready-made programmes and their message gets blocked. For example, a programme made in North America may elicit the response, 'it may work for them but it couldn't work here'.

Most important of all, your programme can be *tailored* to the audience's needs. Broadcast programmes go for general appeal and hence deal in generalities, whereas you can be specific.

The technology for programme-making is now readily available and, in this part, I shall describe how you can use it to compile programmes that will convey a message more vividly and meaningfully than pen or voice ever could and one that, over time, can reach a wider audience more conveniently.

There are ready-made programmes that you might find useful. These can be purchased or hired or you can record programmes as they are broadcast on television.

Decision to Make a Programme

There are two issues that get intermingled at this point. First, there is the *need* for a programme and, secondly, the availability of video-equipment and your competence to use it. The latter should not determine whether a programme is made or not. Rather the decision should be on the likely gains that a programme will achieve. Once these are clarified, the practical details can be attended to.

Here are the likely gains, as I see them, for home-made video-programmes.

● *Time-saving* If you repeat the same 'message' to parents and colleagues, think of putting it on video. For example, we made a 25 minute video of the different specialists in our clinic: doctors, psychologists, social workers, physiotherapists, speech therapists. Each one talked briefly about his or her main functions and the viewers saw them working with families and children. This gave new parents and staff a ready introduction to our clinic services.

● *Reaching more people* If you would like to help more parents or 'teach' more staff but are precluded from doing so by your present commitments, then video-programmes are one way out of the dilemma. This was the thinking behind a series of video-programmes we made on helping the language development of mentally handicapped children. In our services we only had two speech therapists for some 1,000 children and adults. It was impossible for them to give parents the necessary individual attention which research studies such as those by Jean Cooper and colleagues[8] had shown to be desirable. Video-programmes have proved a successful compromise. Parents get some individual attention but the main messages are conveyed by video. If you are unable to work with all the parents in your area, this solution might work for you.

● *Conveying vital messages* If there are issues of vital importance that you want to highlight for parents or staff, then video is more likely to do this than will booklets or talks. The speech therapists in St Michael's House made a video-programme on identifying hearing losses in mentally handicapped adults. Alerting staff and parents to this can change, for the better, the way they interact with the adults.

Likewise, we commissioned a video-film on chromosome abnormalities with the central message that parents should complete their families by 35 years of age, otherwise they run a greater risk of having a damaged child.

● *New techniques* If you want to tell others about new approaches which you have found successful, consider using video to supplement the written or verbal reports you make. One of the most popular programmes I have made, says he modestly, was on the stages in children's development of pretend play and how these could be used in assessing a child's level of cognitive maturity. The unfamiliar quickly becomes understandable with video.

Changing your Role

A more selfish reason perhaps but if you are feeling in a rut and doubt the value of your existing ways of working, then video-production might generate a new dimension to your current professional role. As a researcher, I was somewhat disenchanted by the traditional methods of communicating research outcomes to 'frontline' people, i.e. parents and staff. Journals were patently inadequate and books had a limited appeal. Video has proved an attractive alternative. My role as a researcher has changed in two ways. First, more of my time is spent on implementing rather than discovering new approaches and, secondly, to facilitate this nationally, we run workshops for colleagues working in other parts of Ireland to train them in using our video-programmes within their locality.

I believe all professionals constantly need to re-assess their ways of working so that they can do their job more effectively and productively. It is good for your morale as well as the consumers.

Making a start

Once you have decided to make a programme you can explore ways of doing it. Have you access to the necessary equipment or can you purchase, hire or borrow all or some of it? In fact you may be able to get someone else to make the programme for you, for example:

● *Students* taking courses in video as part of their training, in education, communications or art and design.

● *Third-level or Higher-level institutions* such as universities or higher education colleges have their own television and audio-visual departments.

● *Video-production companies* have sprung up in the major cities. They earn their livelihood from making television commercials or commissioned programmes for industry but they may be responsive to a plea for help from you: a gift in kind. Of course, if you are willing to pay, they are unlikely to say no. The telephone directory should yield their addresses.

● *Access television*; some television companies now offer community workers the chance to produce a programme for broadcasting, e.g. BBC 2, RTE 1 and cable television companies. Many of the resources of the station can be put at your disposal (film crews, guidance on scripting and production, etc.). This option will become more viable when cable television has community access channels.

Components of a Programme

Any programme must be planned in accordance with the message you want to convey; that is obvious. Not so apparent is the diversity of ways in which you can do this. Video easily integrates various potent teaching techniques, such as demonstration, explanation summary captions, replay and analysis. The art of the producer is in judging the most effective ways of communicating the message.

Here are some suggestions.

Demonstrations. To see examples of teaching/therapy or the chance to observe children in natural surroundings is very much more effective than the recording of a person, albeit an 'expert', talking to the camera. Some key points to remember when filming for a programme as distinct for clinic use are:

● *The sound is clear* Paradoxically this is the most problematic aspect of video-recording. Make sure the sound levels are right for all the participants. Check the recording via headphones. Use two or more microphones if need be; although this will require another piece of equipment called a sound mixer.

● *The lighting is good* You need high quality of pictures that will copy. Augment room lighting when recording indoors.

● *Keep the picture in focus* Hard to do when children move around. However, out-of-focus shots are very noticeable in a programme. Extra lighting helps overcome this.

● *Vary the shots* If possible record the same scene from several different angles and experiment with a range of techniques for each shot: close-ups, wide-shots, slow zoom-in, panning, etc.

● *Keep the action on screen* An obvious point, but one sometimes forgotten. If the activity continues out of camera range (the child moves too close) you will have to re-shoot the scene.

Commentary. It is most useful to set the scene for viewers or to provide further explanations. My preference is for the commentator to give a 'voice-over' rather than appear as a 'presenter'. The latter can look rather amateurish. But beware of these common pitfalls when writing the commentator's script:

● Don't tell the viewer about things they can see for themselves, 'Here we see . . .'

● Don't let your commentary over-run into the next picture sequence, e.g. the commentary about work should stop before the workshop sequence ends. However, you can start talking about the next sequence a second or two before it appears. This is a good bridging technique.

● Keep the commentary brief and direct. People are too busy looking at the pictures to concentrate on what you are saying as well. If you really want them to listen, freeze the picture or use a caption which summarises the point.

It is a common fault with the inexperienced programme-maker to include too much commentary. Let your pictures do the talking.

Viewer Involvement. During a 'teaching' programme you might plan to have one or more activities in which the viewers participate. At best this gives them the chance to try out the techniques you have illustrated; at worst, it will help to prevent them falling asleep in front of the television.

Among the activities I have included in programmes are: making a transcript of a child's language, classifying children's play actions into one of five stages and noting the number of language models a teacher gave the child. I recommend you take an activity in these stages:

(1) *A preview* of the scene they will be observing more closely. This familiarises them with the context and prepares them for the exercise.

(2) *Observation* Replay the scene and during this time the viewers should record. If the action is moving very quickly, consider 'freezing' the picture to let the viewers keep up with their recordings.

(3) *Feedback* You must give the viewers some feedback as to the

correctness of their responses. You can do this in various ways, such as replaying the scene for a third time with voice-over commentary, or showing a caption of a correctly completed record form.

There are a number of different judgements involved in setting up a viewer activity. Are the instructions comprehensible or are they so repetitive and simplistic that they waste valuable time? Is it reasonable to expect a naive audience to do this level of activity or is it an insult to their intelligence? Have you given enough time for the feedback to sink in or have you bored them unnecessarily? These questions soon get answered if you observe an audience doing an activity and later hear their reactions. If necessary you might have to go back and remake that part of the programme.

Viewers need to be forewarned of an activity, not least so that they can have pen and paper ready. We include a preliminary caption before the start of the programme.

All the arguments in favour of video apply especially here. Viewer involvement ensures that your programme is instructional as well as entertaining.

Interviews. These are an effective way of conveying people's opinions or relating their experiences. If you are including a number of interviews within the one programme try to vary the background or setting, e.g. have parents in a home-like setting, teachers outside their school and so on. If their comments go on for a time you might insert some pictures which illustrate the point they are talking about.

Group Discussion. This can be compelling television but it can be hard to film a discussion with only one camera and sound might prove a problem. Hence this is *not* advised for the novice programme-maker.

Making the Programme: Planning Content

Planning a video-programme is somewhat akin to giving a talk. Many of the principles described in Chapter 8 apply equally well here. There is, however, one big difference. You need to think in *visual images* rather than words.

● A good starting point is to list the scenes you would like to include in the programme. Some of your clinic video-tapes might prove suitable but, if not, you will have to arrange special recordings.

● Try to have these recordings as natural as possible. If you want to illustrate home-based activities, then record in the home. If you want fathers to participate, ensure fathers appear in the programme. Resist the temptation to do all the recordings in the same setting, a studio or clinic, because it is convenient.

● Children rarely perform on demand. Give them time to settle and *always leave the camera running*. Sometimes you pick up unexpected gems. Any 'wasted' recordings can be edited out later.

● Some children will be more interested in the video-equipment than in acting naturally. We recommend that: all the equipment is set up and running before the children come into the room; some novel toy or material is at hand straight away; the child is ignored by the camera operators and other technicians. The parent or teacher should be the only person who interacts with the child during recordings. At the worst, you can withdraw the child from the room and try again later.

● Keep a 'shot list' of all you have recorded. For each scene, list the name of the child and what they did and note the beginning and end of it by using the counter on the machine. This listing will be useful to you when it comes to selecting the excerpts for the programme.

● Inevitably, you record much more material than you will ever use in the programme. In fact the more you have to choose from the better. You will discover that some scenes are unusable because of poor sound, the child's back was to the camera or the point is not made sufficiently clearly. Apparently the BBC works on a selection rate of 24 to 1; that is 24 hours of recording for a one hour programme. We generally end up with a rate of 6 to 1.

● You can now arrange your selected excerpts in order and decide on other production features such as captions, viewer activity, etc. (where they come and how long they will last).

Although you are not confined to a precise length for your programme, as is the case with television producers, it is good to give yourself a limit. On average, we aim for between 20 and 30 minutes. That is about the tolerance length for an audience and for the producer.

● You also have to draft the commentator's script, bearing in mind the points made previously (p.268).

Assembling the Programme

The final operation is largely a technical one and referred to in the jargon as *editing*. Unlike film, video-tape cannot be cut and reassembled; you are dealing with electrical signals. What you can do is make a copy of these signals in a new order as per your programme script. To do this, you use a second video-recorder, preferably one with an *editing* facility that enables the differing electrical signal from the two recordings to be electronically joined into a unitary signal on the copy tape. The result is a smooth change-over from one scene to another.

Editing can be done quickly if you have only a few sequences to assemble. The more sequences you have, the longer it takes. Three other factors are important: your familiarity with the recordings; the mechanics of editing; and the type of editing machine available. Some of the recent, and sadly more expensive, models make editing very simple. However, under the most favourable circumstances it takes us around one hour to edit four minutes of finished programme. It is a time-consuming job and you begin to appreciate the large team of people involved in producing programmes broadcast on television: read the credits next time!

However, this involvement of time can prove well worthwhile and as I noted before you may be able to get someone else to do all the technical work for you.

Permission for Showing

As a matter of courtesy, we invite the adults who appear in the film or, in the case of children, their parents, to a special first showing of the finished programme. At this, we ask them to sign a permission form which states their agreement to appearing in the programme or to their child appearing. This reinforces the verbal agreement they gave earlier. This form outlines who the likely audiences will be, namely 'parents, staff and students interested in mental handicap'.

The copyright of the film rests with the person(s) who made it and hence the responsibility is theirs to ensure that it is not used in a way which could embarrass or otherwise cause distress to the people who appear in it.

Showing the Programme

For most of us, watching television is often primarily entertainment rather than a learning experience. But, having gone to a great deal of trouble to make an educational programme, you need to consider carefully the most favourable conditions for screening it, so that the viewers get your message. Among the most likely are: (1) as part of a course or workshop; (2) included with an introductory talk and question time; (3) an organised discussion session after the screening.

In each case the viewers are 'primed' to attend to the programme's content; they can have their questions aired and answered and hearing other people's reactions often clarifies their own thinking. Other sections of the book deal with these topics in more detail. The essential point to remember is that the value of any television programme is affected by the milieu in which it is watched.

Ready-made Programmes

Finally, a happy ending for those who doubt their competence as programme-makers. You might be able to use ready-made programmes. These can be obtained in two ways.

(1) *Recording of programmes 'off-the-air'* A video-recorder enables you to record programmes as they are broadcast on television. From time-to-time there will be documentary programmes of relevance to your work. Unfortunately, you do not get advance notice of when suitable programmes will appear. You have to keep an eye on the television schedules and record likely programmes. If they prove unsuitable, nothing is lost as the tapes can always be reused. There are copyright laws regarding the showing of programmes you have recorded. Strictly speaking, these recordings are for your personal use and should only be replayed on the equipment and in the location where the programme was recorded. However, the use of recordings for educational purposes is treated more leniently. But you must never charge admission to view a programme or sell copies of it to other people.

(2) *Hire or buying of copies of video-programmes* Various companies specialise in hiring or selling educational video-programmes. Most of these programmes have been made by national networks and their technical standards are therefore high. However, the programme's content may not be entirely suitable for your needs: titles can mislead. The company catalogues will give a brief description, but you are advised to

preview a programme before purchasing.

Playback. It is relatively simple to playback pre-recorded programmes on a video-recorder. The only technical operation is tuning one of the channels on the television to the video-recorder. This is akin to picking up a broadcast channel via an aerial and is quickly done. The manual for the television or the recorder will give you full details.

During the showing, everyone in the audience should have a clear view of the television. It helps to darken the room so that reflections are avoided. For a large audience you may need a second television or monitor. Nearly all video-recorders have two playback outlets, one for television (RF out), the second for monitors (video/audio out).

Video is undoubtedly *the* communication medium of the immediate future. Already many homes have a video-recorder and professionals must not neglect this resource. The future promises even better facilities — cable television, two-way communication between the home and a central facility, etc. In President Reagan's words: 'You ain't seen nothing yet!'

12

Writing for Parents

The difficulty is not to write but to write what you
mean; . . . not to affect your reader, but to affect him
precisely as you wish.
(Robert Louis Stevenson)

The hardest part is the first sentence. Over 40 minutes have
elapsed since I wrote the chapter heading and all the far I've got
is sharing my difficulties with you. My experience is not atypical,
at least I hope not. Nor can I agree with Stevenson; people do
find writing difficult. They much prefer a telephone call to
composing a letter or a corridor meeting to the writing of a
memo. The free-flow of conversation suddenly dries up as it gets
converted into ink on paper. And that could explain why we use
so many clichés in our professional writing or fall back on
standardised homogenised prose. The result: effective communication is blocked.

Stevenson, however, was right about the purpose of writing: it
is to affect your reader in a precise way. Yet, unlike speech, you
can't rephrase or elaborate your prose to accord with your
reader's comprehension. Writing is too cumbersome for that.
Ernest Gower's advice was deceptively succinct: 'Be simple, be
short, be human.' No better motto for the professional writing
for parents.

Two challenges face us. First, the lack of training given to
young professionals in the skill of writing for parents. It is
presumed that their case notes, essays or teaching reports are
sufficient practice. If anything, the opposite is true; that's where
the bad practices start.

Secondly, there is an over-reliance on face-to-face contacts
between parents and professionals. I believe that this needs to be
complemented with written documents for the following reasons:
(1) *Parents can reflect* It can be difficult to recall, let alone

275

reflect, on all that was said during a face-to-face meeting. A written record can be perused by parents at their leisure and at their own pace.

(2) *Parents can share the information* Written information can be more easily and more accurately shared with other people. For example, a mother updating the father on what the therapist recommends or the parents can share it with other family members or other professionals.

(3) *Parents can be kept informed* Face-to-face contacts are, at best, periodic. In between times, parents will appreciate knowing what's going on, for instance in school, or they could benefit from reminders about what they might be doing. Written communications are the easiest way of maintaining these contacts. The greater the interval between meetings with parents, the more necessary they are.

(4) *The message is credible* 'It's there in black and white.' There is no doubt about what is happening, what's to be done, or what the test results show. Recollection and hearsay are not always reliable and there are times, fortunately rare, when written documentation can even be a safeguard for professionals.

In summary, written communications are not an extra; they are an integral part of any service which espouses partnership with parents.

This chapter contains guidelines on writing for parents and gives ideas about many types of documents; from assessment reports to magazine articles and home-school diaries to course manuals. The final pages list useful books, written for parents. However, these are no substitute for personal correspondence.

To get you tuned in to this topic, you might try this activity. Write a short review of this book, 120 to 150 words, similar to those which appear in professional journals. Then imagine you are writing a letter to a close friend and that you are describing the book to him; again write about 150 words.

Be Simple, be Short, be Human

Which one of the two passages would you describe as simple, short and human? Letter writing is much more like a conversation; whereas your review will have some, if not all, the characteristics of a lecture. But remember, you are already an experienced writer, well able to follow the maxim of this chapter. The guidelines listed below will let you polish up your prose but the key is the image you have of your readers and their needs. Get that right and the words flow.

Guidelines

Know what you want to say Like many elementary things, this is easily overlooked. Ernest Gowers[100] comments:

> Clear thinking is hard work but loose thinking is bound to produce loose writing. And clear thinking takes time but time that has to be given to a job to avoid making a mess of it, cannot be time wasted and may in the end be time saved.

In short, don't commit your confusion to paper.

● *Be yourself* Don't shirk from the word 'I' or the expression of personal opinon.

● *Keep your sentences short* A good maxim is one thought per sentence.

● *Avoid jargon* It is much easier to recognise other people's jargon than your own. Explaining technical terms in simple words may make the text longer but like as not the meaning will be clearer. Incidentally, it also forces you to think through the meaning of your professional jargon.

● *Use no more words than are necessary to do the job* Cut out windy phrases such as '*In the majority of instances*' when you could write '*Usually*' or replace '*At the present time*' with '*Now*'. Go straight into your sentences. There is no need for introductory remarks like 'I should also add' or 'one other thing I should point out'.

● *Be direct* Out of politeness, we often qualify or 'soften' our writings. This can create uncertainty and confusion for parents if they do not appreciate your subtleties. Use positive statements rather than negatives and always avoid double negatives, i.e. 'I don't think his speech has been unaffected by the deformity of his tongue' becomes, 'The tongue deformity has affected his speech.' Avoid conditional tenses of the verb like 'should' and 'would' and words like 'perhaps, maybe, might'. 'Maybe you should try talking less and you might see a difference' becomes 'Talk less and you will see a difference.'

● *Use words with precise meanings rather than vague ones;*

common words rather than the less common. In this sentence, I am *trying* (rather than 'endeavouring') to *show* (not 'illustrate') *how to do this* (instead of 'put this into practice'). Journalists often choose 'first degree' words (those that bring an image to mind) to convey a clear succinct message. Hence the word 'tests' rather than 'assessments', 'reward' rather than 'reinforcement' and 'homework' rather than 'activities to do at home'. If you don't like the connotations of these 'cruder' words, then think carefully about the substitutes you use and how to make them meaningful for the readers.

● *Examples and analogies can enliven your prose* You needn't be serious all the time.

Better Writing

You may or may not be following these guidelines already. One way of finding out is to read again the review you wrote at the beginning of this chapter. Another is to scrutinise some of your past reports or written communications with parents. But a better way is to have the comments of a sympathetic colleague. Often they see your 'mistakes' quicker than you do. Potentially, the best feedback of all comes from parents. It is not easy to elicit their reactions, largely because they blame themselves if they have difficulty following what you have written. Provide opportunities for them to seek clarifications; a follow-up telephone call from you is one possibility.

Illustrations. The use of diagrams, photographs and cartoons not only help get the message across, but makes the text look more attractive and less daunting to the reader. I shall give some examples later on when describing the type of written material parents find useful.

Translations.

Whether a school has only one parent with whom communication in English presents problems, or whether it has 90 per cent, an interpreter should be available to both parents and staff. Often some member of the family, often an older child, can play this role; it is not a good idea to rely on other parents to interpret (though it may occasionally be necessary) because of consideration of confidentiality. Local minority groups may

be able to supply interpreters, if the school has made an effort
to be involved with these groups.

That was the advice of Barbara Tizard and her colleagues,[9] who
go on to add:

> For translations of prospectuses, newsletters and notices,
> similar sources of help including parents can be used. Parents
> will be especially helpful in examining materials for appropriate
> content relevant to their cultures, checking that dates do not
> clash with a religious celebration and that the information
> given covers points which parents are likely to be concerned
> about. (pp.237–8)

Finally, an audio-recording could be sent in lieu of written
communications to immigrant families or to those whom you
suspect will have difficulty reading.

'Write Because you've got Something to Say'

Writing for parents can take many different forms. I shall review
the main ones in this chapter: reports, diaries, newsletters,
articles and so forth. Some, of course, apply more to one
profession than to others, yet Scott Fitzgerald's dictum applies to
all, 'You don't write because you want to say something, you
write because you've got something to say'.

The chapter is divided into three main sections. The first deals
with writing to parents about their child; the second describes
ways of conveying information about available services; the third
gives background material on handicaps aimed at groups of
parents.

Information about their Child

I begin with this because so much of a professional's time is spent
compiling reports, particularly therapists, psychologists and social
workers. What about sharing these with parents? Here is
Elizabeth Newson's[37] view:

> It is interesting that sending reports to parents, particularly
> unabridged reports, is regarded by many clinicians as extra-

ordinary and dangerous. I would personally take the opposite view: that to spend a lot of time assessing a child with great care, and then to send out reports to all sorts of people *with the exception of those who are most closely and permanently concerned with the child*, is bizarre in the extreme, and is only considered reasonable because of the way clinical work has developed historically; if we were inventing it from scratch, would we now, I wonder, include this almost paranoid secretiveness? (p.115; her italics)

Parents have been equally forthright; the Coventry-based parent group Family Focus had this to say in their discussion paper on assessment:

We feel that professionals should give parents detailed written reports of their assessment of any child. Just as it has come to be regarded as good practice for professionals to share such information with each other, so should they expect to share it with parents. (p.193; quoted by Potts[23])

The counter-arguments usually revolve around parental misunderstanding or their disappointment with our tentativeness or the need for confidentiality. The content and clarity of your writing should reduce the risk of misinterpretations, particularly if the parents have been actively involved during the assessments (see p.91). Equally, mothers and fathers find it easier to accept tentative reports if they understand the reasoning behind it, rather than the vague generalities spoken at the end of an assessment.

The issue of confidentiality is more fundamental. Basically, it can be summed up in the mythical question of parents: 'are you doing this assessment for me, or am I doing it for you?' Reports are often commissioned by others (local authorities, health boards or colleagues), in which case the author might want to make confidential comments which might cause pain to the parents. Patricia Potts[23] decries this patronising approach and argues that it

only shows how far professionals have removed themselves from the very issues that have to be confronted. Records are frequently speculative, vague or irresponsibly brief. And they can also be casually damning. Warnock claims that parental access would mean that reports could become less detailed, but it might be sobering for many professionals to examine exactly what the detail presently consists of. (pp.189–90)

In fact, the British DES circular 1/83 on assessment[64] recognises the importance of openness in formulating reliable and worthwhile assessments:

Assessments should be seen as a partnership between teachers and other professionals and parents in a joint endeavour to discover and understand the nature of the difficulties and needs of individual children. Closer relations should be established and maintained with parents and can only be helped by frankness and openness on all sides. (para. 6)

Likewise, the US special education act, Public Law 94-142, requires parents to be involved in the assessment process and specifically includes them as part of the educational planning team.

In summary, shared reports are but another expression of partnership, or its lack.

School Reports. Barbara Smith,[38] a parent and teacher of handicapped children, has this to say, 'I believe it is the right of every parent to receive an annual report and consider that any school not providing parents with one, is failing in their responsibility.' (p.149) Peter and Helle Mittler[15] comment:

The writing of school reports now seems to be much more common than it was some years ago . . . Reports can vary greatly in frequency, style, organisation and information content, from a few brief comments organised along 'subject' lines like a conventional school report in an ordinary school, to highly specific accounts of the child's achievements in attaining goals outlined in an individual programme plan. Used in this way, a report is not merely a record of achievement but the starting point for a joint approach to the development of a further programme of collaboration. (p.29)

Once again, reports are an opportunity for dialogue with

parents as well as a source of information. The former is ultimately more important.

Home-School Diary. Many schools now use a form of notebook or diary that travels between home or school on a daily, weekly or occasional basis. Here are Barbara Smith's[38] views:

> In my experience, diaries seem to be used in three ways: for general items of information (e.g. 'Hello, my name's Barbara Smith and I'm the new teacher . . .'); for more specific information (e.g. 'his calipers [braces] seem to rubbing his leg, will you look at them in school today and see what you think') and for active collaboration on a joint teaching venture (e.g. in a programme on undressing skills, a parental comment one morning was, 'only help last night was shoe-lace which she pulled into a knot'). (p.144)

The two-way flow of communication is valuable to parents and teachers, particularly with children who are unable to recount past events and when school visits are not practical. Nearly all parents appreciate the diary. As one mother told Shirley Rheubottom:[101]

> I liked to come in just two mornings a week — 'cause it was nice to just chat about what [they] had been doing in the classroom, but the other useful thing was [their] notebook. That was very good actually . . . That was sufficient to keep tabs on what she was doing and to be involved. (p.160)

Or this from a mother who had 'terrible problems with Sam feeding'. 'Everyday I have a report . . . I like to know whether he has eaten any dinner . . . if he starts fussing around with his tea at night and I know he has had a big lunch, then I don't push it too hard.' (p.160)

Some notebooks may end up as a one-way communication from teacher to parents, although space is left for parental comments. As one teacher acidly remarked: 'all she [the mother] ever writes is "very good". I think if I told her Johnny has vomited all over me, attacked the assistant and bitten all the children she'd still put "very good"!'

Class Newsletters. This variant of the diary has been tried successfully with larger classes in ordinary infant schools. Barbara Tizard[9] describes the content which particularly appealed to parents in her project:

> besides giving essential administrative information about dates of terms and meetings, [it] should include information about the work of the class, suggestions for home activities related to work being done in the class; copies of songs and rhymes the children are learning; suggestions for weekend and holiday activities; new schemes of work being introduced and of new books or apparatus acquired and information about activities parents may rarely see, like P.E. and music. This kind of information helps parents to make more sense of what their children tell them and to feel in touch with the class activities. (p.147)

She goes on to say that the frequency of production will vary according to the enthusiasm of the teacher and the help he or she gets. She suggests involving the parents, some of whom may well be prepared to type, edit or write.

An alternative is the class notice-board, fixed in a prominent position so that it can be seen by parents as they bring the child to school. But therein lies its limitation, if the children are brought to school by bus.

Home Teaching Recommendations. Parents are more likely to remember, and therefore implement, a therapist's recommendations if they are left a written summary to which they can refer. One of the successful features of the Portage Scheme is the use of activity charts which Peter Wilcox[54] sees as 'fundamental to the success of the teaching programmes'.

> First they contain a statement of exactly what is to be accomplished in very definite and specific terms . . . Secondly, each activity chart must contain complete and explicit directions to be followed, so that parents may refer to them as their guide for teaching. These should specify what materials may be necessary, where the teaching should occur, how to actually present the task to the child, how to reinforce his correct response, how to record and how often to practice.

They must also include a correction procedure describing what to do if the child does not produce the correct response . . . Finally, each chart must contain a simple and clear record of the work and the child's progress. (p.36)

Leaving aside for a moment the amount of detail, there is no doubt that parents appreciate knowing unambiguously what they are expected to do and a written summary undoubtedly helps.

You are the person best able to judge the detail you need to give parents. I personally feel short succinct reports drafted at the end of the meeting and given there and then to the parent are preferable to lengthy narratives which come in the post a week or so later. The recommendations need not be all your own work. Photocopies of relevant sections from books or training manuals can be useful, especially with parents who would not read a whole book.

Nor should your limited artistic abilities deter you from drawing diagrams if they help to get across your meaning.

Information about services

'A leaflet for parents explaining all the different services which are available.'

'There should be more communication so that parents know about services and courses.'

'Comprehensive list of services should be made available to new people.'

These comments are typical of the responses we received from nearly 200 parents of young mentally handicapped children, when we asked them about the improvements they would like to see in the services they were currently receiving.

School Prospectus. A booklet that is attractively produced, and written in an easily readable style, will meet the parent's desire to know more about the school. Illustrations such as photographs of the building, staff and children will enliven the message.

As regards contents, Barbara Tizard's[9] research with parents suggests that they want to know the following:

The names of the teachers, their qualifications and special responsibilities, which classes they teach, the usual number of pupils on roll, the size of classes, age groupings, how children move up, how children are grouped into classes, the names and responsibilities of all ancillary staff should also be included . . . Parents are often mystified by vague phrases such as 'we aim to help all our children reach their full potential'. They will get a better idea of what their children will be doing if the activities and subjects offered are listed . . . we found many parents were concerned about safety procedures . . . and they like to know about the arrangements made for meals. Parents can be told about the role they can play in all aspects of school life. Well chosen examples will give them a clearer idea of the school's expectations and willingness to involve all parents. (pp.143–4)

The production costs need not be great: the school may have its own duplicating facilities or you could use those in teachers' centres or colleges. Alternatively, a local printer may do the job at a special discount. Barbara Tizard[9] concludes that 'most schools have little difficulty in finding or raising funds to cover the cost of producing the prospectus which should be supplied free to all parents' (p.145) and goes on to note that it may well have other uses in building links with the local community, through making it available in public places: libraries, doctors' waiting rooms, clinics, etc.

Services. The predominant reason why parents do not avail themselves of services, is simply that they do not know about them. To counteract this, various local authorities have produced a guide to the services on offer in their area and listing the names and/or addresses. This gives parents an overview of the resources available to them and can be as indispensable to professionals as it is to parents. If there is no such directory available for your locality or the existing one is now outdated, what are you going to do about it? Rod Ballard,[35] a lecturer in sociology and a parent of a handicapped daughter, claims

You cannot have one group of people with rights to something without another group having duties in respect of those rights. Rights in fact imply duties. Our rights (as parents) will cease to exist unless someone tells us what they are. So professional people have a clear and absolute duty to tell us what is available in the form of physical resources. (p.102)

To complement the general description of services, some professionals have produced a guide to the specific services they offer, e.g. the psychological service or speech therapy. This gives the names of people involved, how they can be contacted, what their job entails, how they deal with referrals, what happens afterwards and so on. These guides serve the dual functions of clarification and explanation and if they were more widely available, could minimise the confusion about professional roles to which parents often refer.

Information about Handicap

> The health visitor [public health nurse] tends to know only as much as I do. I would like more help in getting information, i.e. could the home visitor [or social worker] be regularly given lists of available books/pamphlets, which could be passed on to us the parents, so that we may broaden our horizons with regard to our particular interests.

> More information on Down's syndrome should be made available to the public health clinics and to GPs. We found the public health clinics useless — no understanding of the minor physical ailments which accompany the condition.

As these comments illustrate, parents also want to know more about their child's handicapping condition and they rightly expect that non-specialist professionals should also be more informed. This is a relatively neglected area with few professionals willing to commit their knowledge to paper. Admittedly, we have had an increase recently in the number of books published but these tend to be written by specialists employed in universities or research centres. Arguably, they have the time to write but I cannot help but feel that people who are working at the grass roots, are often more attuned to parents' needs and how best to meet them. Moreover, parents and non-specialists may find textbooks rather daunting. They want something shorter and snappier.

Information Sheets. Pertinent facts and guidelines about aspects of handicaps are often dispersed among different sources: books, articles, reports, etc. It can be daunting for a parent to track

Mentally handicapped people are those who have:

1. Low scores on tests and intelligence: Scores on these tests are reported in terms of intelligence quotients IQ. 'Average' people score between 85 and 115. More intelligent people will score higher, for example two people in every 100 will have IQ's over 130. Likewise, some people obtain low scores. If their IQ falls below 70 they may be considered mentally handicapped.

However these tests are not always reliable. Different IQ's can result from different types of tests, from different people giving the test and from the mood of the person on the day they were tested. Hence IQ scores are best given as a range rather than as a single figure, e.g. IQ is between 65 and 75. Also IQ scores do change over time, people may score markedly higher or lower when tested one year later. Thus these tests are not a foolproof way of identifying mentally handicapped people. Nevertheless they are the most commonly used way.

2. Poor social competence: They are unable to look after their everyday needs such as preparing food for themselves, keeping house, looking after their clothes, shopping or working and so on. They need other people to look after their basic needs and to protect them from common dangers.

A person's social competence can be assessed using special rating scales. However these scales only reflect present performance: they cannot predict the person's *ability to learn*. Some people score low because their parents do everything and never give them a chance of learning to look after themselves. But given the opportunity they may quickly learn. Indeed, nearly all mentally handicapped people can be successfully taught social skills to some degree. Hence social competence is a reflection of learning opportunities as well as of learning ability

If a person scores below 70 on an intelligence test and yet is capable of looking after herself and her family, then she is not mentally handicapped. Equally some people (the elderly, physically some people and mentally ill) are unable to look after themselves yet they are intellectually normal. They too are not mentally handicapped. Sometimes though such people are wrongly classed as mentally handicapped

"These two conditions – low IQ and poor social competence – have to be fulfilled before a person is considered mentally handicapped."

Mentally handicapped people can look normal: Unlike physical disabilities a mentally handicapped person can look perfectly normal. The definitions given earlier say nothing about appearance only abilities. Some mentally handicapped people do look different but this is because their whole body is affected as in Down's Syndrome (mongolism). Past experience has shown that such people are mentally handicapped. However there are some Down's Syndrome people who learn to look after themselves and who score close to the average range of intelligence tests. Hen, they should not be considered mentally handicapped even though they still have Down's Syndrome.

Mental handicap is NOT a physical condition: Disabilities are usually defined in terms of a physical defect or abnormality – for example deafness results from a loss of hearing and epilepsy stems from a dysfunction in the brain. This is not the case with mental handicap. It is desc, drive of a person's abilities and capacity to learn

However these learning problems can stem from physical abnormalities and as we shall explain in Fact Sheet 9 a wide range of causes have been established. Nevertheless with many mentally handicapped people, no physical cause is detectable. The handicap is only evident from low intelligence test scores and poor social competence

Mentally handicapped people may learn. Although these people may be slow learners, it must be emphasis that they can learn. Children may be identified as mentally handicapped during their school years but once they leave, get a job and start their own home it is obvious they are no longer handicapped. Their disability was

"Although these people may be slow learners, it must be emphasised that they can learn."

Equally it is possible through training for a mentally handicapped person to master the basic skills of social competence, albeit at the age of 30 instead of the more usual 15 years. Thus these people have grown out of their handicap.

DEGREES OF HANDICAP

Some people are more handicapped than others. In Ireland, mentally handicapped people are subdivided into three broad groups according to the severity of their handicap.

"Unlike physical disabilities a mentally handicapped person can look perfectly normal."

Mild mental handicap: There is usually nothing physically wrong with these people. Their handicap is most apparent during schooling

looking normal

and they attend special schools or special classes. However the majority end up working in ordinary jobs. These people are not handicapped in the usual sense of the word and in other countries they are referred to as slow learners or educationally retarded

Moderate mental handicap: This group usually has some identifiable physical abnormality, such as Down's Syndrome or brain damage. They attend special national schools and the majority go on to work in sheltered workshops or training centres. Only a small proportion at present find ordinary jobs

Severe mental handicap: As the name suggests, these people are much less able to look after

themselves and frequently they have additional handicaps. Children ascertained as severely mentally handicapped are not allowed to go to special care units where they are looked after by nursing or care staff.

Finally, some people are now referred to as *profoundly* mentally handicapped. These are the least able and invariably have other pronounced handicaps – deformities of legs and arms, deafness, blindness or epilepsy. Frequently these people will be in residential care although in proportion are cared for by their families at home

No clear-cut division: According to a recent census of mentally handicapped people in Ireland, for every one person considered to be

severely handicapped there are 2 moderately handicapped and 4 mildly mentally handicapped

These categories should be thought of as rough divisions. There is no foolproof way of allocating people to these groupings and indeed, over time, people can move from one group to another

Fact Sheet 8 gives more details about the characteristics of mentally handicapped people living in the community

Normal feelings: One in every hundred Irish people are mentally handicapped. In terms of abilities, they are different from the rest of us. But this does not mean that

their feelings and emotions are abnormal quite the contrary. They experience the same joys and sadnesses as the rest of us (see Fact Sheet 7). No handicap can mask the human spirit.

Further Information

Contact: National Association for the Mentally Handicapped of Ireland, 5 Fitzwilliam Place, Dublin 2

Figure 12.1: Sample Fact Sheet

these down. An alternative is for you to summarise key facts on one sheet of paper, designed to be read in five minutes or so. The example given in Figure 12.1 is from a series of fact sheets on *Mental Handicap*[102] produced for parents and interested members of the public. Other possible topics are: 'What is Down's syndrome?', 'Looking at books with your child', 'Play for blind children', 'Toy libraries' and so on. Each sheet should give basic information that is applicable to all parents and list sources of help available *in your area*. For instance, if you list books, note also the library or bookshop which stocks them.

Hand-outs. The value to parents of a lecture or talk or even video-programme is all the greater if they can take away a written synopsis of its content. The hand-out is best prepared as a series of key points, rather than continuous prose which some parents find off-putting. Try to incorporate some or all of the illustrations used during the presentation. You may find that course hand-outs can be adapted easily into an information sheet.

Magazine and Newspaper Articles. Another way of reaching parents is through articles in specialist magazines or through the media generally. A bonus with the latter is that it helps to create a better awareness within the public at large.

Among the possibilities are articles in magazines or in the local press aimed at parents or, more generally, women. These could describe local services (the people involved, what they do, etc.) or give an account of new developments, e.g. courses for parents. You might outline general advice about handling children or nurturing their development or it might argue the case for improved services.

You can contact the features editor of the local paper or magazine and outline some of the possibilities you have in mind. He or she might then commission one of their staff to write the piece.

Alternatively, it is quite common for them to receive unsolicited articles and a proportion of them are published. Don't be put off if your first attempts are unsuccessful. Take account of the comments received and submit the article to another publisher. The bonus is that most publications pay for articles they print.

Finally, if you come across articles in magazines or journals which you think would be useful to parents, have them photocopied so that you can loan them out.

Manuals. Somewhat more ambitious, is the writing of a 'training' manual for parents, either in association with a course or to stand on its own. This might deal with a specific topic, e.g. feeding or adapting of toys for physically handicapped children, or it might tackle more general issues such as dealing with problem behaviours. You might create a totally new manual or else make a synthesis from existing books and articles.

The key elements to incorporate into your manuals are:

● *Simplicity of language*. Make it conversational.

● *Illustrations* (photographs or cartoons) If they do nothing else, they break up the text and make the amount of reading seem less daunting.

● *Specific examples* General principles need to be anchored with concrete examples which parents can apply directly to their situation or use as an analogy.

● *Structured text* Short paragraphs with key phrases as headings enable parents to discover the basic messages more easily. Chapters should be short and, if possible, printed on different coloured paper.

● *Complete* Include copies of any record forms which the parents might require. This saves them the bother of drawing up their own and lets them use them straight away.

With modern photocopying facilities, manuals can be professionally produced at reasonable cost. Our first editions are always printed in this way.

It is crucial to get feedback from colleagues or parents. As Ernest Gowers commented, 'never be content with your first draft; always revise it and you will find that practice, though it will not make you perfect, will greatly improve your efficiency.' (p.18) The revised manual could then be commercially printed and sold to recoup your costs.

. . .'And Finally'

The use of quotations and illustrations from other peoples' writings has been quite deliberate in this chapter. It enables me to collect for you the experiences and advice of people with more

experience in this area than I, and their writings — the end
product of revisions and editing — present the information more
clearly, succinctly and definitely than spoken words.

And therein lies the two great advantages of the written word.
I have benefited from other peoples' writings and now you as a
reader are gaining, I hope, from my prose. The next link in the
chain is within your grasp.

'Some Books to be Tasted'

The mid-1970s marked the beginning of what has become a
burgeoning industry: books written especially for parents of
handicapped children. Indeed, this has been paralleled by a pile
of paperback guides for parents in general. Consequently, the
choice for parents has never been wider and Francis Bacon's
astute observation becomes ever more applicable, 'some books
are to be tasted, others to be swallowed and some few to be
chewed and digested'.

There is no such thing as the 'right book' for all parents or
even for all time; fashions change and new approaches evolve.
Hence I am not a believer in parents buying books, at least not
until they have tasted them! It's the professional's job to ensure
they get the opportunity to do this. Among the possibilities are:

● *Library* Asking the public libraries in your area to stock the
books you feel are useful to parents. Moreover, you or they
might produce an information sheet giving details of authors, title
and publisher.

● *Toy libraries* They often loan books to parents on the same
basis as the toys for children.

● *Parents' den* Some schools have set aside a room for parents,
where they can chat, make coffee, etc., and here are displayed
relevant books and magazines. A loan system might be arranged.

● *Extracts* You might photocopy the relevant pages of an article
or book on loan or give the extract to parents. This is especially
useful with less literate parents who may be put off by a whole
book. In fact, with all parents it is best to recommend certain
sections of the book for them to read. The notion that you must
start at the beginning and plod methodically through is still
widespread.

The real art is to select books, or passages within books, that fulfil E.M. Forster's condition 'the only books that influence us are those for which we are ready and which have gone a little further down our particular path than we have yet got to ourselves'.

Parents as Authors

The growing literature of books by professionals for parents is being complemented by books written by parents that professionals might usefully read. Although often written with other parents in mind, these, none the less, give an insight into the perplexities of life with a handicapped child and how parents coped with various services or the lack of them. The best of these, and ultimately you are the only judge, will fulfil Andre Gide's hope 'to read a writer is for me not merely to get an idea of what he says but to go off with him and travel in his company'.

Books for Parents

The following are a selection of some of the many books now available; written especially with parents and the 'lay-reader' in mind. The first two sections deal with children in general; the remainder focuses on children with special needs.

Child Development

Brazelton, B.L. *Toddlers and parents* (Penguin, London, 1979). In the USA *Toddlers and parents: a declaration of independence* (Dell Publishing, New York, 1974).

Evans, J. and Ilfield, E. *Good beginnings: parenting in the early years* (High/Scope Press, Michigan, 1982). In Britain, available from National Children's Bureau, 8 Wakley Street, London EC1V 7QE.

Jolly, H. *Book of child care: the complete guide for today's parents* (Sphere Books, London, 1977).

de Villiers, P.A. and de Villiers, J.G. *Early language* (Fontana/ Open Books, London, 1979). In the USA (Harvard University Press, Cambridge, MA, 1979). [Note: this is one of an excellent series of books under the title *The developing child*, J. Bruner, J. Cole and B. Lloyd (eds)]

White, B.L. *The first three years of life* (W.H. Allen, London, 1979). In the USA (Avon Books, New York, 1975).

Furthering Development

Azrin, N. and Foxx, R. *Toilet training in less than a day* (Pan Books, London, 1977). In the USA (Pocket Books, New York, 1981).

Koch, J. *Superbaby: over 300 exercises and games to stimulate your baby's intellectual, physical and emotional development* (Orbis, London, 1982). In the USA *Total baby development* (Wallaby Pocket Books, New York, 1978).

Mackay, D. and Simo, J. *Helping your child to read and write more* (Penguin, London, 1976).

Matterson, E.M. *Play with a purpose for under-sevens* (Penguin, London, 1975).

Toy Libraries Association *The good toy guide, 1983* (Inter-action, London, 1983).

Information about Handicaps

Anderson, E. and Spain, B. *The child with spina bifida* (Methuen, London and New York, 1977).

Cunningham, C.C. *Down's syndrome: an introduction for parents* (Souvenir Press, London/Brookline Books, Cambridge, MA, 1982).

Lansdown, R. *More than sympathy: the everyday needs of sick and handicapped children and their families* (Tavistock, London, 1980). In the USA (Tavistock/Methuen, New York, 1980).

Nolan, M. and Tucker, I.G. *The hearing impaired child and the family* (Souvenir Press, London, 1981; in the USA from State Mutual Book, New York).

Russell, P. *The wheelchair child*, 2nd edn (Souvenir Press, London, 1983; Prentice-Hall, Englewood Cliffs, NJ, 1984).

Rutter, M. *Helping troubled children* (Penguin, London, 1975; Plenum, New York, 1976).

Scott, E., Jan, J.E. and Freeman, R.D. *Can't your child see?* (University Park Press, Baltimore, 1977).

Stone, J. and Taylor, F. *A handbook for parents of a handicapped child* (Arrow Books, London, 1977).

Wing, L. *Autistic children: a guide for parents* (Constable, London, 1980; Citadel, Secaucus, NJ, 1974).

Guidance on Teaching

Carr, J. *Helping your handicapped child: a step-by-step guide to everyday problems* (Penguin, London, 1980).

Cunningham, C.C. and Sloper, P. *Helping your handicapped baby* (Souvenir Press, London, 1978; available in USA from State Mutual Book, New York).

Finnie, N. *Handling the young cerebral palsied child at home* (Heinemann, London, 1974).

Jeffree, D.M., McConkey, R. and Hewson, S. *Teaching the handicapped child* (Souvenir Press, London, 1977). In the USA *Teaching the handicapped child: a guide for parents and teachers* (Spectrum Books, New Jersey, 1982).

Mitchell, D. *Your child is different* (Unwin, London/Boston, 1982).

Newson, E. and Hipgrave, T. *Getting through to your handicapped child* (Cambridge University Press, Cambridge and New York, 1982).

Specific Suggestions

Baker, B. and various co-authors *Steps to Independence Series: Behavior problems, Early self-help skills, Intermediate self-help skills, Advanced self-help skills, Toilet training, Speech and language Level 1* and *Level 2, Towards independent living, Play skills* (Research Press, Champaign, IL, 1976–1983).

Conant, S., Budoff, M. and Hecht, B. *Teaching language-disabled children* (Brookline Books, Cambric ͺe, MA, 1983).

Cooper, J., Moodley, M. and Reynell, J. *Helping language development: a developmental programme for children with early language handicaps* (Edward Arnold, London/St Martin's Press, New York, 1978).

Gillham, B. *The first words language programme* and *Two words together* (Allen and Unwin, London, 1979 and 1982). In the USA the first of these is published by University Park Press, Baltimore, the second by Allen and Unwin, Boston.

Hastings, P. and Hayes, B. *Encouraging language development* (Croom Helm, London/Brookline Books, Cambridge, MA, 1981).

Irwin, A. *Stammering: practical help for all ages* (Penguin, London/Walker and Co., New York, 1980).

Jeffree, D.M., McConkey, R. and various co-authors *Let me speak, Let me read, Let's make toys, Let's join in* (Souvenir Press, London, 1976–1984; available in USA from State Mutual Book, New York).

Johnston, V. and Werner, R. *A step-by-step learning guide for retarded infants and children: a step-by-step learning guide for older retarded children* (Constable, London, 1980) (first published in the USA by Syracuse University Press, Syracuse, NY, 1975).

Lear, R. *Play helps: toys and activities for handicapped children* (Heinemann, London/International Ideas, Philadelphia, PA, 1977).

McConkey, R. and Price, P. *Let's talk: learning language in everyday settings* (Souvenir Press, London, 1985).

Riddick, B. *Toys and play for the handicapped child* (Croom Helm, London, 1982; available in USA from Longwood, Dover, NH).

Toy Libraries Association Series of booklets on various aspects of play and learning. Address: Play Matters, Seabrook House, Potters Bar, Hertfordshire EN6 2H.

Whelan, E. and Speake, B. *Learning to cope* (Souvenir Press, London, 1979; available in USA from State Mutual Book, New York).

Parents' Experiences

Browning, E. *I can't see what you are saying* (Elek, London, 1972).

Collins, M. and Collins, D. *Kith and kids* 'Souvenir Press, London, 1976).

Copeland, J. *For love of Ann: the true story of an autistic child* (Arrow, London, 1976).

Featherstone, H. *A difference in the family* (Basic Books, New York, 1980).

Hannam, C. *Parents and mentally handicapped children* (Penguin, London, 1980).

McCormack, M. *A mentally handicapped child in the family* (Constable, London, 1978; Verry Best Publishers, Boston, 1981).

Purser, A. *You and your handicapped child* (Allen and Unwin, London, 1981).

Rivlin, R. *A boy called Alan* (Mercier Press, Dublin, 1974).

Smithson, M. *Lesley: the child we choose* (Mencap, London, 1978).

13

Telling Others

> We already know enough about intervention with
> families to be doing more of it. Lest this review of what
> has been tried gives a distorted picture of what is
> available, we need to underscore the present shortage of
> help for parents.
> (Bruce Baker)

This chapter is for day-dreamers; those who 'enjoy letting their minds wander among pleasant imagery', to quote my dictionary. Given all that I have written about working with parents, you'll probably have a good idea of the pleasant images I have in mind for this chapter.

The first is this: that all teachers and therapists will come to regard work with parents as an integral part of their job and not as an extra. The second day-dream is that all parents, no matter in what part of the country they live, will have the *opportunity* of being involved in furthering their child's development through working alongside professionals. The third is that our service administrators and civil servants will provide the resources and systems whereby parental participation can become a reality and that they will treat this as an obligation, not an option.

Perhaps these are impossible dreams; I don't know. We have barely begun to translate them into reality; so who knows what is possible? But of this I am sure. It will need concerted effort by all three groups: parents, professionals and providers. None can impose his or her will on the others; each requires the support of the others; all must sacrifice their selfish ambitions for the sake of the others.

There are, however, certain actions that each group can take to bring some part of these dreams to fruition. I will outline these for each of the three groups. But I stress that I do not consider the listings to be exhaustive. I am sure that in the future we shall discover yet more ways of removing today's obstacles.

295

I appreciate too that young professionals in training or newly qualified will consider that many of these changes go far beyond what they could realistically hope to bring about. Indeed, that goes for most of us, *individually*. But I believe that we need to have a clear idea as to how things might be different and, if that vision is shared by contemporaries and colleagues, then change, even far-reaching changes, can become a reality.

And should you feel that we need people whose feet are rooted in reality, rather than dreamers of dreams, you might ponder on these words of Dag Hammarskjöld, 'Never look down to test the ground before taking your next step; only he who keeps his eye fixed on the far horizons will find his right road.'

Professionals

For professionals, work with parents will ultimately lead to the rewriting of the current job descriptions of teachers and therapists and to a review of the roles we expect them to fulfil in services for handicapped children and their families. The main vehicle for change will be through professional training and development. Here are some examples of how working with parents might feature in this.

Initial training

● Lectures on professional practice will include information on working with parents; descriptions of how it is currently practised and how students could set about making it a reality in their professional life.

● Some staff–student tutorials might deal with attitudes to parents and explore some of the difficulties which students feel they could encounter in working with parents.

● Students might have opportunities to role-play working with parents. Video-recordings could be used to analyse this experience.

● Parents could be invited to talk to the students about their personal experiences of life with a handicapped child and of the services they have received. They might also outline their views on the developments they would like to see in the future. Video-programmes of parents talking can be a useful substitute or supplement.

● During placements in schools or clinics, students should have the opportunity of observing and listening to parents. For example, they could be encouraged to spend some time in the children's home, 'not to describe the family's problems or deficits', as Barbara Tizard[9] points out, 'but to see what she can learn from them, and to relate this to her experiences in school.' (p.118) The much-beloved child-study that features in most training courses could then be rounded-off by a family study.

● As part of their final professional practice, students could be required to work with parents on common learning objectives. They would then be evaluated not only on what they did with the child, but also on their actions with the parents.

Obstacles. The two most frequently mentioned obstacles are, first, the already overloaded undergraduate curriculum and, secondly, the lack of experienced course tutors or leaders. As regards the former, this comes down to a question of priorities which will surface again in the section on role definition (see p.300). The latter is potentially more serious. If the tutors or leaders on initial training courses have little or no direct experience of working with parents they may be unwilling to include this topic within the curriculum.

They could, of course, delegate this aspect of the course to other colleagues who have more experience or they could draw upon the growing number of video-programmes and textbooks which are now available. For example, I hope that tutors or leaders would find this book a useful resource manual which they could work through with students in lectures or tutorials. In fact, the value of the book to students will be greatly increased, if they have the chance to carry out some of the activities and discuss the outcomes with a tutor and/or their fellow students.

Inservice Training

Work with parents requires many additional skills, which it would be unrealistic to cover in the initial training curriculum; running of discussion groups, giving of talks or organising of courses, to name but a few. Moreover, when it comes to practical skills the best way of learning is through testing them out in your work setting. Hence, for the foreseeable future, inservice training opportunities for work with parents will need to be expanded.

● The tutors/leaders of existing postgraduate courses and those with responsibility for inservice training within local services, should consider the points made previously under initial training. 'Old' courses could be adapted as well as new ones created.

● Local authorities, colleges, universities and professional organisations could mount short courses on specific aspects of work with parents: use of video, visiting homes, group work, etc.

● Colleagues within a service who are interested in working with parents could meet together as a 'self-help' group. Members could take it in turns to describe their work with parents and obtain reactions and suggestions from their colleagues. They could try these out in the interval before the next meeting and report on the effectiveness or otherwise of their efforts.

● Teachers and therapists who are experienced in working with parents could organise workshops or courses so that others can learn from their expertise. For example, the team which instituted the Portage Scheme in the Wessex region of England have organised one-week, full-time training courses for personnel in other local authorities. This is a quick and effective way of 'buying in' expertise.

● Another approach is for the service to second people to work alongside the 'experts'. For example, Cliff Cunningham[25] and his team at the Hester Adrian Research Centre offered three-week placements to health visitors (public-health nurses) from the local authorities who had helped fund part of the research. During their placement, they accompanied the project staff when visiting homes, they were trained in the use of charts and assessments and they had regular 'tutorials' with the team. This 'apprenticeship' model of training has much to commend it for novice practitioners.

Individual teachers or therapists might be able to negotiate similar placements with other teams or centres with experience of working with parents.

● Yet another model of training existing staff is one referred to as pyramid training or the training-of-trainers. Here a small group of staff is selected to attend a particular course on the explicit understanding that they will set up similar training courses on returning to their own service. Obviously, the staff must first be allowed time to become familiar with the new approaches, e.g. by using them in their own work setting. Thereafter, there must be a clear obligation on them to organise a training course for local staff and the facilities for so doing must be made available.

We have successfully used this approach in Ireland when it came to sharing our video-courses (see p.231). We trained at least two people from local services in the use of the course materials and they in their turn organised local courses for parents and/or staff. Within one year, over 100 parents had taken the course on language development in some 15 centres throughout the country.

Pyramid training via existing personnel is the only way of achieving rapid and widespread dissemination of new developments. This approach works best if the potential tutors have tangible resource materials (video-programmes, handbooks, recording charts) which they can use on their local courses. In short, they need a course kit.

Obstacles. The foremost obstacle to developing a range of inservice training opportunities is the dearth of experienced tutors/leaders. As Peter Mittler[103] notes:

> simply to be an able practitioner is not enough; people concerned with staff training need a wide-ranging knowledge of their field as a whole, and must be able to relate their own personal and professional interests to developments in related professions.

He adds, almost with a sigh one suspects, 'such people will not be easy to find.' (p.208)

One suggestion is that some of the available inservice resources should be used to train a cadre of tutors/leaders, drawn from experienced service personnel. Moreover, money earmarked for research could be channelled into the development of training packages to aid dissemination. The US government has actively supported these types of activities. Parent training programmes such as the Portage Project were developed, field tested and made available to practitioners with Federal funds. The state departments of education have to develop plans to ensure that the outcomes are widely applied.

Ultimately, some form of national plan will be required to ensure that expertise is available equally in all parts of the country.

Professional Roles

Work with parents will involve rewriting the existing job descriptions of teachers and therapists. Indeed Barbara Tizard[9] would take this one step further and argues that it entails a whole new definition of professionalism.

> This would involve [teachers] seeing themselves as persons with special skills and knowledge, who are able not only to use these skills with children but also to explain their work to a lay audience, to acknowledge the educational contribution which parents can make, and to accept that they may have a valid view on educational matters. (p.118)

Peter Mittler's[22] argument is similar:

> The highly trained professional must in future share and communicate his skills to others . . . indeed learning to give away our skills is one of the most difficult skills that we ourselves have to learn and that we shall teach future generations of our students to learn.

Some examples of how this re-definition of roles might come about, now follow.
● Professionals from different disciplines, but who fulfil similar functions within a service, should have the opportunity of attending common training courses and exchanging their experiences. We need to move away from courses organised solely for one group of professionals, whether it be by universities, colleges or professional organisations. Indeed could these courses not be open to those parents who are able and interested in attending?
● Parents could be invited to attend meetings of professionals, especially when issues of policy and practice are being discussed.
● Teachers and therapists who have worked successfully with parents could write accounts of their experiences for their professional journals or magazines or they could speak at conferences. The impact of these reports can be strengthened by writing them in collaboration with parents. More ambitiously, experienced personnel might organise workshops for colleagues in other localities or they could accept them for short placements.
● Professional representatives who are involved in the validation of university or college training courses should ensure that work

with parents is covered in the curriculum.

● Teachers or therapists who have students on placement should involve them in their work with parents, giving them the support and feedback which will help the learners gain confidence and competence in this sphere of work.

● Each school or therapeutic service could produce an information booklet for parents, describing what it tries to do and how it operates. To date, such public descriptions of professional aims and roles are scarce but a clear statement of your policy will help to frame others' expectations.

● If work with parents is to become a legitimate part of your role, then it cannot always be done as an extra, or outside of working hours. You need to press your 'bosses' to have it included within your job description. For example, teachers with handicapped children in their class might ask for half-a-day a week, free from class responsibilities to meet with parents in their homes or at school.

● Each school and service needs to re-assess its priorities periodically. There may well be aspects of your work which could be dropped or passed on to someone else, thereby freeing the manpower to take on new tasks. In times of ple. :y, however, it is easier to argue for extra resources rather than do the more painful pruning involved in determining priorities.

● It is an enlightening experience to obtain consumers' reactions to your service. This could be done through simple questionnaires but preferably by interviews with parents or guardians. These are best done by a person who is not identified with your service. The parents' comments and wishes should give you valuable feedback about whether or not you are meeting their needs and could have an influence on re-shaping your job description and role. Arguably there is no better stimulant.

I feel it is preferable for professionals to take the initiative in embarking on these consultations, which in my opinion are long overdue. At some point in the future, they could be forced on us, to no one's benefit.

Obstacles. Sally Tomlinson[18] put her finger on the main obstacles to re-shaping professional roles:

> All the professionals involved in special education should, despite their undoubted concern for individual children, recognise that much of what happens in special education is as

much to do with their own particular vested interests as with the needs of the child. (p.277)

Professional self-interest results in defensiveness, demarcation disputes and often duplication of effort. I foresee no easy solutions although I am hopeful that dialogue between professionals, and a greater accountability of them to their clients, will effect positive changes. We might then arrive at the time when we label our professionals by the *functions* they fulfil for clients, rather than by the *personal* qualifications they hold.

Parents

We turn now to look at what parents can do to ensure that they have more and more opportunities for working with professionals. Their obstacle is all too apparent: 'united we stand; divided we fall'. Parents, individually, can do relatively little; they are easy targets for professionals and service-providers who can readily dismiss them as 'trouble-makers' or 'unaccepting parents'. The solution is to meet with other parents in the neighbourhood to join local and national groups. In the past such organisations have achieved major improvements in service provision and I am sure will do so in the future.

● Parent groups could invite professionals from time-to-time to speak at their meetings, describing the work they do and answer parents' questions.

● Parent organisations, through their publications, should inform their members of schemes involving parents which are on-going around the country. Moreover, they could provide them with guidelines to good practice or suggestions about actions they might take locally, illustrating ways in which difficulties could be overcome.

● Parents should make full use of the opportunities now open to them under the law; for example, in respect of their involvement in the assessment procedures laid out in the British Education Act (1983) or in relation to the Individual Education Program Committees established under the Education for all Handicapped Children Act of 1975 (Public Law 94–142) in the United States.

● Parents are now legally entitled to places on the school management boards in many countries. Those who are on the boards should maintain close contact with other parents to ensure that they represent their views.

● Parent groups could become more involved in monitoring the quality of services. The British Mencap society (Royal Society for Mentally Handicapped Children and Adults[104]) is a parent organisation which has published various *Stamina* documents that outline desirable minimum standards for schools, adult centres and residential services.

Many parent groups in North America have been trained in the use of PASS, Program Analysis of Service Systems,[105] which entails a rigorous examination of services against the criteria of normalisation principles. PASS has been used v ·'hin Ireland and Britain, although at present it is mainly professionals who have attended the training workshops.

● Parent groups should press for representation on the policy and planning teams of local and national services. Failing this, they should make written submissions stating their viewpoint and ask to meet the committee to discuss their proposals.

● Parents may need training in advocacy skills. For example, Richard Brightman[106] at the University of California at Los Angeles, USA, has developed a six-session course entitled, 'Parents as Advocates'. He describes the need thus:

> few parents possess either the requisite knowledge of complex special education law or the appropriate assertiveness skills required to fully engage in the IEP process [see above], especially when parent opinion regarding the merits of a given educational program differs substantially from professional opinion. (p.455)

The course coaches parents in the intricacies of the law and how to act assertively. This is done through problem-solving exercises, video-tape analysis and action-orientated homework assignments. The success of this course, indeed its very existence, should encourage the development of similar ones in other countries.

A British example is a study pack produced by the Open University,[107] entitled *Governing Schools*, which is designed to help existing and newly appointed governors of all types of schools in England and Wales, to 'gain knowledge, skills and self-confidence, and to become an effective member of your school's governing body'.

In Colorado, the state department of education sponsors three-day workshops to help parents with a handicapped child learn about the services which are available, how to access them and the responsibilities which the school system professionals have in developing and implementing appropriate programmes. All expenses are paid by the state. The workshops not only enable parents to become knowledgeable about the Federal special education law and state legislation, but also give them the opportunity to share their difficulties and bright moments with other parents. The results have been very favourable — a marked reduction in disagreements with local school staff, parents helping other parents, and overall fewer special education disputes in the state.

Parents and/or professionals could take the initiative in setting up similar courses in their locality.

● Parents could act as advisors or tutors to other parents. This has worked successfully in several places in Britain, most notably the Southend-on-Sea group therapy scheme mentioned before (see p.154). Moreover, the success of the Preschool Playgroup Associations in Ireland and Britain is largely built on the idea of parents helping other parents. However, the recruitment of parents with a handicapped child to work with 'new' parents is better developed in parts of the United States and Canada. For example, the Greater Omaha Association of Retarded Citizens has had a 'Pilot Parent' Scheme in operation since 1970. The pilot parents are carefully selected and given 18 hours training before being matched to new families, usually on the basis of similarity of the children's disability. Their aim then is 'to pilot new parents through the initial difficulties of accepting that their child is handicapped, learning about the handicap, and finding the proper services to aid their child in his or her development'.

Some professionals would immediately see dangers in this approach, but I hope that most would see it as a way of increasing resources and of bringing help to parents in a way which complemented and extended the professional's role.

The underlying philosophy in all these schemes aimed at greater collaboration is that parents are the allies of professionals but, nevertheless, with their own autonomy and powers to negotiate. There is also general agreement that those parents who wish to opt out of closer involvement with services and professionals should have their wishes respected and that this should not reflect badly on them or their children.

Providers

Finally, we come to consider what the people with the power to allocate resources can do to bring about closer working relationships between parents and professionals. The people I have in mind are managers of services, administrators, civil servants and politicians both local and national.

● Providers must determine the needs of the clients they are trying to serve. Dialogues with representatives of parents and professionals, along with the commissioning of surveys of needs, will help to ascertain the gaps in their present services and identify weak aspects.

● Parent representatives should be included on planning and policy committees and consultations offered to all the parents in receipt of services and who may be affected by any proposed changes.

● Managers and administrators need to keep up-to-date with new developments. As Alastair Heron and Mary Myers[57] argue:

> It cannot be too often emphasised that it is almost useless, and frequently harmful and demoralising, to send front-line staff to training courses, only for them to face, on their return, the opposition or simply lack of support of middle management . . . The *first* people to require and receive 'reorientation' are those in administrative positions who have the effective control of the use made of 'duty time' by front-line staff. (p.87)

They further argue that in matters of training, where everything depends on the general acceptance of innovations, the rule must be from the top downwards.

● The funding of 'demonstration' projects, without any long-term commitments, can be a useful way of making innovations. Over-and-above the gains to the clients participating in the project, such schemes can act as a stimulant to the existing services, particularly if staff of the demonstration project are committed to acting as a resource for existing personnel in other parts of the service by organising training courses and arranging placements. Many of the parental-involvement schemes described in Gillian Pugh's[40] book began as research and demonstration projects.

● Service agencies could make application for research grants to finance new developments. Hitherto, grants have been awarded mainly to universities and colleges, but I cannot help but feel that the much-lamented gap between research and practice could be bridged, at least in part, by reviewing the settings in which research is carried out.

Alternatively, service agencies might create a development fund out of their existing budgets to help them fund new approaches to services.

● Extra resources will be needed to enable new services to start and grow. The monies for these could be found from re-allocations of existing budgets and a reappraisal of priorities. However, administrators and politicians may need to lobby for an increase in their allocations. Well-argued proposals backed by facts and figures will stand a greater chance of being accepted.

It may be some consolation for them to be reminded of Sean Cameron's[74] conclusion that parental involvement requires neither new buildings nor a new profession. Paradoxically, many will consider this a mixed blessing. The cost-saving may be obvious but these new arrangements may require administrative and accountability systems that are at odds with the existing arrangements, which were designed for designated professionals working in designated centres.

● Providers may need to explore totally new ways of providing services. For example, the advent of cable television, with its potential for local specialised programming, could bring a whole new dimension to home-based work with parents. All the parents in a district could have direct access to programmes such as phone-ins, interviews, demonstrations of teaching techniques, panel discussions, etc.

Service planners need to be in the forefront in discovering and assessing the potential of new technology. Sad to say, they are often the least inclined to take risks. Perhaps it is this characteristic more than any other that we need to reappraise if our services are to be wholly responsive to parents' needs.

● There is the prospect, already a reality in some countries, of parents becoming the instigators of services and the employers of administrators and professionals. This concept is so very different to that within which most of us have worked but our unfamiliarity should not blind us to its advantages. Among the possible future scenarios are individual contracts between a professional and a family or parent co-operatives employing professional staff on a consultative or part-time basis. These could be funded out of private monies or, indeed, the taxpayers' contributions could be channelled directly to families instead of the present system of financing services. However, this brings us firmly into the realm of politics with a capital 'P' and has implications far beyond work with parents.

Creating Change

This chapter has been about changes; whether they are instigated by professionals or parents or providers or by any combination of the three. I am under no illusion that change comes easily. We are conditioned to being cautious and conservative in our dealings with disabled people. There is, too, a sense of security and stability with the familiar. Indeed I recall some words from the hymn 'Jesus bids us shine' that, as a child, gave me such a feeling of well-being : 'you in your small corner, and I in mine'. It strikes me now that this is the very mentality which precludes partnership.

Rod Ballard,[35] a parent and a professional social worker, in writing about the emotional distance between parents and professionals, relates this story:

A family of porcupines huddled together for warmth when it got cold. When they did this they found that they started to prick each other so they were forced apart, but this of course made them feel cold again, so they came closer until the pricks of each others' quills became just tolerable enough to bear and they became more or less comfortable.

Parents and professionals may extend their quills outwards in relation to each other because they have a personal investment in keeping as far apart as possible to avoid a mutual and painful pricking, a confrontation with reality. My argument is that we need to be pricked, but that this must be within a relationship which is warm, empathetic, trusting and understanding. (p.102)

It is out of discomfort that change occurs. May you never be too comfortable or too thick-skinned in your work with parents.

Appendix: Resources Available in The United States

The Family Resource Coalition (FRC) is a national, grassroots federation of individuals and organizations promoting the development of prevention-oriented, community-based programs to strengthen families. The Coalition identifi∵ ⌐ and publicizes model family resource programs. Its purpose is to fuel the growing movement to make primary prevention services available to all parents.

The Family Resource Coalition was developed to achieve the following goals:

- To assist family resource programs to improve in quality and to increase in number.
- To conduct a public education campaign to make the general public aware of the needs of families with young children and how family resource programs meet many of those needs.
- To help family resource programs to become better advocates for children and families in their states.

Toward this end, the FRC has produced two guides: *Sharing Resources: An Annotated Bibliography of Technical Assistance Materials* (1) and *Programs to Strengthen Families: A Resource Guide* — a book authored with Yale University which provides program descriptions of over 70 family resource organizations (2). These guides contain fuller statements about the programs listed below. The guides, and additional information on FRC services, are available from: The Family Resource Coalition, 230 North Michigan Avenue, Suite 1625, Chicago, Illinois 60601, USA (Phone 312-726-4750).

Extending Family Resources (1)

By Judith A. Moore, Leo A. Hamerlynck, Elizabeth T. Barsh, Susan Spieker, and Richard R. Jones. Contact: Children's Clinic and Preschool, 1850 Boyer Avenue East, Seattle, WA 98112.

The Extending Family Resources (EFR) service delivery model was designed to reduce barriers and family stress related to caring for a developmentally disabled child. In this model, individualized family programs focus on: building the family's support network, training family members to work with the handicapped child, and providing access to a range of supportive services (respite care, transportation, special equipment, etc.).

The Parent-to-Parent Program Organizational Handbook (1)

By Katherine Reynolds and Victoria Shanahan. Contact: University Affiliated Facility, The University of Georgia, 850 College Station Road, Athens, GA 30610-2399.

This is a 94-page looseleaf notebook of materials compiled by the Georgia Parent-to-Parent Program to assist others in developing peer support programs for parents of handicapped children. The handbook covers steps to take in initial organization, volunteer training, publicity, developing a referral system, compiling information on local services, and developing a state-wide organization. It contains an outline of the definitions, causes, characteristics, educational implications and medications involved in major developmental disabilities. A glossary of terms, lists of national advocacy organizations, and references on peer support and developmental disabilities are included.

The Pilot Parenting Program: A Design for Developing a Program for Parents of Handicapped Children (1)

By Fran Porter. Contact: Pilot Parents, Greater Omaha Association for Retarded Citizens, 3212 Dodge, Omaha, NE 68131.

This manual is a step-by-step guide to developing a low-cost, agency-based program for parents of handicapped children. In this model, trained parent volunteers establish supportive relationships with new parents, 'piloting' them through the initial difficulties of accepting and learning about their child's handicap. They help parents find information on handicapping conditions and community resources.

The 99-page book outlines the roles and responsibilities of a steering committee; methods of recruiting, screening and training volunteers; and provides guidelines for handling publicity and referrals, matching new parents with volunteers, program coordination and recordkeeping tasks, and the use of professional consultants.

Project HOPE (Helping Other Parents Through Empathy): A Parent Support Network (1)

By Donald Mott, Vicki Jenkins, Eva Justice, and Rebecca Moon. Contact: Family, Infant and Preschool Program, Western Carolina Center, 200 Enola Road, Morganton, NC 28655.

Project HOPE is a parent-to-parent support network for parents of handicapped children. The program uses trained volunteers who are experienced parents of handicapped children to provide support and information to new parents of handicapped children.

This 26-page paper describes the organization of Project HOPE and includes the rationale for the program, background information, descriptions of the participants, a discussion of the procedures for training the parent outreach volunteers, and a description of community awareness activities and referral procedures. The results of program evaluation are also included, as well as a 20-page appendix of forms, assessment tools, training information and references.

Reaching Out to Parents of Newly Diagnosed Retarded Children: A Guide to Developing a Parent-to-Parent Intervention Program (1)

By Jeff Bassin and Diane Drovetta Kreeb. Contact: St Louis Association for Retarded Children, 1240 Dautel Lane, PO Box 27480, St Louis, MO 63146.

This 39-page booklet outlines the development of parent outreach programs aimed at providing information and support for families of very young handicapped children. The model uses an agency-based office and professional staff to do community outreach work, coordinate and train volunteers, keep records and raise funds. Volunteer parents provide one-to-one peer counseling services. This guide describes methods of recruiting, screening and training volunteers; matching parents with peer counselors; and providing consultation and program coordination services.

Conference Series on Early Adolescence (1)

By Gayle Dorman, Dick Geldof, and Bill Scarborough. Contact: The Center for Early Adolescence, The University of North Carolina at Chapel Hill, Suite 223 Car Mill Mall, Carboro, NC 27510.

The curriculum is designed to help parents better understand their young adolescents (aged 10 to 15). It includes lecture and discussion materials on normal adolescent behavior, risk-taking behavior, sexuality, limit-setting and negotiation, community skills and family interaction. The materials are presented as a series of four one-day, community-wide conferences, but can also be used in planning smaller, more informal parent discussion and support groups.

The 283-page looseleaf notebook outlines the content, purpose, and structure for four keynote addresses and 12 workshops. It includes guidelines for planning and logistics, publicity, training materials, and budgeting; and tips for workshop leaders, handout material, and suggested readings.

The Parent Education Curriculum of Family School (1)

By Joan San Reivich and Yvonne L. Fraley. Contact: Family Support Center, 2 Baily Road, Yeadon, PA 19050.

The Family School Curriculum was developed for parents of handicapped, developmentally disabled, abused, and 'at risk' children. This 123-page manual is written for professionals working (in various settings) with groups of parents of preschool, special needs children. The curriculum covers 78 hours of integrated instruction, presentations, guided discussion, parent-child activities, and experiential exercises. The program is designed to help parents explore topics such as health, nutrition, safety, child development, children's feelings, discipline, trust, and communication.

Parent Training (1)

By Edith Spees, John Poertner, Portia Kennel, and Fran Middleton. Contact: Diann Crawford, Illinois Department of Children and Family Services (DCFS), 1 North Old State Capitol Plaza, Springfield, IL 62706.

Developed and field-tested by DCFS, this program provides parenting skills training for parents 'at risk' of child abuse or neglect — to avoid removal of children from their homes or facilitate the return of children who have been removed. The curriculum offers information and skills-building exercises in important areas of parenting, including: communications, self-esteem, managing stress and anger, and behavior management. It provides opportunities for parents to practice and apply the knowledge and skills they gain, through group discussion, role-play, and homework exercises. The 133-page manual includes instructions for trainers, teaching objectives, outlines, and handout materials for the 8-session course. A companion *Trainer Manual* is designed for helping professionals who are working with DCFS field offices, but is also relevant for professionals in other service agencies. It summarizes child development principles (so that the trainer can integrate these into the curriculum) and discusses adult learning styles and processes. The 102-page manual includes sections on program planning, coordination and evaluation.

Active Parenting, Inc. (1)

2996 Grandview Avenue, Suite 312, Atlanta, GA 30305.

Active Parenting produces a video-based parent education program, based on the work of Rudolf Dreikurs, Alfred Adler, and others. The six-session course covers materials on problem-solving, discipline, and communication skills; ways to encourage independence, responsibility, and cooperation in children; and suggestions for conducting family meetings. The program package includes the video-tapes, a leader's guide to facilitating discussions, and handbooks with written materials and homework exercises for parents.

Active Parenting also trains parent educators and others interested in using the video-based teaching method in parent groups.

Family Matters (1)

Distribution Center, 7 Research Park, Cornell University, Ithaca, NY 14850.

The Family Matters Project at Cornell University has developed a series of research-based training materials for parents, educators, and helping professionals. These workshops promote family strengths, through parental empowerment and cooperative approaches to advocacy. The facilitator's guides describe the structure and format of these workshops.

Cooperative Communication Between Home and School contains leader's guides for a six-session workshop series for parents, two in-service training workshops for elementary school teachers, and a monograph for school administrators. Based on the premise that children benefit when parents and teachers work together, understand each other's view points, and share the educator's role, these materials are designed to develop empathy, problem-solving, and cooperative communication skills between parents and teachers.

Empowering Families: Home Visiting and Building Clusters is a facilitator's guide for in-service training workshops for home visitors, group leaders, and others who are helping families. It includes materials on starting parents networks and working with parents groups.

Communication for Empowerment, a handbook for group facilitators, describes an empowerment-oriented approach and related techniques for leading workshops.

Parents in Touch (2)

Indianapolis Public Schools, 901 Carrollton Avenue, Indianapolis,

Indiana 46202. (Tel: 317-266-4134). Contact: Izona Warner, Project Director

The overall objective of *Parents in Touch* is to improve dialogue among parents, children, and the schools. The district-wide program seeks to involve parents in helping to improve their children's school attendance and achievement. The program's major objectives include: (1) creating public awareness of the shared responsibility between parent and school for student success; (2) training staff to encourage effective parent involvement; (3) maintaining a system for communicating with parents, including parent-teacher conferences; (4) involving community representatives in finding ways to promote parental involvement; and (5) teaching communication strategies to parents to improve their children's achievement. The program offers parents both methods and materials to help achieve these goals.

Parent Education Resource Center (PERC) (2)

Davis County School District, 77 South 200 East, Farmington, Utah 84025 (Tel: 801-451-5071). Contact: Mary Hughes, Director.

The *Parent Education Resource Center* is located in a public school serving handicapped students. The center has an extensive library of books, toys, filmstrips, pamphlets, and education kits on child development and parenting, which are loaned to parents and professionals at no charge. The center offers classes and discussion groups or parenting, including special help to parents of the handicapped, gifted, or under-achievers. Center staff also worked with PTA volunteers to develop an educational program about sexuality for use by parents of elementary students.

Closer Look (2)

Parents' Campaign for Handicapped Children and Youth, 1201 Sixteenth Street NW, Washington, D.C. 20036 (Tel: 202-822-7900. Contact: Barbara Scheiber, Executive Director.

Closer Look instructs parents in problem-solving and advocacy techniques through parent guides and two- to five-day training workshops. Three training curricula have been developed for families: 'Parents Advocating Vocational Education', describing programs for handicapped young people; 'Life Skills Training Program', a model curriculum to help parents and disabled adolescents work together in developing independent living skills; and 'Project Bridge', which assists parents to enhance communications skills. The program is in the process of starting a hotline for parents of learning-disabled teenagers.

Parent Specialist Education Program (2)

Philadelphia Chapter (Rainbow), Inc., Association for Retarded Citizens, 2350 West Westmoreland Street, Philadelphia, Pennsylvania 19140 (Tel: 215-229-4550). Contact: Bonni Zetick, Director.

The *Parent Specialist Education Program* ˙ a community-based program designed to aid parents and professionals who work with people with special needs. The project's goals are: (1) to provide information on how to utilize community resources available to the developmentally disabled; (2) to improve parent-child relations; (3) to encourage parents to advocate on behalf of their children; (4) to reduce isolation by bringing together those involved with developmentally delayed people; and (5) to foster communication and respect among parents and professionals who work with children with special needs.

Child Care Resource and Referral, Inc. (2)

1312 Northwest Seventh Street, Suite H, Rochester, Minnesota 55901 (Tel: 507-288-9388. Contact: Tutti Sherlock, Executive Director.

CCRR sponsors a series of parenting seminars at the workplace. This program makes parent education available to working parents by offering the seminars on-site during regular working hours. Topics include 'Time Management for the Working Parent' and 'Choosing Quality Child Care'.

In addition to providing direct services to parents, CCRR works closely with day care providers. Training is offered and materials and equipment are available for loan from a resource and reference library. CCRR also sponsors a child care food program for licensed family day care homes. Through its advocacy on behalf of parenting and day care programs. CCRR has secured more funds from the state legislature to develop and maintain programs throughout the state that serve parents and children.

Other Resources

Appalachia Educational Laboratory (AEL) Division of Childhood and Parenting, PO Box 1348, Charleston, WV 25325 (304-344-8371).
The Division of Childhood and Parenting researches and develops activities related to parenting and childhood education. Products include:

● Three videotapes: 'It's Never Too Late' (discipline), 'Mixed Emotions' (children's emotions) and 'Guess What' (parents as teachers). The tapes are designed to assist parents in participating in their children's development.
● *Parenting Materials: An Evaluative Annotation of Audiovisuals for Effective Parenting* — evaluations of 154 audiovisual materials.
● *Home Visitor's Kit* — three volumes designed to help potential family workers develop the entry level skills, knowledge, and orientation needed to conduct home-based programs that serve families. Available through Human Sciences, 72 Fifth Avenue, New York, NY 10010.
● *Day Care and Home Learning Activities Plans* — three volume set of more than 900 activities for use by paraprofessionals and parents in day care centers and homes. Includes instructional manual with weekly lesson plans and modifications for special children. Available from Educational Communications, Inc., 9240 S.W. 124th Street, Miami, FL 33176.

Child Welfare League of America (CWLA), 67 Irving Place, New York, NY 10003 (212-254-7410).
CWLA is a federation of child welfare agencies in the United States and Canada devoted to the improvement of care and services for deprived, neglected and dependent children, youth and their families. The League develops standards for services, provides consultation to agencies, conducts surveys and research, sponsors conferences, publishes professional materials, and administers special projects. A catalog of CWLA publications

and services is available on request. Products include: *Resources for Young Parents* — two annotated bibliographies, program models, and interpretive pamphlets on the health, educational and social services that are available for teachers, social workers and health personnel.

ERIC Clearinghouse on Elementary and Early Childhood Education) ERIC/EECE), College of Education, University of Illinois, 1310 S. Sixth St, Champaign, IL 61820 (217-333-1386)

ERIC/EECE, one of 16 ERIC Clearing-houses sponsored by the National Institute of Education, is responsible for abstracting and indexing documents relating to the total care of children from birth through age 12. ERIC/EECE also offers computer search services and information analysis papers in the area of early childhood and in general aspects of elementary education.

The Family Living Series is a set of 24 loose-leaf bulletins (Catalog No. 188) dealing with topics related to child development, parenting and family relations. Sample titles include 'Talking With Your Child', 'Coping With Parental Stress', and 'Helping Children Develop Interests'. Each bulletin is one to three pages long.

ERIC/EECE also publishes a newsletter that carries articles on early childhood education and lists recent publications and bibliographies relevant to parent education.

High/Scope Educational Research Foundation, Family Programs Department, 600 N. River St, Ypsilanti, MI 48197 (313-485-2000).

High/Scope is an independent, non-profit organization that engages in curriculum development for children from infancy through elementary school; operates a laboratory school and conducts workshops and seminars for teachers; sponsors professional conferences; and produces multimedia training packages to supplement face-to-face teacher training. The Family Programs Department of High/Scope operates several parent education projects.

National Congress of Parents and Teachers (PTA), 700 N. Rush St, Chicago, IL 60611 (312-787-0977).

The PTA is a volunteer organization concerned with improving the education and welfare of children and youth. Organized on the local, state and national levels, the PTA performs three major functions: advocacy, service and parent education.

References

1. U. Bronfenbrenner 'Is early intervention effective? Facts and principles of early intervention: a summary' in A.M. Clarke and A.D.B. Clarke (eds), *Early experience; myth and evidence* (Open Books, London, 1976).

2. B.L. White, *The first three years of life* (Star Books, London, 1979; Avon Books, New York, 1984).

3. J.W.B. Douglas, *The home and school: a study of ability and attainment in the primary school* (Panther, London, 1967).

4. R. Davie, N. Butler and H.Goldstein, *From birth to seven; a report of the National Child Development Study* (Longman, London/Humanities Press, Atlantic Highlands, New Jersey, 1972).

5. P. Mittler, 'Parents as partners in the education of their handicapped children'. Paper commissioned by UNESCO, ED/79/conf. 606/7 (UNESCO, Paris, 1979).

6. J. Carr, *Young children with Down's syndrome* (Butterworth, London, 1975; Human Sciences Press, New York, 1984).

7. C.C. Cunningham, 'Early stimulation of the mentally handicapped child' in M. Craft (ed.), *Tredgold's mental retardation*, 12th edn (Baillière Tindall, London, 1979; W.B. Saunders, Philadelphia, 1980).

8. J. Cooper, M. Moodley and J. Reynell, 'The developmental language programme. Results from a five year study', *British Journal of Disorders of Communication*, vol. 14, no. 2 (1979), pp.57–69.

9. B. Tizard, J. Mortimore and B. Burchell, *Involving parents in nursery and infant schools* (Grant McIntyre, London, 1981; High Scope, Ypsilanti, Michigan, 1983).

10. Plowden Report, *Children and their primary schools* (HMSO, London, 1967).

11. J. Newson and E. Newson, *Perspectives on school at seven years old* (Allen and Unwin, London and Winchester, MA, 1977).

12. T. Smith, *Parents and preschool* (Grant McIntyre, London/High Scope, Ypsilanti, Michigan, 1980).

13. M. Fox, *They ge. this training but they don't really know how you feel* (National Fund for Research into Crippling Diseases, Horsham, 1975).

14. R. McConkey and D.M. Jeffree, 'Pre-school mentally handicapped children', *British Journal of Educational Psychology*, vol. 45 (1975), pp.307–11.

15. P. Mittler and H. Mittler, *Partnership with parents* (National Council for Special Education, Stratford, 1982).

16. A. Sutherland, *Disabled we stand* (Souvenir Press, London, 1981; Indiana University Press, Bloomington, Indiana, 1984).

17. B. Zydirveld, quoted in P. Mittler and H. McConachie (eds), *Parents, professionals and mentally handicapped people: approaches to partnership* (Croom Helm, London, 1983; Brookline Books, Cambridge, MA, 1984).

18. S. Tomlinson, 'Professionals and ESN(M) education' in W. Swann (ed.), *The practice of special education* (Blackwell, Oxford, 1981).

19. J. Tizard and S. Mantovani, 'Day care problems' in *Children and society: issues for pre-school reforms* (OECD, Washington, DC, and Paris, 1981).

20. C. Hannam, *Parents and mentally handicapped children* (Penguin, London, 1975).

21. P. Russell, 'The parents' perspective of family needs and how to meet them' in P. Mittler and H. McConachie (eds), *Parents, professionals and mentally handicapped people: approaches to partnership* (Croom Helm, London, 1983).

22. P. Mittler and D. Beasley, 'A multi-national family training workshop'. Report to UNESCO and UN (International League of Societies for Persons with Mental Handicap, Brussels, 1982).

23. P. Potts, 'What difference would integration make to the professionals?' in T. Booth and T. Potts (eds), *Integrating special education* (Blackwell, Oxford and New York, 1983).

24. M. Budoff and A. Orenstein, *Due process in special education: on going to a hearing* (Brookline Books, Cambridge, MA, 1984).

25. C.C. Cunningham, 'Early support and intervention: the HARC infant project' in Mittler and McConachie, *Parents, professionals and mentally handicapped people.*

26. H. McConachie, 'Fathers, mothers, siblings: how do they see themselves?' in Mittler and McConachie, *Parents, professionals and mentally handicapped people.*

27. D. Jeffree, quoted in Mittler and McConachie, *Parents, professionals and mentally handicapped people.*

28. M. van Hattum, quoted in Mittler and McConachie, *Parents, professionals and mentally handicapped people.*

29. Family Focus, quoted in Booth and Potts, *Integrating special education.*

30. L.N. Huang and L.J. Heifetz, 'Elements of professional helpfulness: profiles of the most helpful and least helpful professionals encountered by mothers of young retarded children' in J.M. Berg (ed.), *Perspectives and progress in mental retardation*, vol. 1 (University Park Press, Baltimore, 1984).

31. Court Report, *Fit for the future: report of the Committee on Child Health Services* (DHSS, London, 1976).

32. S. Beveridge, 'Developing partnership: the Anson House Preschool Project' in Mittler and McConachie, *Parents, professionals and mentally handicapped people.*

33. J.N. Richardson, *Julie? She's a love: a study of 76 young mentally handicapped children and their families* (Scottish Society for the Mentally Handicapped, Glasgow, 1979).

34. E. Newson and T. Hipgrave, *Getting through to your handicapped child* (Cambridge University Press, Cambridge and New York, 1982).

35. R. Ballard, 'Early management of handicap: the parents' needs' in T.E. Oppe and F.P. Woodford (eds), *Early management of handicapping disorders* (Associated Scientific Publishers, Amsterdam, 1976).

36. I. Scheffler 'Philosophical models of teaching' in R.S. Peters (ed.), *The concept of education* (Routledge and Kegan Paul, London, 1967, and Boston, 1970).

37. E. Newson, 'Parents as a resource in diagnosis and assessment' in Oppe and Woodford, *Early management of handicapping disorders.*

38. B. Smith, 'Collaboration between parents and teachers of school-age children' in Mittler and McConachie, *Parents, professionals and mentally handicapped people.*

39. J. Bruner, *Under five in Britain* (Grant McIntyre, London/High Scope, Ypsilanti, Michigan, 1980).

40. G. Pugh, *Parents as partners: intervention schemes and group work with parents of handicapped children* (National Children's Bureau, London, 1981).

41. M.L. Kellmer Pringle, *The needs of children* (Hutchinson, London, 1975).

42. D. Wilkin, *Caring for the mentally handicapped child* (Croom Helm, London, 1979; available in USA from Longwood, Dover, NH).

43. J. McEvoy and R. McConkey, 'Play activities of mentally handicapped children at home and mothers' perceptions of play', *International Journal of Rehabilitation Research*, vol. 6, no. 2 (1983), pp.143–51.

44. J. Hattersley and L. Tennant, 'Parents workshops in Worcestershire' in G. Pugh, *Parents as partners* (National Children's Bureau, London, 1981).

45. B. Baker, 'Intervention with families with young severely handicapped children' in J. Blacher (ed.), *Families of severely handicapped children: research in review* (Academic Press, New York, 1984).

46. B. Baker, D.B. Clark and P.M. Yasuda, 'Predictors of success in parent training' in P. Mittler (ed.), *Frontiers of knowledge in mental retardation*, vol. 1 (University Park Press, Baltimore, 1981).

47. C. Garland and S. White, *Children and day nurseries* (Grant McIntyre, London/High Scope, Ypsilanti, Michigan, 1980).

48. S. Sandow and A.D.B. Clarke, 'Home intervention with parents of severely subnormal pre-school children: an interim report' in *Child: Care, Health and Development*, vol. 4, no. 1 (1978), pp.29–39.

49. M. Powell and E. Perkins, 'Asian families with a preschool handicapped child — a study', *Mental Handicap*, vol. 12, no. 2 (1984), pp.50–2.

50. R. McConkey and J. McEvoy, 'Parental involvement courses: contrasts between mothers who enroll and those who do not' in J.M. Berg (ed.), *Perspectives and progress in mental retardation*, vol. 1 (University Park Press, Baltimore, 1984).

51. J. Carlyle, 'A paediatric home therapy programme for developmental progress in severely handicapped infants', unpublished report, Royal Devon and Exeter Hospital, 1979.

52. C. Kiernan, quoted in Pugh, *Parents as partners*.

53. E. Newson, quoted in Pringle, *The needs of children*.

54. P. Wilcox, 'The Portage Project in America' in Pugh, *Parents as partners*.

55. J. Key, J. Hooper and M. Ballard, 'A parental perspective on the Honeylands Home Visiting Project for severely handicapped infants provided by three mothers of older handicapped children' in *Child: Care, Health and Development*, vol. 5, no. 2 (1979), pp.103–9.

56. Warnock Report, *Special educational needs? report of the committee of enquiry into the education of handicapped children and young people* (HMSO, London, 1978).

57. A. Heron and M. Meyers, *Intellectual impairment: the battle against handicap* (Academic Press, London and Orlando, Florida, 1983).

58. J. Smith, A. Kushlick and C. Glossop, 'The Wessex Portage Project: a home teaching service for families with a pre-school mentally handicapped child', unpublished report, Health Care Evaluation Research Team (no. 125), Winchester.

59. S. Webster and co-authors, *The Portage guide to home teaching* (NFER/Nelson, Windsor, 1975).

60. P. Newell, *ACE special education handbook: the new law on children with special needs* (Advisory Centre for Education, London, 1983).

61. O. Hargie, C. Saunders and D. Dickson, *Social skills in interpersonal communication* (Croom Helm, London/Brookline Books, Cambridge, MA, 1981).

62. Rectory Paddock School Staff, *In search of a curriculum*, 2nd edn (Robin Wren, Sidcup, 1983).

63. D. Brynelsen, 'Infant development programmes in British Columbia' in Mittler and McConachie, *Parents, professionals and mentally handicapped people*.

64. Department of Education and Science Circular 1/83, *Assessments and statements of special educational needs* (HMSO, London, 1983).

65. C. Cunningham, 'Aspects of early development in Down's syndrome infants', unpublished PhD thesis, University of Manchester, 1979.

66. J.H. Flavell, 'Stage related properties of cognitive development', *Cognitive*

Psychology, vol. 2, no. 4 (1971), pp.421–53.

67. D.M. Jeffree and R. McConkey, *PIP Developmental Charts* (Hodder and Stoughton, London, 1976).

68. S. Furuno and co-authors, *Hawaii early learning profile (HELP)* (University of Hawaii, Hawaii, 1979).

69. S. Rogers and co-authors, *Early intervention development profile* (University of Michigan Press, Ann Arbor, 1975).

70. R. Evans and co-authors, *National Children's Bureau developmental guide* (National Children's Bureau, London, 1976).

71. D.M. Jeffree and S. Cheseldine, *Pathways to independence: checklists of self-help, personal and social skills* (Hodder and Stoughton, London, 1982).

72. H. Gunzburg, *Progress assessment charts* (SEFTA publications, Bristol, 1966).

73. R.D. Struck, *Behavior Characteristics profile* (Vort Corporation, Palo Alto, 1979).

74. R. McConkey and P. Price, *Let's talk: learning language in everyday settings* (Souvenir Press, London, 1985).

75. R. McConkey and F. Gallagher, *Let's play: a videocourse on nurturing the play of handicapped children* (Ulster Polytechnic and St Michael's House, Dublin, 1984).

76. S. Cheseldine and R. McConkey, 'Parental speech to young Down's syndrome children: an intervention study', *American Journal of Mental Deficiency,* vol. 83, no. 6 (1979), pp.612–20.

77. P.W. Dowrick, 'Self-modelling' in P.W. Dowrick and S.J. Biggs (eds), *Using video: psychological and social applications* (Wiley, New York and London, 1983).

78. R. McConkey and H. Martin, 'The development of object and pretend play in Down's syndrome infants: a longitudinal study involving mothers', *Trisonomy 21* (in press).

79. R. McConkey and H. Martin, 'Mothers' play with toys: a longitudinal study with Down's syndrome infants', *Child: Care, Health and Development,* vol. 9, no. 3 (1983), pp.215–26.

80. K. Lewin, 'Group decision and social change' in E.E. Maccoby, M. Newcomb and E.L. Hartley (eds), *Readings in social psychology,* 3rd edn (Holt, Rinehart and Winston, New York, 1958).

81. J. Rogers, *Adults learning,* 2nd edn (Open University Press, Milton Keynes, 1977).

82. G. Gaskell and P. Sealy, *'Groups' Block 13 of Social Psychology Course,* (Open University Press, Milton Keynes, 1976).

83. R.F. Bales, 'Task roles and social roles in problem solving groups' in E.E. Maccoby *et al.* (eds), *Readings in social psychology,* 3rd edn (Holt, Rinehart and Winston, New York, 1958).

84. Open University, *Group notes* (Community Education, Open University Press, Milton Keynes, 1983).

85. R. McConkey and B. McCormack, *Breaking barriers: educating people about disability* (Souvenir Press, London, 1983; Indiana University Press, Bloomington, Indiana, 1984).

86. M. Mellor, School for parents, 'Group experience for parents of the mentally handicapped: parents as group leaders and therapists', unpublished paper.

87. C.C. Cunningham and D.M. Jeffree, *Working with parents: developing a workshop course for parents of young mentally handicapped children* (National Society for Mentally Handicapped Children; NW Region, Mancester, 1971).

88. T. Attwood, 'The Croydon workshop for parents of severely handicapped,

school-age children', *Child: Care, Health and Development*, vol. 5, no. 3 (1979), pp. 177–88.

89. J. Gardner, 'School-based parent involvement: a psychologist's view' in Mittler and McConachie, *Parents, professionals and mentally handicapped people*.

90. R. McConkey, 'New approaches to parental involvement in preschool education', *Educational Review*, Occasional publication 9 (1983).

91. R. McConkey and M. O'Connor, 'A new approach to parental involvement in language intervention programmes', *Child: Care, Health and Development*, vol. 8, no. 3 (1982), pp.163–76.

92. J. Wolfson, 'Parent education: the Open University experience' in *Children and society: issues for pre-school reforms* (OECD, Washington, DC, and Paris, 1981).

93. Community Education, *Parents talking: family relationships* (Open University, Milton Keynes, 1983).

94. D. Mitchell (ed.), *Your child is different* (Unwin, London, 1982).

95. B. Baker and co-authors, *Steps to Independence Series* (9 titles) (Research Press Company, Champaign, Illinois, 1976–83).

96. L.J. Heifetz, 'Behavioral training for parents o. retarded children: alternative formats based on instructional manuals', *American Journal of Mental Deficiency*, vol. 82, no. 2 (1977), pp.194–203.

97. E.J. Lovell, 'Parent-infant programs for preschool deaf children: the example of the John Tracy Clinic', *Volta Review*, vol. 81, no. 4 (1979), pp.323–9.

98. S.L. Judson and R.L. Burden, 'Towards a tailored measure of parental attitudes: an approach to the evaluation of one aspect of intervention projects with parents of handicapped children', *Child: Care, Health and Development*, vol. 6, no. 1 (1980), pp.47–55.

99. R. McConkey, J. McEvoy and F. Gallagher, 'Learning through play: the evaluation of a videocourse for parents of mentally handicapped children', *Child: Care, Health and Development*, vol. 8, no. 6 (1982), pp.345–59.

100. E. Gowers, *The complete plain words* (Penguin, London, 1973).

101. S. Rheubottom, 'Handicapped child = Taxi' in Mittler and McConachie, *Parents, professionals and mentally handicapped people*.

102. R. McConkey and B. McCormack, *Fact sheets on mental handicap* (Health Education Bureau/St Michael's House, Dublin, 1983).

103. P. Mittler, *People not patients: problems and policies in mental handicap* (Methuen, London and New York, 1979).

104. Royal Society for Mentally Handicapped Children and Adults, *Minimum standards for local services* (MENCAP, London, 1977).

105. W. Wolfensberger and L. Glenn, *Program analysis of service systems (PASS 3)* (National Institute of Mental Retardation, York University, Toronto, 1975).

106. R.P. Brightman, 'Training parents as advocates for their developmentally disabled children' in Berg, *Perspectives and progress in mental retardation*.

107. Community Education, *Governing schools* (Open University, Milton Keynes, 1980).

Index